# THE ACCIDENTAL REVOLUTIONARY

## Essays on the Political Teaching of Jean-Paul Sartre

## Jules Gleicher

UNIVERSITY
PRESS OF
AMERICA

Copyright © 1982 by

**University Press of America, Inc.**

P.O. Box 19101, Washington, D.C. 20036

Printed in the United States of America

ISBN (Perfect): 0-8191-2836-8
ISBN    (Cloth): 0-8191-2835-X

# TABLE OF CONTENTS

# PREFACE

(I)f I have ventured amiss--very well, then
life helps me by its punishment. But if I
have not ventured at all--who then helps me?

Kierkegaard, The Sickness Unto Death,
Part First, III, A. (a) (2).

## I

There are truths that can be shouted, and others
that can only be whispered. Nowhere are the consequences of this observation so manifest as in the
sphere of political rhetoric. And not even so out-
spoken and iconoclastic a political activist as Jean-
Paul Sartre is immune from its force.

At a recent scholarly conference on Sartre and
biography,[1] Hazel Barnes called attention to Sartre's
discretion, perhaps even insincerity, in his own and
Simone de Beauvoir's accounts of peculiarly personal
and delicate autobiographical episodes. The question,
naturally enough, occurred, "What scope should one
give to possible Sartrean insincerity in works of a
more public character?" Not much, Ms. Barnes insisted--
Sartre was, after all, the philosopher of translucency
par excellence--, except, of course, for "the polemical
writings."

While the term "insincerity" ought, in this context, to be replaced by one less apt to predispose us
against a thinker who deserves our initial respect,
we must still ask just which writings qualify as "polemical." Clearly, the pro-Communist tracts of the 1950s;
but what else? What of, say, a work like The Flies?
But that anti-Vichy, anti-Christian play seems hardly
reticent. On the contrary, given the circumstances of
its composition and first staging, what stands out is
its remarkable boldness.

It may be necessary at this point to offer a corollary query to our opening statement: If some truths
are shouted, what whispers does the shouting conceal?
In the case of The Flies, and the subsequent works as
well, I suggest, an anti-egalitarian strain which is
markedly at odds with the surface teaching. While
this is not the only focus of the following essays, it
is, for the reader, as good a point of departure as any.

v

## II

It will be noticed that my coverage of Sartre's activities stops at 1961. This in part reflects my belief that the sequel merely elaborates already developed themes. It is also an attempt to correct for the kind of distortion that recent events may produce in the way we view remoter ones. At the risk of sounding macabre, I would state the matter thus: If, instead of living to the ripe age of seventy-five, Sartre had shared the fate of Kierkegaard or Nietzsche, and effectively departed the world while in his forties, how would we know him? Surely not as a Marxist; nor as a quasi-Marxist, pseudo-Marxist, or Marxist manqué. Perhaps too not even as an Existentialist. Our relative neglect of the later Sartre is thus an attempt to recover an original perspective on his earlier (and perhaps ultimately more interesting) works.

It will also be noticed that I did not interview Sartre or Simone de Beauvoir, and can thus not lay claim to any privileged "inside" information. My textual interpretations will have to stand or fall as textual interpretations. For this offense, I shall only invoke Sartre's own expressed skepticism on the value of interviews and personal knowledge of an author whose works one is exploring.[2]

## III

The essays in this volume were first composed between 1973 and 1975. After the publisher was either insightful or charitable enough to judge their content worthy of public declaration, I discovered, to my gratification and annoyance, that, except for some matters of detail, I could not substantially improve them. My chief interests having since migrated, I leave to others, better qualified than myself, the task of using, correcting, or discarding these reflections, as their best judgment shall direct.

Whatever the shortcomings of my own efforts, there are certain debts that I must gladly acknowledge: Professors Joseph Cropsey, the late Herbert J. Storing, and Paul Ricoeur, of the University of Chicago, read and commented on an early draft of this study at a time when their cooperative assistance was of most vital interest to me. Many of the ideas were first developed among the informal seminar group on philosophy and literature then clustered around Professor

George Anastaplo. (Chapter 4 especially retains the rhetorical flavor of this first setting.) I could not have wished for kinder conditions of debut than those provided by that spirited band of young searchers and researchers. Professor Eugene Genovese, in his capacity as editor of <u>Marxist Perspectives</u>, provided some very helpful comments on a part of chapter 5 which appeared as an article in that journal. Among my colleagues at Rockford College, Professors Paul Gottfried, Dain Trafton, and Donald Walhout gave special encouragement to my publication efforts. I have also received generous financial support from the College's Mary Ashby Cheek Fund. Mrs. Karen Brechlin typed the first part of this manuscript with interest and enthusiasm, and when circumstances compelled the discontinuation of her efforts, Miss Amanda Hudson completed the task with proficiency and great patience. Throughout, my friend, wife, and companion, Joan Kapstein Gleicher, has kept me mindful of the shore that lies on the opposite side of despair, while doing her best to keep me on the right side of sanity.

IV

I wish to dedicate this volume to my mother and to the memory of my father and uncle.

Rockford, Illinois
August 11, 1982

[1]"Sartre and Biography: A Symposium," the University of Chicago, October 2-4, 1981.

[2]"A Conversation with Jean-Paul Sartre," <u>Ramparts</u> 12 (February 1974), p. 39.

## 1. INTRODUCTORY OVERVIEW

> Though the Water running in the Foun-
> tain be every ones, who can doubt, but
> that in the Pitcher is his only who
> drew it out?
>
> Locke, Second Treatise, 29

### I

In an age of specialization, Jean-Paul Sartre presents the enticing spectacle of the Renaissance Man of
letters. His works cover a wide variety of subject matters, in virtually every genre of prose writing. Philosophical treatises, plays--both serious and farce--,
novels, short stories, public speeches, topical essays,
and articles of literary and artistic criticism have
issued from his pen. An extensive, but not exhaustive,
bibliography of his writings and public statements, published in 1974, listed no fewer than 586 items.[1] Even
during the last five years of his life, after having
announced, under the strains of long-failing health,
the termination of his writing activities,[2] he continued, with characteristic perseverance and intre-
pidity, to make public statements about, and to exert
personal influence upon, his political environment.

It should therefore not surprise that the present
study is not a comprehensive account of Sartre's
thought. Rather, it examines a number of his works
with a view to answering the question, What was Sartre
trying to teach his readers and auditors concerning
public life,[3] and why?, and it traces the development
of certain key themes and concepts through successive
phases of his career. This study is therefore a part
of a part of the story. But neither is its chosen
focus merely random. The special importance of ethical-political teaching to Sartre's thought is attested
to both by Sartrean Existentialism's general reputation as a "philosophy of social engagement" and by
Sartre's own testimony. In his laudatory foreword to
Francis Jeanson's early commentary on his philosophy,
for instance, he especially commends the young Jeanson
for grasping its fundamentally ethical direction, and
for correctly seeing that in his system "ontology
cannot be separated from ethics."[4]

But if we may take for granted the general importance of ethics to Sartre's philosophy, we must be

1

less certain about the correctness of any single characterization of a Sartrean ethical or political teaching. In the same prefatory letter, Sartre also praises Jeanson for having avoided "the error of judging the work of a living author as if he were dead and his work forever arrested."[5] Sartre, that is, always was, and wished others to be, alert to the possibility that he might change his mind, both with respect to emphasis and to substance. And change has indeed been a key issue of Sartrean criticism, with attention usually focused upon a supposed "radical conversion" to Marxism, which would have occurred sometime during the early 1950s.[6] Sartre seemed to confirm such a view in an important interview in 1969, in which he characterized his intellectual development as a passage from individualism to "the true experience, that of society." At the same time, however, he implicitly questioned the "truth" of the social experience by defining freedom as "the small movement which makes of a totally conditioned social being someone who does not render back completely what his conditioning has given him." On the subject of Marxism, he suggested that the history of Soviet Russia is theoretically problematic, and referred to the thoughts of Mao as "pebbles" in the Red Guard's heads and to the Cultural Revolution as a kind of madness. And he announced a remaining task of his career to be the composition of a political testament which would show how he came to be "remade other" by politics and explain "why I was to write exactly the contrary of what I wanted to write."[7] In the absence of such a statement, any interpretation of Sartre's public career can be only hypothetical. But that interpretation is needed, this last remark emphatically indicates. To that end, it will be helpful to provide at the outset a brief overview of Sartre's career as a political writer.

## II

Prior to World War II, neither Sartre's life nor his writings evidence a special concern with politics. His political opinions seem in the main to have consisted of disaffection from the prejudices of the Right and disgust over the affectation of bourgeois life, sentiments by no means unusual for a sensitive young bourgeois intellectual. But unlike his boyhood friend, Paul Nizan, who found his way early into political activism, Sartre's sentiments did not, for instance, prevent him from visiting and studying in Nazi Germany during the 1930s. His pre-war writings consist of phenomenological studies of the emotions and the imagination, written in the involved and remote style of academic philosophy; a collection of short stories; and the novel Nausea.[8] The first are almost wholly devoid of political references, indulging only such an occasional passing remark as that he had long considered historical materialism to be a "fruitful" working hypothesis.[9] In the fiction one finds the aforementioned criticism of bourgeois life and of the Right, made chiefly through ridicule and character-assassination. For example, Lucien Fleurier, the grand bourgeois protagonist of the short story "The Childhood of a Leader," is a rabid anti-Semite, participates in a sordid homosexual adventure, and regards his prospective wife as a mere chattel. But one also finds here and in Nausea expression of the philosophic premise (which later receives extensive elaboration in Being and Nothingness, Sartre's philosophic magnum opus), that man is the unique meaning-assigning being in a meaningless universe, and fictional portrayal of some attitudes toward that premise. But Sartre takes these reflections in no particular political direction. To the protagonist of the short story "The Wall," who had been fighting for the anarchist cause in the Spanish civil war, politics loses all relevance in the face of imminent death. And Antoine Roquentin, of Nausea, after indulging in caustic remarks on the bourgeoisie and on socialist "humanism," ends up retreating into the realm of the imaginary by resolving to write a novel in order to overcome his meaningless existence, in order to enable him to "remember my life without repugnance."[10]

The war years brought a change in Sartre's perspective. Captured during the first German assault in 1940, Sartre spent most of his short military career in a prisoner-of-war camp. There, he quickly became a kind of spiritual leader among the prisoners, many of them young recruits. Simone de Beauvoir, Sartre's life-long friend and companion, reports that at about this time he acquired a sense of "duty to the younger generation." He wished to avoid a repetition of the post-World War I feeling among the young veterans, "that they were a 'lost generation.'"[11] He escaped from the camp, with relative ease, early in 1941, and shortly thereafter was discharged from the military. Returned to occupied France, he tried to make good his newly discovered sense of public purpose in the Resistance, but the cadres, many of them controlled by the Communists, had little use for this bourgeois intellectual who was a student of German philosophy.

Sartre thus found himself forced, more or less by default, to ply his better talents, those of the writer.
In this capacity, he published a play, The Flies, and
did editorial work for clandestine journals. But these
were the actions of a still relatively obscure author,
whose immediate influence was, and was expected to be,
only local.

Post-war events changed all that. In the aftermath of the Liberation, the world was betaken with a
sudden and passionate interest in things French, and
Sartre found himself transformed, virtually overnight,
into a great celebrity. Simone de Beauvoir reports:

> A celebrity and a scandal at the same
> moment, it was not without uneasiness that
> Sartre accepted a fame which, exceeding all
> his old ambitions, also contradicted them.
> Although he had wanted posterity's approval,
> he had not expected to reach more than a
> very small public in his lifetime. A new
> fact, the advent of "one world," transformed
> him into an author of world fame; he had ima-
> gined that Nausea would not be translated for
> many years; as a result of modern techniques,
> the rapidity of communications, his works were
> already appearing in a dozen languages. It
> was a great shock for a writer reared in the
> old tradition, who had viewed the solitude
> of Baudelaire, of Stendhal, of Kafka, as the
> necessary price of their genius. . . .
> And [the] price [of this inane glory]
> was high. He received worldwide and unex-
> pected attention, but saw himself robbed of
> that of future generations. Eternity had
> collapsed. . . . His books, even if they were
> read, would not be the ones he had written;
> his work would not remain. . . . He [accepted
> this total catastrophe] in his Présentation
> which opened the first number of Les Temps
> Modernes in October [1945]. Literature had
> shed its sacred character, so be it; hence-
> forth he would posit the absolute in the
> ephemeral; imprisoned in his own epoch, he
> would choose that epoch against eternity,
> consenting to perish entirely along with it.[12]

The long and active career as a publicist which Sartre
then began as editor-in-chief of the periodical Les
Temps Modernes, immersed him in the politics of the

Fourth and Fifth Republics. But his political stands have always been critical, proceeding from the outside, from where he thought the intellectual could be most useful. Except for a brief and unsuccessful flirtation with electoral politics in 1948, he never sought nor held public office.

Most of Sartre's post-war life has involved him, in various capacities, with the radical Left. While we shall give these events thematic attention in a later chapter, a few remarks are appropriate here. Taken simply in themselves, many of his political activities--his participation in peace conferences with the Soviet Union, his opposition to France's attempt to retain Algeria, and later to the American involvement in Vietnam--seem unremarkable for a European intellectual. What is curious is the supposed "fit" underlying these stands, between a Marxist world view and his enunciated doctrine of Existentialism. For where Marxism views man as essentially and ineluctably an economic being, Existentialism posits man as a radical freedom, as beyond all essence, as possessing, in the words of one commentator, "a freedom more acute than, possibly, has been seen in two thousand years of philosophy."[13] Where Marxism sees in the unfolding of history a promise of the decisive fulfillment of man's being, Existentialism regards human endeavor as in some fundamental sense necessarily futile, and man as "a useless passion."[14] And while Marxism proceeds upon what appears to be a thoroughly plebeian ethic, Sartre seems to teach, at least in his early political writings, a highly individualistic notion of heroism, which requires distinguishing oneself from the common many.

III

This chronology has given rise to a number of conjectures concerning the articulation of Sartre's career. Taken in its strongest sense, the aforementioned thesis of a "radical conversion" to Marxism implies that there are essentially two Sartres, whose sometime similarities are more a matter of coincidence than of continuity. If, on the other hand, there is a unifying element to the disparate events in Sartre's public life, the natural place to look for it would be in his prepolitical--his "private"--writings, those composed before the rhetorical demands of speaking to a large and opinionated audience would have imposed upon him the necessity of trimming his sails to the prevailing public currents. In its most extreme form, this view would regard the whole of Sartre's Marxism as essentially a feint, designed to win over an important but recalcitrant body of intellectual opinion by insinuating his philosophy into it. The contrary view to this takes Sartre's Marxism as the logical culmination, in the public realm, of the immanentizing ontological project described in an embryonic, individualistic form in <u>Being and Nothingness</u>.[15] These three positions would regard the relation of early to late Sartre as, respectively, one of fundamental irrelevance, crucial contradition, or imperfect expression.

We might also delineate a fourth view, which draws upon the preceding three as follows: Sartre's early philosophic position renders the entire question of ethics hopelessly problematic; Sartre either always was, or quickly became, aware of this; thus, his subsequent public teachings comprise successive attempts neither to perfect nor to refute this position, but to obscure it from public attention, even to the eventual extent of lending credence to the thought of a radical break. While I incline toward this fourth alternative, I stop short of endorsing it fully, simply because the early evidence is inconclusive on the degree of Sartre's own awareness of the ethically problematic character of his more strictly philosophical position. It seems to me, however, that this fourth thesis confers a greater underlying coherence and intellectual respectability upon the succession of his public statements. I offer it, therefore, not as dogma, but as a working hypothesis. Pursuing this interpretation, we may also anticipate certain parallel theses: Sartre's public teachings successively lower the advertised standard for humanity; this development reflects a democratic tendency somehow present in his philosophy from the beginning; and behind these teachings is a personal project of self-advertisement, Sartre's desire to establish himself in some political capacity or other.

This study has four foci. We begin with certain key passages from <u>Being and Nothingness</u> which indicate the directions of a Sartrean political teaching and attempt to provide such a teaching with a metaphysical foundation. The three succeeding chapters explore what I regard as his three significant political teachings, those associated with the ideas of heroism, humanism, and Marxism. This involves looking at three different kinds of sources--a play, a public lecture,

6

and a series of polemical writings--covering nearly twenty years of Sartre's life. Finally, I offer some concluding remarks concerning Sartre's status as a political philosopher. While it may seem odd to devote as much attention as I do to The Flies, I believe this apportionment to be justified both by the play's peculiar biographical position, as the first thematically political work that Sartre published, and by its dramatic character. The examination of an inspirational teaching that is effected through the gradual unfolding of a plot seems to me to call for the long interpretive road of textual commentary. Conversely, I do not analyze at any length Sartre's systematic development of a science of society in The Critique of Dialectical Reason because my prime concern is with Sartre as a public teacher, rather than as a social scientist writing for technicians. My approach is thus a calculatedly naive attempt to proceed from "the things themselves."

## NOTES

[1]Michel Contat and Michel Rybalka (eds.), The Writings of Jean-Paul Sartre, trans. Richard C. McCleary (Evanston: Northwestern University Press, 1974).

[2]Jean-Paul Sartre and Michel Contat, "Sartre at Seventy: An Interview," New York Review of Books, August 7, 1975, p. 10.

[3]Throughout this study I use the terms "political" and "public" virtually interchangeably. I wish thereby to signify that my guiding conception of politics is not limited to considerations of parties and offices of government, but rather reaches to those ruling conceptions which give form to a society and substance to men's everyday dealings with each other. Thus, a shaper of men's opinions may be a political figure even though he had never sought nor occupied any political office. One consequence of this usage, which I readily acknowledge, is a blurring of the traditional distinction between politics and ethics.

[4]"Letter-Foreword," to Francis Jeanson, Sartre and the Problem of Morality, trans. Robert V. Stone (Bloomington: Indiana University Press, 1980), p. xxxix. This work originally appeared as Le Problème moral et la pensée de Sartre (Paris: Editions du Myrte, 1947).

[5]Ibid.

[6]For the genesis and possible meanings of this phrase, see infra, p. 27.

[7]"The Itinerary of a Thought," in Between Existentialism and Marxism, trans. John Mathews (New York: Random House, Pantheon Books, 1974), pp. 34, 35, 56, 58, 64, 63. Emphasis supplied. This article first appeared in New Left Review, no. 58 (1969).
In his 1975 interview with Michel Contat, Sartre announced that he had abandoned the project of writing a political testament, and declared what he had already written to be "the essential." "Sartre at Seventy," pp. 12, 14.

[8]See Contat and Rybalka, vol. 1, pp. 37-71.

[9]The Transcendence of the Ego: An Existentialist Theory of Consciousness, trans. Forrest Williams and Robert Kirkpatrick (New York: Farrar, Straus and Giroux, Noonday Press, 1957), p. 105. This work originally appeared under the title "La Transcendance de l'égo: esquisse d'une description phénomenologique," Recherches philosophiques, no. 6 (1936-37).

[10]The Wall and Other Stories, trans. Lloyd Alexander (New York: New Directions, 1948), pp. 238, 252-53, 256, 260-63; 199-226; 268-70; 33-34. Nausea, trans. Lloyd Alexander, rev. ed. (New York: New Directions, 1964), pp. 170-82, 62-75, 238.

[11]Simone de Beauvoir, The Prime of Life, trans. Peter Green (New York: World Publishing Company, Lancer Books, 1962), p. 516. This book originally appeared as La Force de l'âge (Paris: Libraire Gallimard, 1960).

[12]Idem, Force of Circumstance, trans. Richard Howard (New York: G. P. Putnam's Sons, 1964), pp. 40-41. This book originally appeared as La Force des choses (Paris: Libraire Gallimard, 1963).

[13]Wilfrid Desan, The Tragic Finale: An Essay on the Philosophy of Jean-Paul Sartre, rev. ed. (New York: Harper and Row, Harper Torchbooks, 1960), p. 107.

[14]From BEING AND NOTHINGNESS by Jean-Paul Sartre. Copyright (c) 1956 by Philosophical Library, Inc. Jean-Paul Sartre, Being and Nothingness: An Essay

on Phenomenological Ontology, trans. Hazel E. Barnes (New York: Simon & Schuster, Inc., Washington Square Press, 1966), p. 784.

[15]See, e.g., Thomas Molnar, Sartre: Ideologue of Our Time (New York: Funk and Wagnalls, 1968).

## 2. ANGUISH AND BAD FAITH:
## ONTOLOGICAL FORM, ETHICAL CONTENT

To strive against the whole world is a comfort,
to strive with oneself is dreadful.

Kierkegaard, Fear and Trembling, Prob. 3.

I

Being and Nothingness, published in 1943 but in
preparation for over a decade, is the culmination of
Sartre's pre-war writings and typifies his pre-war
concerns. It is not a work destined for wide public
consumption, but rather is, in appearance and in substance, a piece of academic philosophy, fraught with
jargon--some of Sartre's own, some of it, as with
the terms "Being-for-itself" and "Being-in-itself,"
borrowed--and with convoluted argumentation. Its fundamental task is to describe man's metaphysical, or as
Sartre has it, ontological,[1] situation. This involves
him principally in descriptions of what he regards as
most fundamental to the human being, structures of consciousness. These descriptions consist largely of, but
are not limited to, man confronting inert matter.
Because the universe also consists of other conscious-
nesses, Sartre includes a discussion of man's Being-
for-others. But this structure of consciousness is not
taken up thematically by way of the political. There
is no inquiry into the nature of justice or rights as
such in Being and Nothingness. There are, however,
important political implications to be drawn from the
work's phenomenological descriptions.

In his 1969 interview, Sartre described his pre-
occupation at the time of the composition of Being and
Nothingness as "provid(ing) a philosophical foundation
for realism," "giv(ing) man both his autonomy and
his reality among real objects, avoiding idealism without lapsing into a mechanistic materialism."[2] The
work's scope is further indicated by its critical-
synthetic approach. For what Sartre attempts to do
is to refine and revise--to purify--various powerful
intellectual strands present in the first third of the
twentieth century, and to synthesize them. Thus, he
brings together a radicalized version of Husserl's
phenomenological method,[3] a set of concepts borrowed
from Hegel, and some of the existential concerns of
Heidegger, in a work which includes among its undertakings a critique of Freudian psychology and its re-
placement by an existential psychoanalysis, and phe-

11

nomenological descriptions of the Marxian categories "bourgeoisie" and "proletariat."

The absence of discussions of right and justice in Being and Nothingness is not necessarily a defect. By its own terms, it was intended as the first half of a two-part work. The sequel was to be an ethical treatise, which Sartre in fact never wrote. But we may also suspect that Being and Nothingness's non-discussion of political philosophic concepts and the eventual abandonment of the ethical sequel, Sartre's expressed intention to write it notwithstanding, are consequences of an ontology that excludes such projects in principle.[4] In particular, we think of his concept of "ethical anguish" and of the character of Being-for-others. The former is the true reflection that "my freedom is the unique foundation of values, and that nothing, absolutely nothing justifies me in adopting this or that particular value, this or that particular scale of values."[5] This concept seems on its face to rule out the possibility of rational discourse on justice, rights, and the good. "Values" are not discovered through such discourse, but rather are adopted by freedom as the necessary but impossible horizon of our acts.

Being-for-others is a complex affair. In the main, however, Sartre's discussion tends to the conclusion that the relation of one consciousness to another is fundamentally antagonistic. The Other is the constant threat to my projects within my field of instrumentalities. He may rob me of my instrumentalities, turning them to his use, and, insofar as I am a body, make me an instrument within his projects. The individual relationships of love and hate which Sartre describes all have as their aim the suppression of the Other's antagonistic freedom. But because the Other is fundamentally given to consciousness as a freedom, these attempts all fail. As an objection to the possibility of politics, and hence of philosophizing about politics, however, this antagonistic relationship is not decisive. True, it practically precludes the harmonious communion of consciousnessess. But such preclusion, far from spelling the death of politics, may indeed be its precondition. It is because we cannot enjoy harmonious communion with each other--or, if we can, only rarely and under extraordinary circumstances--that ruling and being ruled are generally necessary.

However this may be, Sartre, for his part, has not

12

let the ontological character of <u>Being and Nothingness</u>,
or these particular limitations on the possibility of
political discourse, prevent him from using the ontological treatise as an occasion for political criticism. Indeed, he weaves political criticism and ontological exposition into a complex, and sometimes con-
fusing, fabric, paralleling similar efforts in literary
form in <u>Nausea</u> and the short stories. We shall consider the dual concepts of bad faith and anguish, which
together constitute a watershed of Sartrean ontologico-
ethical criticism.

II

The chief text on bad faith is the chapter of that
title, part 1, chapter 2, of <u>Being and Nothingness</u>,
which sets out demonstratively to answer the somewhat
arid question, What must man be in his being in order
that he have "the possibility of denying himself?"[6]
In order to answer this question, Sartre chooses to examine a single, concrete negative human behavior. Thus,
the question may also be formulated, "What . . . must
[consciousness] be . . . if the human being is to be
capable of bad faith?"[7] His choice of this particular
negative behavior, is, however, not merely arbitrary,
for the chapter's peculiar exposition of bad faith
provides Sartre's ontology with an ethical cutting edge.
The peculiarity lies in the disjunction between the abstruse explanation of what bad faith is and the many
accessible, vivid, and memorable instances of it which
Sartre provides; such that the reader who might in
the end not be able to define or to understand bad faith
could still recognize it all around him. The chapter's
structure contributes to this conjecture that it is
designed to promote a moral predisposition. Having
stated the ontological problem of bad faith toward the
end of the previous chapter, Sartre does not provide a
direct response until the closing section of the present chapter. In the interim, he offers terminological
distinctions, numerous and striking examples, and
polemical démarches. While this may be sound tech-
nique, working from the phenomena themselves toward
principles of assured relevance, he seems, at the very
least, to overstate his ontological case. The dis-
cursive context of the chapter's two longest coherent
parts are, moreover, attacks on positions of known
ethical import, Freudian psychology and a liberal ideal
of sincerity.

Sartre's first attempt at a definition of bad

13

faith is through ordinary language. Following an identification frequently made, he early on "willingly
grant[s]" that bad faith is "a lie to oneself."[8]  But
he then indicates that this concession, far from solving
our conceptual problem, is only its beginning. For it
is not at all clear how such a lie to oneself is possible. The difficulty lies in the nature of the lie.
For lying is a transcendent behavior, which depends upon
the existence of the Other. The liar knows to be a
lie what the duped person takes to be the truth. In
the case of bad faith, however, liar and duped are one
and the same person. But if the person knows his lie
to be a lie, he will not be duped by it, and the lie
will fail. Ordinary language thus offers at best only
a vague approximation, a kind of metaphor.

Nor does Sartre find recourse to the unconscious
to be especially helpful. For in order to account for
the complex defensive behaviors which a person in bad
faith employs in order to protect his bad faith, advocates of the unconscious must posit within the human
psyche a "censor" engaged in a project of disguise,
which knows the forbidden truth in order to conceal it,
to not-know it, that is, which is in bad faith. Thus,
Sartre concludes, "[p]sychoanalysis has not gained anything for us since in order to overcome bad faith, it
has established between the unconscious and consciousness an autonomous consciousness in bad faith. . . .
Proponents of the theory have hypostasized and 'reified'
bad faith; they have not escaped it."[9]

Ordinary language fails adequately to describe bad
faith because the latter lacks the clear consciousness
of a lie. But neither is bad faith a behavior of the
unconscious. What, then, is it? The examination of
this problem leads Sartre to offer a variety of formu-
lations--"flight from freedom," "flight from anguish,"
"believing in order not to believe and not believing
in order to believe," "vacillation between transcendence
and facticity"--all highly technical, and all requiring
explanation in terms of the general schema of Sartre's
ontology. Let us therefore quickly review that schema.

## III[10]

Sartre divides Being, in the first instance, into
two basic parts: Being-for-itself and Being-in-itself.
Being-for-itself is conscious being, concretely, man.
(This concretization is only partially accurate, since
man is also, as we have already noted, Being-for-others.)

Being-in-itself is non-conscious being; most obviously, inert matter, but also whatever can be treated as inert matter by Being-for-itself--the bodies of other Beings-for-themselves, for instance, or the Being-for-itself's own body, or its own past. Of Being-in-itself, all that one can say is that it is. In order for Being-in-itself to be any thing--to be a "this," or to "be there," or "therefrom" or "thereto"--Being-for-itself must act upon it. Being-for-itself is the source of all perspectivity, determination, causation. But Being-for-itself, for its part, is constituted by its object. The being of consciousness is precisely the consciousness of being. What distinguishes conscious-ness from its object is a kind of psychic distance which Sartre calls "Nothingness." This peculiar con-stituting-negating relation between Being-for-itself and Being-in-itself is the basis for such paradoxical statements as that the being of consciousness is to be what it is not and not to be what it is. That is, Being-for-itself is Being-in-itself in the mode of not-being, and it is not Being-in-itself in that it is always "beyond" the Being-in-itself which constitutes it.

The Being-for-itself of which Sartre usually speaks is not a transcendental Ego, but what he, in a radicalization of Descartes, calls "the pre-reflective cogito," the instantaneous center of perception. This primitive consciousness is prior to any "I"; the "I" is rather the unifying object-pole of temporalized consciousness reflecting upon itself, or consciousness as the constant object of reflection over time. The "I" is Being-for-itself treating itself as Being-in-itself. But insofar as the consciousness being re-flected upon as an "I" is Being-in-itself, the con-sciousness which reflects upon it is beyond it. As beyond Being-in-itself, Being-for-itself is radically free; it is an imperium in imperio. While man, as a being-in-the-midst-of-the-world, as a corporeal being, is conditioned, or situated, in various ways, as Being-for-itself he is not determined by the situation to be a particular consciousness rather than another, that is, to assume this or that particular attitude toward being. While this meaning of freedom, the freedom to assume an attitude, may seem highly restrictive and technical, even trivial, Sartre evidently regards it as the linch-pin of all human endeavor.

Finally, if any quality can be said to character-ize the general activity of Being-for-itself, it would

15

be restlessness. Through doing and having, the two grand categorical conducts of human reality, Being-for-itself constantly strives to appropriate Being-in-itself. But Being-in-itself is transphenomenal; it always overflows our consciousness of it. Moreover, the implicit end of this striving, the appropriation of all of being as consciousness of being, the transformation of Being-for-itself into the In-itself-for-itself which Sartre calls "God," is in principle impossible. Man's most fundamental most final end is absurd. "Man is a useless passion."[11] We may now return to the problem of bad faith.

IV

That problem, we recall, is how consciousness can instantaneously lie to itself. However grave this problem may be theoretically, the numerous examples Sartre gives show that the existence of bad faith is not a problem empirically--it happens all the time. They also reveal the basic elements of Being-for-itself of which bad faith makes use, namely, being-what-one-is-not, or facticity, and not-being-what-one-is, or transcendence. Bad faith takes facticity as simple identity, and transcendence as simple contradiction. Rather than see itself as a situated freedom, the consciousness in bad faith either claims to be absorbed into its situation or denies its real relation to it. Bad faith treats Being-for-itself as though it were Being-in-itself; it mistakes the nature of Being.

In the chapter's third part, Sartre offers a theoretical account of bad faith as a kind of belief, that is, as consciousness of an object grasped as an absence or indistinctly. But there are some objects of consciousness which, by virtue of their very being, can only be so grasped. The error of the consciousness in bad faith is improperly to distinguish those objects of consciousness which can be grasped clearly from those which cannot; and so to err on the basis of a deliberate decision concerning the nature of being generally; and also so to err with the prejudicative awareness that this is a falsification of being. The operative premise of this account seems to be that "deep down" we all intuitively know--cannot help but know--what we are.

Whatever theoretical problems still remain in this explanation, the assimilation of bad faith to belief has a great practical effect. It shifts the burden from the question, How is bad faith possible? to the question, How is it possible not to be in bad faith? For bad faith is "an immediate, permanent threat to every project of the human being."[12] It is not, in the end, something that comes about after a long and complicated process, but rather "a spontaneous determination of our being. One puts oneself in bad faith as one goes to sleep and one is in bad faith as one dreams. Once this mode of being has been realized, it is as difficult to get out of it as to wake oneself up."[13]

This explanation makes of bad faith something relatively innocent, and renders suspect Sartre's use of the term as a moral category. Bad faith may be something for which we are "responsible," insofar as it emerges from our being and nowhere else; but it is not evidently something that we ought to do anything about, no more than we ought to do anything about falling asleep and dreaming. But Sartre's ubiquitous use of the term as a pejorative seems undeniable. Bad faith's general ethical character, as it emerges in the "Patterns of Bad Faith" section, is that of role-playing, some of it innocuous (e.g., the "role" of being sad), but much of it pathologic. None of the examples that Sartre gives could accurately be described as the playing of a noble role. Further, the examples of the convicted man's confession of guilt and the coward's denial of his cowardice raise the question of the relation of bad faith to the traditional virtues, especially the political virtues.[14] For if bad faith is not only present in, but absolutely essential to, the standard judicial procedures and the disposition toward courage which are among the necessary conditions of any political community, then the ethical critique of bad faith radically calls into question the status of political community as such.

The aspect of role playing is perhaps best illustrated by the famous example of the café waiter. This café waiter, Sartre observes, through his exaggerated gestures and excessive solicitousness of the customers is obviously playing at something; but at what? A moment's reflection reveals that he is playing at what he is, being a café waiter, and he is the café waiter by playing at it:

The child plays with his body in order to explore it, to take inventory of it; the waiter in the café plays with his condition in order to realize it. This obligation is

not different from that which is imposed
on all tradesmen.  Their condition is
wholly one of ceremony. . . . [Such roles
constitute] precautions to imprison a man
in what he is, as if we lived in perpetual
fear that he might escape from it, that he
might break away and suddenly elude his
condition.[15]

The mention of imprisonment recalls a remark at
the chapter's beginning, concerning another kind of
negative behavior, the prohibition or veto, in which
the human being arises in the world "as a Not" (un Non).
Of this behavior, Sartre says, "[I]t is as a Not that
the slave first apprehends the master, or that the
prisoner who is trying to escape sees the guard who is
watching him."[16]  The prohibition and bad faith are
both permutations of human self-negation, but with the
crucial difference that in the case of bad faith the
enslavement or imprisonment does not require an identi-
fiable master or jailer.  It is the typical form of
oppression in a modern society, in which social conditions are characterized by substantial equality and
impersonality.  The waiter and other tradesmen are not
so much the victims of class conflict and exploitation
as they are of a more subtle, and largely self-imposed,
manipulation, which cuts them off from the development
of their presumably more human faculties.  "A grocer
who dreams is offensive to the buyer, because such a
grocer is not wholly a grocer."[17]

The array of examples of bad faith also refers to
other, more traditional, moral qualities.  For instance,
bad faith entails a kind of mental and moral sloth.
The coquettish woman who disarms her suitor's intentions
by abstracting from herself as body, by pretending to
be "all intellect," seeks to "postpone the moment of
decision as long as possible."[18]  And Sartre declares
as a general matter that bad faith "stands forth in
the firm resolution not to demand too much, to count
itself satisfied when it is barely persuaded, to force
itself in decisions to adhere to uncertain truths."[19]
Again, the examples of the homosexual who refuses to
acknowledge his homosexuality, insisting that his case
is different, betokens bad faith's personal dishonesty.
This dishonesty receives an institutional dimension in
the judicial procedure which demands of a man that he
confess his guilt in order to receive pardon, even
though by that confession he constitutes himself as no
longer the culprit whom he confesses to be.  And in all

18

cases, bad faith involves the peculiar kind of cowardice consisting of the avoidance of ethical anguish. We encountered this term earlier, but a fuller account is now in order.

V

Anguish is the experience of existential freedom, "the mode of being of freedom as consciousness of being," awareness of the openness of one's horizons, "my consciousness of being my own future, in the mode of not-being," "the reflective apprehension of freedom by itself."[20] Ethical anguish is the experience of the openness of one's ethical horizons, the consciousness that "my freedom is the unique foundation of values and that <u>nothing</u>, absolutely nothing, justifies me in adopting <u>this</u> or that particular value, this or that particular scale of values."[21] This experience is, however, in the nature of a special act. In order to have it, "I must place myself on the plane of reflection."[22] Typically, we act before positing our possibilities, in an urgent world already rife with values which we tend to accept without question. "[I]n this world where I engage myself, my acts cause values to spring up like partridges."[23] Bad faith is a flight from anguish, but necessarily involves a primitive awareness of anguish in order to flee it.[24] "Authenticity," the "self-recovery of being which was previously corrupted,"[25] to which Sartre refers in a note at the end of the "Bad Faith" chapter, is, then, a recovery of anguished being. Anguish and bad faith thus form the two poles of <u>Being and Nothingness</u>'s ontologico-ethical schema.

Sartre provides a number of examples to illustrate anguish. When I stand on a precipice, I may experience fear at the prospect of slipping or falling over the edge, but this refers only to my being an object-in-the-midst-of-the-world, susceptible to universal determinism. I experience anguish, on the other hand, at the possibility of hurling myself into the abyss. And this becomes my possibility only because reflection reveals my other possibilities, of taking precautions against falling, as inconclusive, as having an efficacy which is sustained only by my freedom. I thus feel anguish at the thought that my life is unjustified and completely in my own hands. This is anguish in the face of the future. Anguish in the face of the past occurs in the case of the gambler whose earnest resolution to quit gambling melts when he approaches the

19

gaming table. At that moment he realizes in anguish that the past, in the form of his resolution, has no necessary hold upon the present, and that he must continually and freely renew that resolution for it to be effective.

But Sartre's account of anguish seems not to give these examples their due. They seem not only to show the reflective apprehension of freedom, but also to imply an ethical context as a necessary precondition and constitutive element of anguish. The gambler feels anguish not only because he realizes his resolution's fragility, but also because he senses both its importance and its correctness. Without these latter elements, indeed, anguish seems to be absurd, not worth itself. We would hesitate, for instance, to call "anguish" the realization of our freedom in the making of such insignificant and morally neutral choices as that between different kinds of desserts.[26] The anguish involved in confronting habitual ethics is that one may freely have chosen, and may freely choose, to live wrongly. Sartre's ethically relativistic account of these anguished moments slights at least half of their phenomenality, and so flies in the face of his general principle, that "appearance lays claim to being."[27] Why, we may ask, does the appearance of "values" imply their true being any less than is the case with any other kinds of appearance? Sartre's answer seems to be that "[v]alue derives its being from its exigency and not its exigency from its being."[28] That is, value can be revealed only to an active freedom, which makes it exist as value solely by recognizing it as such. But recognition may mean either the original positing or assignment of meaning to something, or the acknowledgement of a meaning that is already there. While Sartre evidently wishes to refer the recognition involved in anguish to the first of these alternatives, his examples point to the second. (Indeed, he acknowledges as much, albeit perhaps inadvertently, for in discussing the precipice example he notes that "fortunately" the temptation to suicide which anguish reveals to me as my possibility is itself inconclusive.[29] Why should this revelation be fortunate, if not with reference to the a priori goodness or desirability of continuing to live?) The examples of anguish thus reveal the reflective apprehension of freedom, not as truly fundamental, but as secondary, as relative to some already given value.

Conversely, it is not obvious why a truly funda-

20

mental reflective apprehension of freedom would be
experienced as anguish. On its face, it seems equally
plausible that such a reflection would occur as joy,
or nausea, or curiosity. But the identification of
freedom with anguish does make sense in terms of the
ethical polarity of anguish and bad faith. For if the
flight from freedom is a flight from anguish, that is,
from an agonizing experience, then bad faith has a
prima facie sensibility as a kind of flight; whereas
it is paradoxical to speak of "flight from joy," somewhat strange to speak of "flight from curiosity," and
quite mundane to speak of "flight from nausea."
"Anguish" evokes the idea of noble suffering, and
"flight from anguish" cowardice. The ethical content
of bad faith has thus referred us to an alternative
ontological conception, anguish; but we **can** discern
behind that conception a prior notion of virtue.

Sartre may seek a middle ground between the priority of choice and the priority of value in his concept
of the original project. He notes:

> All these **trivial** passive expectations
> of the real, all these commonplace, every-
> day values, derive their meaning from an
> original projection of myself which stands
> as my choice of myself in the world. But
> to be exact, this projection of myself to-
> ward an original possibility, which causes
> the existence of values, appeals, expecta-
> tions, and in general a world, appears to
> be only beyond the world as the meaning and
> the abstract, logical signification of my
> enterprise.[30]

But this only re-locates the problem. It does not
account for why, or whether, we would feel anguish
when the original project itself came into question.
Alternatively, if the original project itself is
never put into question, but may merely change from
time to time, then a fundamental compromise is introduced into the principle of man's freedom.

VI

To recapitulate, the identification of freedom
with anguish seems to rest on two grounds. First,
within the framework of the entire construction, it
makes intelligible both bad faith as a flight from
freedom and the overcoming of bad faith as an heroic

or virtuous act.   Secondly, it seems to be confirmed by certain experiences to which Sartre can point, such as those of the cliff-walker and the gambler.   But an examination of these examples has shown the basis of their anguishedness to be not only the reflective apprehension of freedom as the ground for the efficacy of all human projects, but also the givenness of ethical values as the horizon for such projects.   Similarly, the comprehensibility which the concept "anguish" gives to the concept "freedom" in the construction "flight from freedom" carries with it a serious complication. For that comprehensibility seems to rest upon the palpable supposition that anguish is unpleasant.   But just what is it, then, that the consciousness in bad faith is fleeing when it flees anguish?   Is it fleeing its own freedom, or is it fleeing the unpleasure of reflecting upon its freedom?   The latter is strongly suggested by the pre-reflective character of bad faith, for it is simply paradoxical that a pre-reflective event like bad faith should comprehend, as one of its "moments," so complex an event as the reflective apprehension of freedom.

Sartre attempts to deal with this difficulty, in his theoretical account of bad faith, through a personification of bad faith and a metaphoric use of the verb "to know" apropos of bad faith's "knowledge" of anguish.   Bad faith as an "it" thus becomes the agent of the consciousness which is in bad faith.   And the belief of bad faith implies nonbelief because to believe is to know that we believe, and to know that we believe is to know that we only believe.   Sartre admits that this use of "to know" strains the description, but he excuses himself with the thought that non-thetic consciousness "is in its very translucency at the origin of all knowing."[31]   As an explanation, however, this seems insufficient.   It seems rather that one would have to posit not only the origin of knowledge in non-thetic consciousness, but also the end of non-thetic consciousness in knowledge.   That is, in order to account for the appearance of belief as mere belief, one would have to say something like, "Man by nature desires to know."[32]   But it is precisely for its implicit natural teleology, for its involvement of the soul in any "veiled appeal to finality," that Sartre has condemned Freud's psychology as an "explanation by magic."[33]   We seem to be able to read his criticism of Freud against Sartre himself:   In order to explain bad faith, he has established within non-thetic consciousness a censor-like knowing consciousness, which acts according to principles of natural teleology.

If, on the other hand, it is anguish's unpleasure that bad faith flees, then the pre-reflective apprehension of anguish at least makes sense impressionistically. One avoids anguish as one might avoid an annoying sensation in one's foot, and one falls into bad faith rather as one might unthinkingly adopt a compensating limp. But in this case we implicitly posit within the human being a kind of determinism, a calculus of psychic pleasures and pains, which seems, if not to refute, then at least to qualify the meaning of man's fundamental freedom. Man thus returns to nature. To be sure, such determinism is not so total as to preclude our ever remaining in, or even embracing, anguish. But it does emerge as the matrix within which human freedom expresses itself as disengagement. Again we may ask, will such disengagement be experienced as anguish? And again, the answer occurs that it may be so experienced, but it need not be. In particular, if the disengagement were to occur in the course of an intellectual activity, such as an inquiry into the fundamental character of being, then would it not be experienced more as wonder or fascination?[34] This comes closer to what we are apt to feel when we read, and attempt to follow the argument of,Being and Nothingness itself. It therefore seems significant that when Sartre mentions his own anguish, it is not as the inquirer into Being, but as one who writes a book of inquiry into Being, that is, as the performer of an action that is in-the-world, which places him in relation to others:

> I have been "wanting to write this book," I have conceived it, I have believed that it would be interesting to write it, and I have constituted myself in such a way that it is not possible to understand me without taking into account the fact that this book has been my essential possibility.[35]

Thus, while moments of anguish are not typical of everyday experience, neither are they the rarest of moments. Indeed, Sartre's examples evidence a desire to place the fundamental apprehension of man's being within the grasp of every man. For who has not faced the decision whether to reveal himself to others through some action, or sensed the fragility of some resolution or renunciation? Even the occasional tempta-

23

tion to suicide may be close to universal.  In the
concept of anguish, Sartre appears to seek a synthesis
of two strivings, that for a resolute alternative to
bad faith which may make possible a kind of nobility,
and that for democracy.  Whether these two strivings
are compatible, and if so at what cost, is an abiding
question in Sartre's successive political teachings.
Before we move to those teachings, however, some
additional points must be stated concerning the character of bad faith and that recovery of being which
he calls "authenticity."

VII

As an ethical critique, Sartre's discussion of bad
faith may be criticized as both too broad and too narrow.  Is a concept, we may ask, which attempts to be
as comprehensive as bad faith too comprehensive to be
useful?  Do we really assist our understanding by attributing to the diverse behaviors depicted in this
chapter a single regulative principle expressed in
terms of "structures of consciousness"?  Or is bad
faith not perhaps in this respect like Spinozan Substance, which, by being implicated in everything,
explains nothing?  Sartre's examples, on the other
hand, lead us to wonder whether the real thrust of his
ethical complaint might not be something other than
bad faith, something more particular, of which bad
faith is a component, like the mediocrity or amour
propre of bourgeois life.  It seems significant in
this regard that, while Sartre feels free to avail
himself elsewhere in Being and Nothingness of examples
taken from other times--in the discussion of motiva-
tion, for instance, he reaches back to the times of
Clovis and Constantine[36]--, all the examples in the
"Bad Faith" chapter which are not simply timeless are
distinctly contemporary.  If the ontological description does in fact skew the ethical point, then we may
be warranted in looking elsewhere for a more pertinent,
and perhaps a more coherent, account of the behaviors
and attitudes which he here portrays as ethical ills.
In the absence of an ethical treatise, this means
looking chiefly at Sartre's fictional and polemical
works, which not only purport to examine the problem
but also proffer solutions.

The appropriateness of looking to such sources is
suggested not only by default but also by a certain
incongruity within Being and Nothingness itself.  That
incongruity has to do with what Sartre calls "the

24

spirit of seriousness" (l'esprit de sérieux). In its broadest signification, this term refers to a whole way of life, that kind of bad faith consciousness which regards itself as rooted in ponderous necessity, which

> apprehends values starting from the world, and which rests in the reassuring, substantiation of values as things. In this spirit I define myself starting from the object by leaving aside a priori as impossible all undertakings in which I am not involved at the moment; the meaning which my freedom has given to the world, I apprehend as coming from the world and constituting my obligations.[37]

But more particularly, it refers to a certain style of philosophizing and to the relation between philosophizing and the recovery of anguish. It refers to that philosophizing which takes itself as a necessary activity, indicated by the nature of things, rather than as an activity, like any other, whose value derives solely from the fact that it is chosen. A philosophy not infected with this spirit, an authentic philosophy, would know itself as so chosen, and would feel free to avail itself of greater substantive and stylistic openness.

To all appearances, Being and Nothingness is not so open. In its premises and in its style, it appears to be part of a respectable modern tradition of ponderous metaphysical treatises, a "serious" work. But Sartre mitigates, even perhaps fundamentally recasts, this appearance in the passage I have cited, in which he refers the writing of Being and Nothingness, not to the necessity of discovering the truth, but to his personal project of self-revelation. But Being and Nothingness's ponderous style renders it accessible only to a few. This constitutes its incongruity, made especially pointed by the democratic desideratum which we found to be implicit in the concept of anguish. If such a discrepancy is excusable in the case of ontology, where the subject matter may be intrinsically esoteric, it seems to be much less so in the case of ethics, which considers questions touching the generality of men as a matter of course. For such questions a more accessible form of writing than the treatise may be appropriate, especially for a philosopher whose confessed aim is to publicize himself.

Both this incongruity within <u>Being and Nothingness</u> and the logic to the Sartrean system of a free-wheeling style of philosophizing have been noted, with disfavor, by Herbert Marcuse. Noting philosophy's "essential inadequacy . . . in the face of the concrete human existence," he accuses Sartrean Existentialism of attempting to square the circle, with the consequent production of hybrid monstrosities:

> According to Sartre, the "esprit de sérieux" must be banned from philosophy because, by taking the "réalité humaine" as a totality of objective relationships, to be understood and evaluated in terms of objective standards, the "esprit de sérieux" offends against the free play of subjective forces which is the very essence of the "réalité humaine." By its very "style" philosophy thus fails to gain the adequate approach to its subject. In contrast, the existentialist style is designed to assert, already through the mode of presentation, the absolutely free movement of the <u>Cogito</u>, the "Pour-soi," the creative subject. Its "jouer à être" is to be reproduced by the philosophical style. Existentialism plays with every affirmation until it shows forth as negation, qualifies every statement until it turns into its opposite, extends every position to absurdity, makes liberty into compulsion and compulsion into liberty, choice into necessity and necessity into choice, passes from philosophy to <u>belles lettres</u> and vice versa, mixes ontology and sexology, etc. The heavy seriousness of Hegel and Heidegger is translated into artistic play. The ontological analysis includes a series of "scènes amoureuses," and the existentialist novel sets forth philosophical theses in italics.[38]

Sartre's short answer to this caricature, and to Marcuse's concluding observation that the contemporary "experience of the totalitarian organization of the human existence forbids to conceive freedom in any other form than that of a free society,"[39] might be in turn to accuse the revolutionary of being infected by the spirit of seriousness. This, both for his glib assumption that a free society is possible, and for taking that goal as somehow dictated by the nature of things, rather than being the product of his own conscious choice. But Sartre is not altogether hostile to Marcuse's formulation. His task is rather to explore the possibility of a free society from the perspective of the recovery of anguished being.

In this light, we may comment upon a rather famous footnote in Being and Nothingness. Having developed Being-for-itself's relation to the Other as fundamentally, and to all appearances inescapably, antagonistic, Sartre notes: "These considerations do not exclude the possibility of an ethics of deliverance and salvation. But this can be achieved only after a radical conversion which we cannot discuss here."[40] Marcuse and others take Sartre's subsequent pro-Marxist writings and stands as a fulfillment of this hypothesized radical conversion.[41] But it is by no means evident from the text of this note that the projected conversion was to be one in Sartre's own outlook. Equally plausible is the thought that the radical conversion requisite to an ethics of deliverance and salvation must occur either in human relations generally or in the prevailing attitude of would-be deliverers and saviors. In the latter case, what would be involved is not Sartre's radical conversion to political radicalism but political radicalism's radical conversion to Sartrean philosophy. The latter possibility is more consistent with Being and Nothingness's consistently self-assured tone. However aware Sartre may have been of the work's partiality, he voices not a doubt in it about the fundamental correctness of its assertions. It may be worth noting that there are two notes in Being and Nothingness which defer discussion of important topics, this one and the note at the end of the "Bad Faith" chapter concerning authenticity. It seems as reasonable to assume that the two deferred discussions would reflect upon and amplify each other as that "pure ontology and phenomenology [would] recede before the invasion of real history, the dispute with Marxism, and the adoption of the dialectic."[42] We return, then, to authenticity and the radical escape from bad faith.

While there is no systematic discussion of authenticity, the critique of bad faith permits us to anticipate something of its character. As the examples of bad faith displayed certain vices, so the overcoming of bad faith suggests corresponding virtues. The lamenting of the kind of social manipulation that

27

stifles nonsalable talents implies the desirability of
developing those talents, and perhaps too of rendering
to each the opportunity to mind his own business, at
least insofar as this may permit him to "dream."[43]
The criticism of personal indecision and of the determined adherence to uncertain truths suggests the pref-
erability of knowing one's own mind on the basis of an
unremitting mental rapacity, especially concerning the
constitution of mind itself, or man's fundamental cos-
mic situation. This, and the reviling of personal and
institutional dishonesty, imply a premium on a stark
introspective honesty. And the demonstration of how
the ordinary notions of courage and cowardice imply
each other points to an alternative notion of courage
which involves the apprehension of oneself in anguish.
What Sartre seems implicitly to laud and to prescribe
are his own versions of courage and justice, an existential honesty which may in the end displace traditional wisdom, and a marked immoderation in matters
intellectual and perhaps also moral.

## VIII

How is all this to come about? Sartre refers the
recovery of anguish, abandonment, and the sense of
responsibility that one feels for sustaining the world
and oneself, as a way of being-in-the-world, to what
he calls "moments of conversion," moments of "an abrupt
metamorphosis of my initial project."[44] These are

> extraordinary and marvellous instants when
> the prior project collapses into the past in
> the light of a new project which rises on
> its ruins and which as yet exists only in
> outline, in which humiliation, anguish, joy,
> hope are delicately blended, in which we let
> go in order to grasp and grasp in order to
> let go.[45]

It is important to note that such moments are not
acts of will. For the will operates only within the
horizon of an original project. Thus, the will "can
reach only details of structure and will never modify
the original project from which it has issued any more
than the consequences of a theorem can turn back
against it and change it."[46] But if conversion is not
an act of will, neither is it simply something which
comes from without to a passive consciousness. For
this would introduce into consciousness what for Sartre
is an impermissible determinism. Like bad faith, the

28

moment of conversion must be a spontaneous self-determination. Is its occurrence, then, simply a matter of chance? In principle, it seems that the answer must be, Yes. Conversion can, in principle, occur at any time, under any set of circumstances. But as a being-in-the-world, man will experience his conversions, like everything else, in relation to things in the world. I feel the temptation to suicide when on the precipice, or to gamble when at the gaming table.

Finally, we may ask, after the moment of conversion, after the recovery of being in anguish, abandonment, and responsibility, what then? If what follows is the immediate adoption of some new original project, such that our subsequent actions are comprehensible within the formulation, "I am an X," then we seem quickly to have fallen back to the level of bad faith. If, on the other hand, we remain suspended in radical self-doubt, immersed in the reflective apprehension of our freedom, then the plenary character of this thought would seem to foreclose the possibility of any further thought or concrete action. As a moment in a real human life, therefore, the moment of conversion turns out to be a strictly momentary moment; and the subsequent emancipated life, lived under the aegis of the glimpse of freedom obtained therein, to be "free" only equivocally. From a strictly ontological viewpoint, such a life will be neither more nor less free than one lived completely in bad faith. Yet practically, it does make sense to call such a converted life "different," to call it "changed" and "free," insofar as it subsumes the discovered insight concerning freedom into itself. What this seems to require is the unconscious, subconscious, or "pre-judicatively conscious" presence of a supervening knowledge, as a constitutive element in our everyday, unreflectively conscious life. In the end, we are again referred to the problem of the primacy of knowledge.

# NOTES

[1] Sartre distinguishes ontology from metaphysics, as inquiry into the What?, as opposed to the Why?, of Being. It may be the case that for Sartre the metaphysical question is in principle unanswerable. See Being and Nothingness, pp. 785-95; Desan, Chap. 9 ("The Conflict with Metaphysics").

[2] "Itinerary of a Thought," pp. 36, 37.

[3] The radicalization consists in the suppression of the concept of the transcendental ego, a position which Sartre had staked out in Transcendence of the Ego. See also Ronald Aronson, "Interpreting Husserl and Heidegger: The Roots of Sartre's Thought," Telos 13 (Fall 1972): 47.

[4] See, e.g., Desan, chap. 10 ("The Choice of Sartre, or Existential Subjectivism").

[5] Being and Nothingness, p. 76

[6] Ibid., p. 87. "Denying" could also be read "negating."

[7] Ibid., p. 85.

[8] Ibid., p. 87.

[9] Ibid., pp. 94, 95.

[10] The following summary attempts to encapsulate the argument of Being and Nothingness, pp. 3-30, 119-58, 238-98, 559-784.

[11] Being and Nothingness, p. 784.

[12] Ibid., p. 116.

[13] Ibid., p. 113. Emphasis in original.

[14] Ibid., pp. 107, 111.

[15] Ibid., p. 102. Emphasis in original.

[16] Ibid., pp. 86-87.

[17] Ibid., p. 102.

[18] Ibid., p. 97.

[19] Ibid., p. 113.

[20] Ibid., pp. 65, 68, 78.

[21] Ibid., p. 76. Emphasis in original.

[22] Ibid., p. 75.

[23] Ibid., p. 76.

[24] Ibid., p. 83.

[25] Ibid., p. 116.

[26] Sartre is not unaware of this problem, but he offers no coherent, principled solution. See Jean-Paul Sartre, L'Existentialisme est un humanisme (Paris: Editions Nagel, 1946), p. 100.

[27] Being and Nothingness, p. 24.

[28] Ibid., p. 76.

[29] Ibid., p. 69.

[30] Ibid., p. 77.

[31] Ibid., p. 114.

[32] Cf. Aristotle, Metaphysics, 980a22.

[33] Being and Nothingness, pp. 94, 95.

[34] Cf. Plato, Republic, 329d, 608d.

[35] Being and Nothingness, p. 75. Emphasis in original.

[36] Ibid., pp. 559-61, 575-79.

[37] I have preferred the translation of this passage which appears in Robert Denoon Cumming (ed.), The Philosophy of Jean-Paul Sartre (New York: Random House, Vintage Books, 1965), p. 129. Cf. Nietzsche, Thus Spoke Zarathustra, Part 3, Chap. 11.

[38]Herbert Marcuse, "Sartre's Existentialism," in Studies in Critical Philosophy, trans. Joris de Bres (Boston: Beacon Press, 1973), pp. 189, 186.

[39]Ibid., p. 189.

[40]Being and Nothingness, p. 534.

[41]Marcuse, p. 189.

[42]Ibid.

[43]Being and Nothingness, p. 102.

[44]Ibid., p. 598.

[45]Ibid., p. 612.

[46]Ibid.

## 3. THE FLIES: THE MYTH OF POLITICAL HEROISM

> The slenderest knowledge that may be obtained
> of the highest things is more desirable than
> the most certain knowledge of the basest.
>
> St. Thomas Aquinas, Summa Theologica, I.1.5.

### I. Preliminary Observations

"We were never more free than under the German
Occupation." So Sartre, with characteristic irony,
paid tribute to his countrymen following the Liberation. The French had been free because, in the face
of constant deprivation, oppression, and propaganda,
every act of resistance took on an added dimension of
meaning. "(E)ach accurate thought was a victory; . . .
each word became precious as a declaration of principle; . . . each gesture had the weight of a commitment." The possibility of torture and death pushed
each person's freedom to its limit, and the fact that
each résistant, by his secret knowledge, could doom
ten or a hundred comrades revealed this freedom as
"total responsibility in total solitude."[1]

The Occupation years may have been, again ironically, a time of extraordinary political freedom too.
For the political horizon was then open in a way that
it has not been since. The hated foreigner had to be
expelled, of course, and the collaborationist regime
swept aside. But what direction French politics
should then take, what principles should then guide it,
were questions which could be considered unencumbered
by the necessity for loyalty, or loyal opposition, to
a respectable regime containing an established configuration of political forces. While the Communists
might attempt to dominate the underground organization,
the Resistance belonged by right to all Frenchmen.
Because revolution was not the exclusive preserve of
any party, one could, for the time being, think truly
revolutionary thoughts. It was in this climate that
Sartre composed and helped to stage The Flies in the
spring of 1943.

While The Flies is Sartre's first published play,
it is not the first play he ever wrote and staged.[2] That
play was entitled Bariona, or the Son of Thunder,
and the circumstances surrounding its composition provide some instructive background to our investigation
of The Flies. Ostensibly a Christmas pageant, Sartre

33

wrote it while a prisoner of war in a German camp toward the end of 1940, to be performed by and for the benefit of his fellow prisoners. While the events of the Nativity provide the appropriate setting, the play's real concern is with an attempted revolt against the Roman occupation of Judea. The play's religious face gave it the respectability needed to pass the camp censors, but its more sincere message was reportedly not lost upon its prisoner audience. When he wrote The Flies, then, Sartre's past "career" as a playwright consisted of writing for one audience while writing around another.[3]

This biographical datum invites the thought that The Flies too is essentially a piece of wartime propaganda, an anti-Vichy tract put into the garb of classic drama--an updated version of the Oresteia--in order to pass the censors. This view receives support from Simone de Beauvoir's account that Sartre's original object in deciding to write a play in 1943 was "to remind [Frenchmen] of rebellion and freedom" through a plot both "technically unobjectionable and transparent in its implications."[4] Following the Liberation, Sartre himself made no secret of this facet of the play.[5] Then too, the internal evidence of The Flies' anti-Vichy character is considerable. Despite its classic setting, its dialogue is not at all in high classic style, but rather in colloquial, sometimes even vulgar, modern French. It contains a number of deliberate anachronisms which point its audience away from the mythical Greek setting. In Act 1, for instance, Orestes' tutor remarks with sneering surprise at the Argive houses' lack of conspicuous front windows, an absence not unusual in ancient Greek architecture. He refers "back" to the geographer Pausanias, who lived in the Second Century A.D. And the character Jupiter incants the names of post-classic deities (pp. 32:18-20; 40:4; 54:20; 74:20).[6] The play depicts demeaning scenes of public remorse and confession, which were, at the time of its production, the official policy of the Pétain administration. Most pointedly, perhaps, one of its characters is Jupiter, a Roman God[7] whose pervasive presence constitutes one of the chief props for the tyrannic regime that rules this Greek city. This particular piece of symbolism is unlikely to have been lost on any French viewer of The Flies in German-occupied France.[8]

But these unmistakable references to Vichy surely do not exhaust the meaning of these devices. Modern

34

language and anachronism direct our attention to modern times generally as well as to the particular year of the play's production. And public confession is, as we know, not exclusive to any single tyranny. Perhaps in tacit recognition of this consideration, Sartre did not neglect The Flies in subsequent years. He commented favorably on its 1948 performance in Berlin, where it was condemned by the journals under Russian license; attended its Polish opening in 1957; and was present at its premier in Czechoslovakia late in 1968. But there is also something peculiar about its substantive condemnation of tyranny. All of the obviously anti-Vichy barbs, for instance, occur in the first half of the play. Thereafter, there is a partial retraction of the tyranny's alleged oppressiveness, and even the tyrant himself emerges in a more sympathetic light. Orestes' victory turns out in the end to be not chiefly his overthrow of Aegisthus, but of Jupiter, who for his part becomes less the patron of a particular tyrant than a spokesman for a principle of rule justified by a version of Platonic-Christian theology. Insofar as Orestes' example aims at galvanizing Frenchmen into joining the Resistance, it does so on grounds both broader than and somewhat removed from those of the typical résistant.

Judged practically as a piece of anti-Vichy propaganda, moreover, The Flies may have to be regarded as a failure. Simone de Beauvoir tells of its immediate reception:

> How tense I was when the curtain went up! It was impossible to mistake the play's implications; the word Liberty, dropped from Orestes' mouth, burst on us like a bomb. The German critic of Pariser Zeitung saw this very clearly, and said so. . . . Michel Leiris praised The Flies in a clandestine edition of Les Lettres françaises, and emphasized its political significance. Most reviewers pretended not to have noticed any such allusion; they pitched into the play viciously, but, so they alleged, on purely literary grounds: it was an unsuccessful imitation of Giraudoux, it was wordy, obscure, and plain dull. . . . [T]hey damned the production, the sets, and the costumes The public did not flock to see The Flies.[10]

The Flies, then, was subjected to a kind of censorless censorship. The hostile critics short-circuited its potential political impact by ignoring its content while focusing upon stylistic considerations, a ploy that could succeed only within a general aesthetic climate that emphasized style over content. (It was perhaps the bitter memory of this conspiracy of silence that fed Sartre's later attack on stylistic orientation, and his call for a literature of engagement and a literary criticism concerned primarily with content.)[11]

While many of Sartre's plays are about politics, The Flies may be his most political play. Its plot revolves around a political act of the most fundamental order--an act of tyrannicide, followed by a change of regime. Interestingly, however, despite its vivid depiction of the substance of tyranny, the word "tyranny" or its derivatives never occur in the play. While this may indicate no more than that tyranny, where it exists, is never called by its proper name, the play does include a thematic discussion of the activity of ruling. The conjunction of these two facts, and the gloomy content of that discussion, raise the question, whether ruling as such might not be, in Sartre's estimation, essentially tyrannical. This, at any rate, appears to be the play's overt political teaching, a teaching surely apt to give it a certain respectability in the eyes of individualistic and anarchistically inclined intellectuals. But this anarchistic interpretation fails to account for a manifest project of political founding in Orestes' speech to the Argives at the play's conclusion. The anarchic implications of the critique of ruling may thus be only provisional. Alternatively, if that critique does represent Sartre's final political truth, then Orestes' positive political dispensation must be explained in relation to it.

A more promising suggestion about the play's meaning has been made by Walter Kaufmann, who is struck by the presence in The Flies of themes and references taken from Nietzsche. Kaufmann cites several passages to evidence the wholesale borrowing both of general ideas and of particular phrases from perhaps as many as eight of Nietzsche's books.[12] But having amassed this evidence, Kaufmann proceeds to take it nowhere. He notes that this Nietzscheanism renders The Flies unique within the Sartrean corpus:

36

. . . The Flies is at variance not only with
the Marxist philosophy of Sartre in his fif-
ties, less than twenty years after he wrote
this play, but also with the philosophy of
the famous lecture, "Existentialism is a Humanism," delivered in 1946, only three years
after The Flies. . . . Nor do we find the
ethic of The Flies in Being and Nothingness
. . . or No Exit . . . which were finished
the same year. We find it only in The Flies
and in the writings of Nietzsche.[13]

In order to resolve this anomaly, he offers a psycho-
logistic conjecture:

In keeping with Socrates' ancient charge
against the poets, Sartre, when he wrote The
Flies, perhaps did not fully know what he was
doing; his inspiration may have been partly
unconscious, as he projected images and im-
pressions received when reading Nietzsche.[14]

As an explanation this is highly unsatisfying.
Apart from our general suspicion of easy recourse to
the unconscious to explain whatever is puzzling in a
philosopher's writings, Kaufmann's own evidence is
simply too strong for it here. The Flies' Nietzscheanism is not, by Kaufmann's own account, a matter of
a few chance phrases. Rather, it goes to the very
substance of the play's teaching. Even granting a subconscious influence in this case, we are left to marvel
at why an influence so pervasive and emphatic here
would fade so quickly and completely in Sartre's other
writings. Rather, Kaufmann's impressive observations
suggest that we look again at these other writings,
reading them in the light of this supposed peculiarity
of The Flies. In the case of Being and Nothingness
we may note, following Marcuse, that work's attack on
the esprit de sérieux, which echoes Part 3, chapter 11,
of Zarathustra, and Sartre's allusion, at the start
of the "Bad Faith" chapter, to the negative behavior
of ressentiment.[15] Although Sartre mentions Nietzsche
by name only twice in that work,[16] this relative
silence is not conclusive. Sartre is not always quick
to acknowledge his indebtedness to other thinkers; and
the intellectual climate of 1943, within which Nietzsche's name, perhaps even more than Heidegger's, was
associated with Nazism, would have made any such explicit acknowledgement somewhat indiscreet. In Sartre's
later works, he does indeed turn toward other dominant

influences. But we shall attempt, in the sequel chapters, to trace the sometimes waxing-sometimes waning continuity of The Flies' central theme which Kaufmann so convincingly associates with Nietzsche.

The substance of this Nietzscheanism, as Kaufmann develops it, may be reduced to five focal issues: (1) the opposition of "my way" to "the way," that is, the emphatic assertion of man as his own giver of fundamental values; (2) the importance of having the courage of one's acts, and therewith an attack on the spirit of remorse and revenge; (3) the project of taking upon oneself a people's guilt, but not punishment, as the proper project of a hero, even of a god; (4) a peculiarly naturalistic and anti-Christian view of death; and (5) the teaching that loneliness and despair are indispensable preconditions to a truly human life. But The Flies departs from Nietzsche in at least three major respects: First, Sartre seems to present these teachings as parcel to a democratic political project. While Zarathustra speaks of "the way of the creator" as proper to the distinguished few, Orestes proclaims[17] "[E]very man must invent his [own] way" (p. 105:29). And he appears to facilitate this teaching at the play's end by abdicating the Argive throne, leaving the citizens in what may be described as a pre-civil state of natural equality, to fashion their future institutions collectively. Secondly, Orestes for the most part lacks Zarathustra's evident joyousness.[18] The character who most conspicuously urges and expresses joy is Electra, and she later discredits herself through her repentance. And thirdly, relatedly, Orestes does not teach eternal recurrence. Rather, it is Electra who thinks of herself as a destiny. She dreams of the dual assassination for fifteen years before it is actually carried out, and it is the departure of events from her recurrently preconstructed scenario that first sours her on their act. Her unwillingness to face an open future, Clytemnestra's fatalism about the recurrence of character types, and Jupiter's eternal condemnation forever to perform the same slow and somber dance before men suggest a rejection of recurrence as a mythic archetype for human life (pp. 70:8-10; 71:23-24; 89:21-22; 90:2-7; 50:8-11; 52:12-25; 53:7-8; 86:36-37; 87:6-7). Orestes does, however, preserve a kind of amor fati by embracing his act as the eternal substantiation of his being (p. 91:21-34). Sartre thus adopts Nietzschean themes selectively and with significant modifications.

Should The Flies have been entitled Orestes?
Manifestly, the play depicts Orestes' crucial development and actions. Except for a brief section at the
beginning of Act 2, he is always onstage, a ubiquity
not approached by any other character. The title,
however, points elsewhere, to the situation of Argos,
and invites us to consider the play's action as it
affects the city. The flies are the Furies, the goddesses of remorse. As flies they appropriately sym-
bolize the Argives' guilt, which dwells upon their
failures and depravities as flies feasting upon carrion. Even at the play's end, this guilt is still an
available possibility, and Orestes' act is, from the
city's perspective, still an open question. The
Argives could keep the flies, or bring them back, by
taking Electra, who after Orestes' abdication could
make a legitimate claim to the throne, as their new
ruler. The play's title, then, indicates the imma-
nence of guilt, and its attendant ethical-political
structures, as a human possiblity.

The title is also, as Kaufmann notes, reminiscent
of Nietzsche's "flies of the marketplace."[19]   But
while Zarathustra exhorts his listener to flee from
the public realm and into his solitude, The Flies
is manifestly the story of Orestes' engagement in the
political liberation of Argos. But it also presents
his journey through this political engagement, from
one "exile" to another (pp. 42:15; 105:15, 16). His
relation to the city is, to say the least, equivocal.
At the play's end he is more alone than ever, more
alone even than Zarathustra, who still enjoys the
company of his animals. Sartre emphasizes this solitude, in a departure from the ancient versions of the
Oresteia, by not including a Pylades among the dramatis
personae. Sartre's Orestes is uniquely friendless,
and his one hope of friendship, with Electra, fails
disastrously.[20]   Despite his temporary detour from
Zarathustra's teaching, in the end he returns to it
all the more forcefully.

Besides Nietzsche, the title recalls the plague
of flies in Exodus, especially since the play's
imagery also invokes other of the Egyptian plagues.
The face of the statue of Jupiter is "splotched with
blood." Jupiter predicts in Act 1 that in another
fifteen years the flies "will have attained the size
of small frogs," and he compares the old townswomen
to lice. Orestes observes that Clytemnestra's face
looks as though it had been ravaged by hail. After

the assassination, the flies blacken the walls of the
throne room, and slip between the lamps and Electra's
eyes, casting her into darkness.  In Act 3, the Furies
threaten to keep her always in darkness by amassing
themselves between the sun and her "like a cloud of
locusts."  And at the very end, Orestes' Pied Piper
myth implicitly invokes the idea of the slaying, or
at least the removing, of the young (pp. 31:s.d.;
34:8-9; 36:6; 50:15-16; 92:4-6; 97:32-33; 111:8-20).
But there is a crucial difference between this last
plague and the others.  The others all proceed from,
or signify the power of, Jupiter; this one proceeds
from Orestes.  His detour through the city permits
him in the end to rival the God's power.  The Flies,
then, depicts not only a city's political liberation,
but a man's apotheosis.

The play is set in a succession of more or less
public places:  a public square, the outdoor site of
a religious ceremony, the throne room of the royal
palace, a temple.  But we quickly learn that the public places have been corrupted:  The streets are
deserted; the houses lack readily visible windows;
the square and throne room are dominated by the hide-
ous statues of Jupiter (pp. 32:8, 18-20; 31:s.d.;
78:s.d.).  Argos displays not only guilt but also the
degeneration of sociality.  The first half of the play
occurs outdoors, the second half indoors.  At the very
end, with the opening of the door of the temple of
Apollo, the outdoor invades the indoor through the
agency of the sun, which has been transformed from the
source of grueling heat to that of bright light
(pp. 32:9-10; 109:32).  The transformation of the open
realm requires an adventure which occurs within en-
closures, a movement through interiority.

While The Flies is a dramatic unity, whose major
themes are interwoven throughout, its plot is largely
episodic.  Act 1 introduces us to Orestes, to the city,
and to all the major characters except Aegisthus.  It
focuses on the contrast between the Argives' peculiar
possession and Orestes' peculiar dispossession.  Act 2
is divided into two tableaux, which focus alternately
on the external and internal facets of politics and
heroism.  It is in the context of Argive politics that
we first see Aegisthus, whose person is fundamentally
assimilated into his public function.  The referred-
to outer facet of politics is Aegisthus' public display
of rulership over the Argives, and its inner the substance of his private dialogue with Jupiter.  For

40

heroism this order is reversed.  Its inner facet is
Orestes' conversion, the play's central event; and
its outer his political act, the dual assassination of
Aegisthus and Clytemnestra.  The third Act focuses upon
Electra's inauthenticity and the confrontation between
Orestes and Jupiter.  Orestes' speech to the Argives
at the play's end returns us to the political, but in
a way that is crucially informed by these preceding
episodes.

## II.  Act I

### Orestes and Argos

The Flies begins, reminiscent of Aeschylus, with
a procession of Argive women, dressed in black, offering libations (p. 31:s.d.).[21]  Unlike Aeschylus' libation bearers, however, these women are all old, Electra
is not among them, and their libations are not to
Agamemnon's ghost but to the statue of Jupiter which
dominates the public square.  This statue presents a
terrible aspect, its face smeared with blood, its large
white eyes gazing down in an unseeing stare.  Recalling
the elaborate discussion of "the Other's look" in Being
and Nothingness, we may say that the statue seems con-
trived to produce in its worshippers the feeling of
being looked at, objectified, fixed in their finitude,
guilty.[22]  This devout libation of the old women contrasts with the young Electra's irreverent "libation"
in the third scene.  As Electra then declares, the old
are dear to Jupiter because they resemble the dead, a
resemblance evident not only in physical appearance
but also in their stagnant political attitude.  The
old Argives, especially the old women, are Aegisthus'
most loyal subjects.  Ironically, they are in this
respect less antiquarian than Electra, who reveres the
memory of Agamemnon (pp. 44:10-45:12).

When Orestes enters with his tutor, he startles
the women with his first words, "Hey, good women!"
(p. 31:1-3).  The greeting is significant both for
its mild display of Orestes' irreverence and for its
literal irony.  For these women are of doubtful goodness, as their hostile reaction to the strangers indicates, nor are they especially womanly.  Despite the
tutor's attempt to address an inquiry to them with a
bit more grace than his master, the women spit in the
travellers' direction and run away, leaving their
religious offering unfinished.  The play's opening
vignette depicts not only the Argives' xenophobia,

but also the disruption of an act of piety, a minor prefiguration of Orestes' major feat, the overthrow of Jupiter.

The tutor launches into a tirade against Argos, which reveals that their coming there was at Orestes' insistence. He compares Argos unfavorably to "more than five hundred capitals, as many in Greece as in Italy, with good wine, hospitable inns, and crowded streets" (p. 32:1-3). The tutor is a man who values the comforts of simple material pleasures and the easy-going sociality of friendly crowds. He has no particular national loyalty -- Greece and Italy are equal at offering the mentioned comforts. He has been unable to obtain directions because of the Argives' fear of strangers, the emptiness of the streets, and the city's oppressive climate. His complaint makes no distinction between the city and nature--all things should serve human convenience. The sun is even the worst offender (p. 32:9-10). While the tutor will reveal himself more fully after Jupiter's first appearance, these opening remarks provide a glimpse into Orestes' intellectual background. The tutor is the modern man par excellence. Not bound by the conventions of any particular city, he places no value on citizen virtue. His vision of human possibilities, while perhaps as broad as the world, aims no higher than comfortable self-preservation and the titillation that comes of observing human variety. Despite Orestes' revulsion toward this "smiling skepticism" (p. 40:15-16), he is nonetheless very much informed by it. Orestes is an intellectual, and as such he can bring to bear upon the Argive situation a detached perspective, born of the tutor's cosmopolitanism, which no Argive can provide. The City's liberation requires the intrusion of this outside element.

For the time being, Orestes merely answers distractedly, "I was born here. . . ." The tutor's response is a non-committal "It appears" (p. 32:11-12). We learn later that the tutor had himself revealed the circumstances of Orestes' origins to him only a few months earlier (p. 43:18-19). He here seems to hedge on this revelation. Particular origins are unimportant to the tutor. But there may be an additional reason for his reticence. The travellers have just come from Delphi, apparently in great haste (pp. 33: 20-24; 34:13-14). Had Orestes received an indication from the oracle concerning his right as heir to the Argive throne, it would be consistent with the tutor's expressed outlook to attempt to undermine its significance by debunking the reliability of oracles as such. As a second line of attack, he might also wish to cast doubt upon its supposed factual premise, that Orestes is that heir.

The tutor makes two further attempts to solicit the information they desire, both unsuccessful. One is to an unseen person behind a door, who slams it in his face before he can complete his question. The other is to an idiot, who is incapable of answering. It is only on this third try that we learn that he is looking for "King Aegisthus' house" (p. 33:1-2, 4).[23]

At this point, Jupiter, apparently trying to catch their attention, passes across the stage several times. The tutor recognizes him as the remarkably bronze-bearded traveller who seems suspiciously to have followed them step by step from Delphi. For the first time, the tutor notices the flies, which had been absent from his earlier catalogue of complaints (p. 33: 25-27; cf. p. 32:6-10). Possibly Jupiter has just brought them onto the scene, as an excuse for conversing with Orestes, upon whom they fall as though recognizing him. When the tutor comments on their noisiness and size, Jupiter injects himself into the scientific observations by telling of their origin. They were attracted to Argos fifteen years earlier, that is, at the time of Agememnon's assassination, by "a powerful odor of carrion" (p. 34:6-7), and have been growing fatter ever since. He predicts their continued growth for another fifteen years. After an uneasy pause, the tutor asks the stranger his name, and Jupiter identifies himself as Demetrios of Athens. The implicit reference to Demeter, Goddess of growth, underscores the perverse nourishment in which the God has just expressed thinly concealed glee. More seriously, it answers the tutor's complaint about the sun by pointing to the Gods', or nature's, indifference to man's well-being. The prosperity of flies is as precious to nature as that of man.

Cries arising from the palace, signalling the start of the festival of the dead, provide Jupiter, in this guise of a frequent visitor to Argos, with the occasion to lecture Orestes on the city's history and political character. His lengthy remarks consist of a description of Agamemnon's assassination, an interrogation of one of the old townswomen, and an exhortation to a hypothetical Orestes not to disturb the city's order.

The account of Agamemnon's death emphasizes the conspiratorial atmosphere that pervaded the city; and the citizens' quiet, even perversely pleasurable, complicity in the assassination. It evokes, as it seems geared to do, Orestes' anger and disgust. It also contains a Jovian political teaching. Agamemnon's great mistake was to prohibit public executions, to deny the people the occasional violent spectacle that distracts them from their own deaths and **relieves their** provincial boredom. Aegisthus, by implication, is a better ruler because he promotes ceremonies of distraction, in which each citizen can revel in his neighbor's misery. From an anti-Jovian viewpoint, then, the Argive death cult is blamable not because it fosters consciousness of death, but because it diverts attention from, and fosters an incomplete consciousness of, one's own death, a consciousness the full implications of which are kept hidden by the false solace of others' suffering.[24]

Jupiter's rude and imperious questioning of the townswoman, whom he displays as a kind of animal specimen, ostensibly aims at vindicating the Gods' justice by showing how they have turned the Argive tumult "to the profit of the moral order" (p. 35:34). This curious appeal to piety becomes obscured by another, implicit, intention, that of emphasizing to Orestes the Argives' ignobility. Responding to Jupiter's prodding, the old woman protests her powerlessness to have prevented Agamemnon's murder. She merely locked her door and relished the king's cries. But, she assures him, she and her whole family are now constantly repenting. Even her six-year-old grandson is "penetrated by the sentiment of his original sin" (p. 37:11-12). After letting the woman go, Jupiter remarks favorably on her "good, old-fashioned piety, solidly based on terror"(p. 37:16-17). Her use of the term "original sin" indicates the relevant nonpagan thrust of his caricature. Our prior observations about the guilt-inducing quality of the statue apply in principle more powerfully to an invisible God who knows and sees all, and Himself remains mysterious and inaccessible.

The exhortation, a speech which Jupiter says he would make to Orestes were he by chance to appear at the city's gates, combines these two appeals to nobility and piety with several others. The appeal to

44

nobility is implicit in his contrast between Orestes'
strength and vitality, which would fit him to be a
captain of a good fighting army, and Argos' deathly
character; and in his characterization of the Argives
as great sinners. Orestes would not be able to share
in their "grievous enterprise" of repentance, which
he should respect, "for you have not had a part in
their crime, and your impertinent innocence separates
you from them like a deep abyss." The appeal to piety
lies both in the mentioned call for respect and in the
emphatic assertion that "fear [and] bad conscience have
a delectable scent in the Gods' nostrils. . . . Would
you wish to deprive (these pitiable souls) of divine
favor?" And what could Orestes offer them? Merely
the mediocrity, peace, and boredom of provincial life.
There are, moreover, risks in disturbing the unstable
order of a city and of souls--"If you touch them, you
will provoke a catastrophe. . . . A terrible catastrophe that will fall back upon you" (pp. 39:11, 13-14,
20-22, 27-29).

Orestes is about to respond to these arguments when
the tutor admonishingly clears his throat. Orestes
prudently terminates the conversation with the avowal
that Argos "doesn't concern me" (p. 39:34). But, we may
note, there are tensions among Jupiter's various appeals
which provide a basis for rejecting his warning. The
very fortitude which Jupiter mentions at the beginning
may permit Orestes to brave the consequences alluded to
at the end. And if he is brave in the deepest sense,
perhaps nothing short of confronting the Gods themselves will suffice. The tension between the depravity
of Argos and the mediocrity of other provincial places
might induce him to seek a third alternative rather than
a reversion to Agamemnon's "little provincial city which
was indolently bored under the sun" (p. 34:30-31).
Likewise, the implied dignity of the Argives' "grievous
enterprise" runs afoul their characterization as fearful and full of bad conscience. Yet the human necessity
that their activities have a dignity may point the way
out of their plight. Perhaps only enterprising qual-
ities--courage; resolution; self-awareness; candor;
most of all, not seeking to please the Gods--can produce a genuine enterprise. Again, each of the experi-
ential arguments is true in itself: Orestes cannot
share in the Argives' repentance, at least not while
he remains "innocent." Nor can the Argives escape the
weight of their past deeds. But these limitations
merely condition rather than foreclose any future
action. Orestes might establish a bond with the Argives

45

through some new act, and the Argives might accept
their past rather than seek to escape it.  In the final
analysis, it is perhaps Jupiter's central, conditional
appeal--"Go away if you love them" (p. 39:15)--which
is crucial.  Orestes need not love the Argives.  Nor
have they revealed themselves as especially lovable.
It was perhaps in quest of even one lovable person in
Argos that he had asked Jupiter what Agamemnon's daughter, Electra, thinks of "all this."  But Jupiter had
quickly dismissed Electra as "a child," and Orestes had
let the matter pass (p. 38:17-19).[25]  Ironically, he
does eventually follow this exhortation to go away, but
only after working through the other Jovian arguments'
contradictions.

Throughout this encounter, Jupiter has attempted
to make Orestes feel that all divine power was against
his proceeding further in any political project.  Reflecting on the change which the past fifteen years has
wrought in the Argive temperament, he had, in an apparent slip of the tongue, pronounced them dear to "my
heart."  And when Orestes had asked incredulously
whether the Argives' scene of blood, flies, and terror
could possibly be pleasing to "Jupiter," he had replied
expansively that "the Gods" have grievous secrets.
Now, before leaving the scene, he emphasizes the extraordinary forces against which a heroic Orestes would be
pitted by giving a "parlor trick" display of a magical
charm for ridding oneself of flies.  Orestes, duly
impressed, exclaims, with unconscious irony, "By
Jupiter!"  (pp. 37:33-34, 38:4-11; 40:4-8).

Jupiter's departure shifts the horizon to the
human realm.  The tutor warns, "That man knows who you
are."  And when Orestes wonders aloud whether the stranger is indeed a man, he responds heatedly that there
are only men, and conjectures that "[t]hat bearded one"
is one of Aegisthus' spies (p. 40:11-12, 18).  The
tutor cannot admit the possibility of the divine.  An
earthly explanation, no matter how intricate, must be
supplied for all phenomena.  For if Jupiter were indeed
a spy for Aegisthus, the spy network would have to
extend as far as Delphi and include fly-charming in its
repertoire.  Orestes' eventual commitment must be
understood as standing upon and turning against the
tutor's self-assured rationalism, with its materialism,
cultural relativism, and idealization of detachment.
His ten-year tutelage has provided Orestes with book-
learning and archeological sight-seeing; but the pal-
aces, sanctuaries, and temples have been presented

46

apart from the ideas of the political and the sacred
which they presuppose. Indeed, the extensiveness of
these readings and travels was designed to debunk any
such higher ideational content, "to familiarize you
with the diversity of human opinions, . . . showing
you again in each circumstance how there is nothing
so variable as human manners" (p. 41:28-31). The end
of this training is the tutor's notion of a free man:

> . . . young, rich, and handsome, wary as an
> old man, freed from all servitudes, and all
> beliefs, without family, without fatherland,
> without religion, without trade, free from
> all engagements and knowing that one must
> never engage oneself, a superior man finally,
> capable to boot of teaching philosophy or
> architecture in a large university city
> (p. 41:32-38).[26]

From this description, Orestes should have not only an
old man's way of thinking, but also the uselessness of
one who stands at the end of life, or of history, who
can only look back at a chronicle of folly. If the
"philosophy" which he could teach is akin to the architecture which stands on a par with it, it would rather
be philosophies or intellectual history. His lifetime
study of men in their diversity culminates in the rejection of man in his unity as a subject of serious
contemplation.

As with Jupiter's speech, the tutor's view contains a contradiction which points Orestes beyond it.
For the detachment of the scholarly life at which his
tutelage aims markedly contrasts with the loving, even
religious, description of its execution. What gives
the tutor's teaching vitality for him is the fact that
it is his, "the fruits of my wisdom and the treasures
of my experience" (p. 41:26-27). Flowering into a
doctrine of non-engagement, its root is an intense
personal engagement. For Orestes, however, who receives it at second hand, the wisdom of relativism
itself partakes of the drab status of the multiplicity
of curiosities which it scrutinizes. Orestes' disgust
at the tutor's critique of the commonly valued things
of the world--a disgust which does not deny its truth--
displays the plight of the post-relativist generation,
or century, for whom the truths of relativism have
become a commonplace, unexciting and therewith ener-
vating.

But there is another side to the manifold manners
of mankind, a side of which the tutor does not take
note, namely, the universality of manners of some kind
or other.  Thus, Orestes longs for the sense of comfort
and of purpose that emerges within particular horizons.
He expresses a romantic envy for those men "who are
born engaged," whose lives are predetermined; or those
whose hearts are weighted down with "disturbing and
earthly images" because of some unnamed childhood event,
apparently the first reflection upon their situation.
He muses elliptically that "their life was changed
because, one day, in their childhood, at five, at
seven . . ." (p. 42:6, 12-14).  Orestes already knew,
when he was seven, that he was "exiled," de trop;
that the sights, sounds, and odors around him "belonged
to others"; that he deserved no memories of his own
(p. 42:15-19).[27]  He implies that those who are fully
situated, "who possess houses, beasts, servants, and
fields" (p. 42:20-22), are fit to have this reward.
But recalling the old woman's grandson, "who is going
on seven . . . and already penetrated by the sentiment
of his original sin" (p. 37:9-12), we may see the flaw
in this implication.  For that boy might well stand to
have these things, and yet he experiences himself as
guilt and repentance, as de trop in another way.  The
Argive situation is akin to Orestes' in a way of which
he is as yet unaware.

For the time being, though, Orestes dwells upon
the more palpable distance between himself and Argos.
Looking at the palace door before him, he constructs a
set of scenarios from his would-be childhood as prince
of Argos:  as a young child, pushing vainly against its
heavy portals; as an adolescent, sneaking through it by
night to seek girls; at his majority, crossing its
threshold on horseback.  But upon closer observation,
the door assumes the academic quality of any of a number of the architectural relics which he and the tutor
have studied all over Greece.  The door, the palace,
the city, he concludes, are not really his.

On this basis he resolves to leave Argos.  The
much-relieved tutor admits the fear which he had har-
bored, that Orestes would attempt to expel Aegisthus
and take his place.  Orestes admits the desire to
"tear him off my father's throne" (p. 43:31), but
rejects the thought because he does not share enough
memories with the Argives to rule them.  Deposition
and rule are, for him, linked, and his presumed in-
ability to perform the latter acts as a veto on the

48

former.  Dynastic concern, and perhaps the oracle too,
take second place to a more general political reason.
He attributes that reason, that "a king must have the
same memories as his subjects," to "the bearded one."
But Jupiter has himself cast doubt on this supposed
necessity by conjecturing that Aegisthus does not
repent, that is, that he and his subjects remember
Agamemnon's assassination in fundamentally different
ways.  Orestes, for his part, reveals the fragility of
this supposed need for a common history through his
unfinished thought, that if he could but gain a share
in their memories, terrors, and hopes by a single act,
even "if I had to kill my own mother. . . ."  Again,
he envisions a familial act, matricide, as parcel to
a political project, gaining the "right to the city."
But he abandons this line of thought as "dreams," and
announces plans to go to Sparta, where he has friends
(pp. 43:35-36; 37:22-24; 44:5, 2, 7).

## Electra and Clytemnestra

Electra now enters the scene to offer her "libation" to Jupiter.  Her speech to the statue and her
actions before it contradict the entire aspect that
Argos has turned toward Orestes, and which has informed
his judgment that he has nothing in common with any of
the Argives.  Her opening word, "Garbage!" carries the
weight of a three-fold denial (p. 44:11).  The idol to
which it is addressed is garbage, "white wood" which
could better be used as kindling, its sanguinary dec-
oration "raspberry juice" (pp. 45:7, 12; 44:12).  As
waste matter it is not frightening, merely repulsive.
Insofar as she endows it with life, it is to attribute
to it a perverse attraction to the old women in their
decay.  Appropriately, she brings it garbage.  And
her invective, coming on the heels of Orestes' stated
departure plan, indicts him.  He too would be "garbage," wasted matter, were he to reject Argos.  If not
a direct contradiction of Orestes' emphasis on common
memories, her remarks and her example at least point
away from the importance of the past.  Her construction
of a scenario, in which her proud, swaggering hero
comes "with his great sword," splits the idol in two,
and reveals it for what it is, rather anticipates a
future (p. 45:2).

Seeing Orestes for the first time, Electra is
startled, but when she learns that he is a foreigner
she welcomes him.  His earlier intrusion on an act of
piety had engendered hostility.  His current appearance

49

during an act of blasphemy is followed by benevolence
and conversation. He identifies himself by his alias,
Philebus of Corinth. When she tells him her name, he
orders the tutor away. Just as Jupiter's departure
was necessary for the exchange between Orestes and the
tutor, so the tutor's exclusion is necessary for that
between Orestes and Electra. The horizon of discourse,
having already shifted from the divine to the cosmo-
politan human, now shifts to the particular. Electra,
though unlike the other Argives, is very much of Argos.
Her defiance is conditioned by it, and thereupon largely
hinges its frailty.

The ensuing conversation reveals much of Electra's
charm, her character, and her limitations. Orestes,
fascinated at the sight of his long-lost sister,
praises her evident beauty. This surprises her. She
is unused to being called beautiful, and hence unused
to thinking of herself as such. She proceeds to complain of her drudgeries as servant to the royal couple.
Her account is personal, even intimate, showing a
fascination with the erotic. When she does the couple's
laundry, she imagines the king "shar[ing] his couch"
with Clytemnestra. She describes Clytemnestra primarily
in her physical aspect, as a tall, stout woman, with
dyed hair, honey-scented white hands, and fat, warm,
"greedy" lips; and only secondarily as her mother
(p. 46:6, 35). Yet the maternal influence is strong
enough to shape her self-image: "I am an infection,
a plague: the people here will tell you so. I have
no friends. . . . Ask my mother. I would discourage
the tenderest hearts" (p. 47:4-5, 8-9).[28] She claims
to have been beaten, but the event which she describes
as most objectionable, Clytemnestra's good-night kiss,
is at least an outward show of parental affection.
She is naively calculating. Having first ascertained
that Orestes will not denounce her for her sacrilege,
she boldly invites him to do so. On the basis of her
friendlessness, she calculates that she is too weak to
run away. But the unpleasantness of her life in Argos
induces her to calculate an end to it through the outside agency of her hero, the idol-smashing Orestes.
Orestes, for his part, takes her answers at face value,
and grows doubtful about leaving Argos. Her descriptions, her deportment, her "dishpan hands" (p. 46:7-
13) all provide what he had lacked--a real Argive to
whose concrete existence he may be a witness, who
apparently does not share the Argive temperament.

Electra now interrogates "Philebus" on Corinth.

She asks whether it is a beautiful city, whether he is proud of it, and then what it means to be proud of one's native city. Orestes mechanically answers the first two questions, but cannot provide the lesson in politics requested by the third. As the tutor has noted, Orestes is "without fatherland." While he has some conception of what rulership requires, his thoughts have not penetrated to the substance of citizenship. Electra therefore returns to the line suggested by her first question, the things that make a city beautiful. She asks about things that she would find personally pleasant: Are there shaded places in Corinth where everyone, boys and girls together, go walking in the evening, talking and laughing until late at night? Orestes again answers mechanically, letting Electra construct Corinth for him. These pleasantries are foreign to him too. But there is a serious intent to her questions. She seeks some point of reference from which to judge Argos, herself, and especially her hope. She explains that the Argives are devoured by fear, and she by hate. And she expresses her hope through her conception of Orestes' situation:

> . . . suppose a Corinthian youth, one of those youths who laugh in the evening with the girls, finds, upon returning from a journey, his father assassinated, his mother in the murderer's bed, and his sister in slavery; would he slink away, the Corinthian youth, would he back away, bowing, to seek consolation in the company of his girl friends? or rather would he draw his sword and split the assassin's head? (p. 48:24-31).

Orestes again professes ignorance. He of course recognizes his own situation, but he is aware of certain crucial differences. He does not laugh in the evening with girls; apparently he has never had anything to do with girls (cf. pp. 42:30-31; 107:7-8). He is not merely returning from a journey, but is a life-long exile, sneaking into his natal city pseudonymously. He has no memory of his assassinated father, nor of his adulterous mother. His sister is as yet only a recent acquaintance, and her condition is not obviously one of slavery. Electra's fictitious example premises an immediacy which the Argive royal family's situation lacks for Orestes. Most importantly, her example abstracts from the political. Orestes is not simply the son of a cuckolded and murd-

51

ered father. He is the heir to a murdered king whose
assassin occupies the royal throne. The act to be
contemplated is for him not fundamentally one of familial revenge but of political succession, and this he
has already ruled out. The situation of a moment
earlier is reversed. It is now Orestes' political a-
wareness, rather than his political ignorance, that
keeps him from answering Electra. Further questioning,
however, is foreclosed by Clytemnestra's entrance.

Clytemnestra is decidedly repulsive, an embodiment
of bad conscience. She wallows in self-pity, taking
every opportunity to proclaim her remorse (pp. 50:6-7,
27-28, 35-37; 51:3-16, 31-33; 52:passim). The cause
of that remorse is of quite secondary importance. In
her age, appearance, and attitude, she stands in ironic
contrast to Electra; ironic, because of her and Orestes'
prophetic observation of the two women's similarity
(pp. 50:9-17; 52:29-31). Her self-revelations are thus
implicitly revelations about Electra too.

Her very first words are an evasion of responsibility: "Electra, the king orders you to prepare for
the ceremony" (p. 49:5-6). As she soon explains,
"I long ago gave up ordering you in my name" (p. 49:
31-50:1). One receives the impression that Electra
must have long been defiant toward her, but she soon
belies this notion: "Electra detests me, and I am not
unaware of it. But for fifteen years we have kept
silent, and only our looks betrayed us" (p. 53:1-3).
She does not originate; she transmits and insinuates.
What she transmits are political orders, from "the
king," directed to a public function, "when the people
requires a picture of our family life for its edifi-
cation" (p. 49:19-20 [Electra speaking]). Electra
understands the political usefulness of such displays,
but rejects the authority from which they proceed:
"What have I to do with Aegisthus' orders? He is your
husband, mother, your very dear husband, not mine"
(p. 50:3-4). Aegisthus-as-king is lost in the thought
Aegisthus-as-non-husband. It appears that Electra
would submit to a husband's commands, or perhaps in-
sinuate herself into such commands as Clytemnestra
later does into those of Aegisthus (cf. p. 81:9-11).

Electra at first reacts with silent, withdrawn
peevishness. But Clytemnestra resolves no longer to
put up with this common behavior of hers, for she has
just observed from her window "another Electra, with
grand gestures, with eyes full of fire" (p. 49:11-12).

It is not apparent just how much of the previous action
she has witnessed. But however little it may have been,
it marks the beginning of Orestes' objective engagement
in Argos. For he has catalyzed an unusual behavior on
Electra's part, which has in turn affected her relationship with Clytemnestra. Willy-nilly, Orestes has
entered into the Argive "history." The present scene
deepens this engagement. Emboldened by Clytemnestra's
revelation and by Orestes' presence, Electra moves
from coy silence to sarcasm to blunt opposition in answering her mother. When Clytemnestra irritatingly
declares that Electra is like herself, Electra **decisively** draws Orestes into the exchange by calling
upon him to judge. Orestes, too honest not to answer,
remarks that Electra's face contains "something like
a promise of a storm" of the sort that has already
ravaged Clytemnestra's (p. 50:15-17).

Orestes' prophecy temporarily focuses Clytemnestra's attention upon him, and she interrogates him
on his background. He announces himself as the traveller Philebus of Corinth; he is eighteen years old;
his father is dead. To her questions concerning his
mother--her age and whether he loves her--he maintains
a disturbing silence. And when she asks why he has
left her, he answers that he is going to enlist among
the mercenary troops at Sparta. Perhaps the mention
of mercenaries reminds her of the **failure** of her own
maternal affection in having permitted the infant
Orestes to be turned over to Aegisthus' mercenaries;
for she continues with a set of largely rhetorical
questions, ostensibly seeking to discover Orestes'
reason for detouring through Argos, but which quickly
descend into a proclamation of her guilt. Electra
angrily identifies what Clytemnestra is doing as "our
national game . . . of public confessions." And she
describes this national occupation in terms which
emphasize its self-consciously gamelike quality, and
the fragility of the politics built around it. She
speaks of the merchant who "drag[s] himself on his
knees through the streets, rubbing his hair with dust
and yelling out that he is an assassin, an adulterer,
or a prevaricator," but only does so "after having
lowered his shop's iron curtain." Argos is, it seems,
a bourgeois city first, and only secondarily a guilt-
ridden city. She mentions "the rule of the game"
whereby one is "only to judge them for the sins that
they confess: the others are nobody's business, and
they would be annoyed at you for discovering them."
But she notes that the people are growing bored with

53

this game, since "each knows by heart the others' crimes." The most vulnerable ones are those which must be told most often, the "official crimes, crimes of founding" (pp. 51:18, 20-23, 34-38, 23-25, 25-27).

As though in response to this observation on the public confessions, Clytemnestra reveals something of which she has hitherto given no indication whatever, that it is not the death of "the old lecher" Agamemnon that she regrets but the abandonment of young Orestes (p. 52:3-4). This crime and the moralistic tone in which she describes it contrast markedly with her self-excoriation an instant earlier as "a prostitute" (p. 51:32). It seems ready-made to captivate her young auditor, who so resembles Orestes as he would have been (cf. p. 52:7). Electra interjects, "It seems to me, mother, that you had a daughter too. You have made a dishwasher of her. But that sin doesn't torment you very much" (p. 52:9-11). Electra thus betrays a serious moral disproportion in her outlook, stemming from her self-absorption. Her being made to wash dishes seems to her as serious a cause for repentance as her brother's delivery into the hands of murderers. An altercation follows between mother and daughter over just what it is that each hates in the other, in which Clytemnestra predicts that someday Electra will drag behind her an irreparable crime. Through this whole exchange "infant Orestes" is completely forgotten.

Noting that it is the young stranger's presence that has precipitated this "dogfight," Clytemnestra expresses her wish that he leave the city. She can only state this as a wish, since "[t]he city's laws make it a duty for us to offer you hospitality" (p. 53:4-5, 5-6). Unfriendly as Argos has already shown itself to be, it is a city and as such has come to observe certain formal amenities. Hospitality toward strangers, a necessity for any city which seeks to have friendly relations with its neighbors, seems to be a survival from Argos' more conventional days. Perhaps the formal abolition of this custom would have constituted too great a shock to that stability in the laws which is necessary to sustain the habit of obedience. In any event, such limitations of the political upon itself will provide both Orestes and Electra with the breathing space necessary to overthrow the regime. Clytemnestra reminds Electra of Aegisthus' order, and describes his punitive power. Electra again defies the order, and describes for Orestes the

ceremony about to take place. Her description of the
festival of the dead speaks to the mentioned flaws of
public confession. The dead are let out of the earth
for a day, and haunt the living in intimate and pervasive capacities. Remorse must be total in their
presence; there are no secrets from them. Coming out
only once a year, the confession one makes to them is
not stale, but intermittently new, including each past
year's wrongs. But their return to the earth restores
the normal way of life as a blessing. The festival of
the dead is public confession at a fever pitch, which
makes a relief of the more usual Argive oppression.

Clytemnestra declares that the king has ordered
Electra brought to the ceremony by force if necessary.
Faced with this possibility, Electra agrees to appear,
and urges Orestes to attend. Clytemnestra in turn begs
him "by your mother" to leave (p. 54:7). Left alone
onstage, Orestes ponders these words. The situation
parallels that at the end of the second scene, when he
had broached the idea of matricide. The formerly empty
notion has now acquired some concrete substance, perhaps even some appeal.

Jupiter reappears, offering to obtain horses for
Orestes' and his valet's departure. But Orestes declares that he is no longer leaving. After a moment's
reflection, Jupiter throws himself upon Orestes as his
host in Argos, offers to find him lodgings, rids him
of his flies, urges that he tell his life history to
his new companion, and again alludes to his divinity[9]
by referring to the story of Telemachus and Mentor.
The Act which began with the minimally dignified,
though self-serving, piety of the Argive women, ends
with the eager, pandering obsequiousness of the self-
serving God.

III.  Act II, First Tableau

The Festival of the Dead

Act 1 has presented a progress of Orestes' curiosity. He begins with the desire to see Argos, apparently entertaining, but not firmly committed to, the
thought of reclaiming his father's throne. But this
wish can as yet have little concrete meaning for him.
His concrete desire may be no more than to see how
Argos is governed, perhaps to test the oracle, and to
ascertain what personal links he may have to the city.
Any political project is subordinate to this plan

55

of discovery.  By the middle of the Act his failure to
discover any such links, in the form of memories,
coupled with the evidence presented to him of the Argives' ignobility, and perhaps also with Jupiter's
arguments concerning the Gods, acts as a veto over any
contemplated political plan.  His encounters with Electra and Clytemnestra provide him with alternative links
to an Argive present, but only enough to sustain curiosity.  His decision to remain in Argos at the Act's
end is only a decision to see the ceremony of the dead,
made on the strength of Electra's request, of his desire to see more of her, and perhaps of his repulsion
toward Clytemnestra.  In Act 2 he moves from curiosity
to commitment, obtaining along the way the sought-for
exposure to Argive politics.

        The first tableau of Act 2 occurs on a mountain-
side above the city, at the cave of the dead, near a
temple and a ceremonial platform from which Aegisthus
will officiate.  The cave, as the site for resurrection
of the dead, again signals the play's relation to
Christianity.  A crowd of Argives mills around the
ceremonial platform, awaiting Aegisthus' arrival.  The
vignettes which occur during this waiting period are
rather revealing of the ceremony and of the Argives'
confused beliefs.  A woman straightens her little boy's
necktie and reminds him to cry on cue.  When he declares his fear, she observes approvingly, "That's how
one becomes a good man" (p. 57:9).  The ceremony is
dominated by a concern for appearance, for the merely
ceremonial.  Two citizens exchange the hope that the
good weather will make the dead less terrible than
they were the previous year, when it rained.  The dead
are believed to be susceptible to the natural elements.
Two other citizens consider what their feelings will
be the following day, once the dead have returned to
the earth.  On the one hand, the ordeal will be over.
But then one can begin to anticipate the next year's
festival.  The horrors of this death cult seem never
to be past.  The ceremony's anti-social character
begins to emerge when another citizen cautions against
speaking aloud about the dead, lest one of them might
have sneaked through a flaw in the rock and already
be among them; they eye each other suspiciously.  A
confrontation between an old woman and a young one
illustrates the festival's function as an occasion for
cruelty, and repeats the contrast between youth and
age which Electra had emphasized (cf. pp. 44:15-23;
52:26-28).  The young woman expresses nervous impatience for the ceremony to begin soon.  The old one

insultingly identifies the source of the young one's fears to be her recently deceased husband, whom she had been cuckolding for ten years. The suffering of each is made bearable by gloating over the misery of others, especially of those who are most vulnerable, like this recent widow about to undergo her first encounter with her wronged dead one. A man agrees with the young woman's impatience, and expresses irritation at Aegisthus for the delay. But another sympathizes with Aegisthus, who will have to "pass twenty-four hours in a tête-à-tête with Agamemnon" (p. 59:1-2). No one publicly expresses any doubt that the dead would do anything other than haunt the living, or suggests that anyone among the living would be immune to haunting.

Jupiter, Orestes and the tutor enter, Jupiter leading them to where they can better see the proceedings without themselves being conspicuous. Each displays his own perspective at this point through a brief exchange of remarks. Orestes sarcastically takes note of "the citizens of Argos, the very loyal subjects of King Agamemnon" (p. 59:11-12). Formerly unable to give an account of citizen pride, he nonetheless has a conception of citizen loyalty. But that conception abstracts from the substance of rule. The loyalty which the Argives supposedly owed Agamemnon is apparently based only on the fact that he happened to be their king. The tutor points up the problem of such conventionalism by setting beside this standard of the citizen his own standard of natural man. He calls the Argives' ugliness and fear "the effect of superstition," and contrasts their pallor with his own rosy complexion (p. 59:15). Had Agamemnon fostered such superstition, would he still have deserved his citizens' loyalty? Jupiter, in turn, ridicules this standard from the perspective of divine incorruptibility. The "poppies" on the tutor's cheeks

> will not keep you from being a dung heap, like
> all of them, in Jupiter's eyes. Go on, you
> befoul the place, and you don't know it. At
> least their nostrils are filled with their
> proper odors, they know themselves better
> than you (p. 59:20-24).

The tutor's entire philosophy is called to task in the name of a traditional philosophic maxim. Because he fails to take adequate account of his own finitude, he does not know himself. And, not knowing himself in this fundamental respect, he cannot know man. To the

57

tutor this critique is devastating. From this point
on, until his brief reappearance at the end of Act 3,
after Jupiter's final departure, he remains silent.
For the remainder of this tableau Jupiter displaces
him as Orestes' admonisher and servant (pp. 59:36-
60:2; 61:36-62:2; 63:30-33; 68:10-13; cf. pp. 38:19-25;
39:31-32). But his implied critique of Orestes'
conventionalism survives this exchange.

At the suggestion of one of their number, the
crowd now calls upon Aegisthus to begin the ceremony.
A woman faints at the thought of her hated dead husband coming to take possession of her. Orestes voices
the thought that someone must tell the people something to remedy their madness. His political impulse,
perhaps in response to the tutor's critique, is to
publicize the latter's enlightenment as a remedy for
superstition. But Jupiter cajoles him with the thought
that one woman's fainting is not worth troubling himself over. A man in the crowd falls into a fit of
self-deprecation, for which Jupiter quietly praises
him. But some other men set his hysteria into calculative perspective by telling him to save his story
until later, "when they will be there" (p. 60:11).
When the crowd seems at a peak of desperation over
Aegisthus' continued absence, he appears, followed by
Clytemnestra, the high priest, and the palace guard.

Another set of exchanges sets into relief the
ceremony's religious character. Aegisthus' first
statement is a reminder to the crowd of their abasement, supported with an oath to Jupiter. Turning to
Clytemnestra, he quietly acknowledges that they will
have to begin without Electra, and announces, sans
oath, that her punishment will be exemplary. "Jupiter"
and the wrath which he supports are largely show,
meant for public consumption. Responding to Aegisthus'
delay in beginning the ceremony until the guards have
located Electra, the high priest remarks to him on the
crowd's extreme restiveness, a piece of essentially
calculative advice which sets his subsequent religious
actions into context. The separation of Church and
State, suggested by the presence of the high priest
as a separate character, is more apparent than real.
The high priest is essentially Aegisthus' accomplice.
The guards return, unable to find Electra, and Aegisthus finally orders the ceremony to begin.

The guards remove the rock from the mouth of the
cave, and the priest calls upon the dead to arise from

the earth. He then dances himself into collapse, per-
mitting Aegisthus, who formally announces the dead's
presence, to take over. For the second time, Orestes
decides to intervene. This attempted intervention is
more personal than the earlier one. Then, he had
stated in general terms, "Someone must tell these
people. . . ." Now he declares that he himself is
going to do something (pp. 59:36; 61:36). Again,
Jupiter prevents him, but this time through a mysterious kind of intimidation. He orders Orestes to look
him in the face, and tells him, "You have understood.
Silence for the present." What has Orestes understood?
Apparently not that his companion is a God, for he
asks, "Who are you?"(pp. 61:38; 62:1-2). But this
grave gesture doubtless adds some depth to his extra-
ordinariness, hitherto revealed only as rudeness, buf-
foonery, and fly-taming. The most recent reference to
this look was in the rebuke to the tutor: "[A rosy
complexion] will not keep you from being a dung heap,
like all of them, in Jupiter's eyes" (p. 59:20-21).
Perhaps this formidable look conveys better than all
argument the message of human finitude, and thus the
futility of the kind of public enlightenment which
Orestes was about to attempt. In any event, he is
temporarily humbled, and does not announce another
political project until after his **conversion**.

Aegisthus now displays his rabble-rousing talents,
exciting the people's sense of misery. He goes among
them, discoursing about the dead, allocating certain
of the dead to certain of the living, describing a
dead soul, and reminding his listeners of the effect
that the dead are to have upon them. The living receive the dead according to their particular wrong-
doings: the unfaithful wife is haunted by her husband,
the negligent son by his mother, the hard-hearted
usurer by his debtors, the strict parents by their
children. Can there be enough dead to suffice for all
the living under this arrangement? Would the debtors
have to choose, for instance, between haunting their
wives and haunting the usurer? Or would the dead
children have to not be at the feet of one parent in
order to be at the feet of the other, since the men
and the women are physically separated at this moment?
(Cf. p. 60:29-30.) This problem does not perplex the
Argives, for whom the dead function essentially as
reflective extensions of themselves. Again, the explicit description of a dead soul is one of self-
contained, immovable passivity:

59

> . . . a torrid noon, without a breath of wind,
> nothing budges there, nothing changes there,
> nothing lives there, a great pale sun, an
> immobile sun consumes her eternally (p. 62:24-26).

This central image is descrepant with the previous
descriptions of the dead as embracing and stretching
their hands out to the living. (Would a "torrid noon"
have hands?) It also seems inconsistent, though less
blatantly, with the succeeding account of their effect,
which is to look upon the living with "millions of
fixed and hopeless eyes," to render them "naked" and
"awkward" (p. 62:33 - 63:1). The look of incorruptible
omniscience evokes self-consciousness of nakedness,
of their "original sin." After the crowd reveals the
effect of this speech through a kind of chorus, expressing the general sentiment, "Pardon us for living
while you are dead" (p. 63:4-5, 16-17, 24-25), Aegisthus concludes by directing their attention to himself.
He announces that "the greatest of the dead is going to
appear, he whom I killed with my own hands, Agamemnon"
(p. 63:28-29).

The mention of Agamemnon's name breaks the spell
which Jupiter had cast upon Orestes. Drawing his
sword, he exclaims that he will not permit Aegisthus
"to mix my father's name into your monkey business
(p. 63:30-31). There is no hint of a political project
in this third outburst. It seems entirely personal.
But what is Agamemnon to Orestes? Since he has "not
the least memory" of the Argos of his infancy, it is
likely that he has none of Agamemnon either. Rather,
the formula "father" seems to obtain meaning for
Orestes through this very act of defense. Orestes, in
effect, adopts Agamemnon. Insofar as mere ancestry
may exercise a mystical influence upon him, it is an
influence in its last flush. Orestes never again
relies upon it as the basis for his acts. But in
assuming a horizon through a self-assertion which is
not fully rational he here prefigures his later political act. Jupiter's response in this instance is completely un-divine. He restrains Orestes bodily. The
God is forced to act within the human horizon, the
only occasion in the play when he does so; and his
success seems as much to be caused by Electra's sudden
appearance, which diverts everyone's attention, as by
any superior physical strength.

Startled by Orestes' outburst, Aegisthus turns,
only to see Electra, dressed in white. He rebukes her

for dressing in a way that is apt to offend the dead, denounces her as "the last descendant of an accursed race" (p. 64:12), the Atrides, and threatens her with harsh punishment. While his diatribe apparently works its effect upon the crowd, which pronounces the verdict "Sacrilege!" (p. 64:18), his line of attack indicates how much Electra has disoriented him. For having just announced the appearance of Agamemnon, it ill becomes him to deride Atreus' line. For the moment, however, he rides the crest of the people's religious outrage, piously proclaiming of her gaiety, "She laughs, and her dead father is there, with congealed blood on his face. . . ." But Electra exposes his vulnerability, asking indignantly, "How dare you speak of Agamemnon?" (p. 64:26-27, 28). She now stands rhetorically where Orestes had stood a moment earlier, but with two differences: "Agamemnon" has some concrete meaning for her, and she lacks a drawn sword. Her only means of action is persuasion, and the fate of her oration to the crowd marks the possibilities and the limits of that means.

Electra appeals to myth, convention, and nature. She exploits her immediate rhetorical advantage, arguing that she is in a better position than Aegisthus to know what is apt to please Agamemnon's ghost. She even suggests having had contact with him, and having assurance of his pleasure at her proud display. The argument retains the existence of the dead, but gives them a new, sympathetic aspect. Insofar as the dead represent possibilities of the living, she invokes these more human possibilities within her auditors. The young woman wonders aloud whether Electra might be telling the truth. The others reject this possibility, but they are already softened. They no longer menace Electra, but earnestly request that she go away. Instead, she asks what they are afraid of. "I look around you," she says, "and I see only your shadows" (p. 65:13-14). Short of denying the existence of the dead altogether, this rhetorical question implies that their nonpalpability renders them unfearsome. Next she reminds them of another way of life, as it is lived in other cities. The focus of attention has shifted, by way of the things that are visible, from speculation about the dead to description of the living. This thought culminates in an appeal to nature: "O mothers of Argos, do you understand? Can you still understand the pride of a woman who looks at her child and who thinks, 'Is it I who have carried him in my bosom?'" (p. 65:21-24). Both convention and nature indict the way of life under Aegisthus' regime.

Aware of this political implication, Aegisthus
orders Electra to be silent, threatening her with
violence. The crowd's responses, however, indicate
that Aegisthus is no longer fully in control. The
citizens are divided on whether Electra should continue to speak. But the vulnerability of her position is
indicated by those who favor her. They wish her to
continue to speak because " (i)t is Agamemnon who in-
spires her" (p. 65:30). Her partisans are still taking
their cues chiefly from her first argument. Her persuasion remains within the matrix of superstitious
belief. She again pictures life in other places, now
expressly contrasting these scenes with the Argives'
own unfreedom even to move around for fear of jostling
the dead. In an ostensive denial of the power of the
dead, she stretches out her arms, begins to dance,
and asks, "Where are the dead? Do you believe that
they are dancing with me, in time?" (p. 66:8-9). Finally, she appeals to the dead directly to give some
sign if they disapprove of her actions, but otherwise
to remain silent. By this formulation, she stacks the
deck in her favor. But the internal flaw of her joint
appeal to Iphigenia and Agamemnon (p. 66:13-14), two
spirits who might be expected to demand divergent
attitudes, indicates a weakness in this final appeal.
Her dual invocation is safe only on the assumption
that the dead are indifferent to the circumstances of
their dying, or, if they care, that they are powerless
to act. In either case, invoking a sign is useless.
But if they do care and can act, Electra dooms herself.
By implication, so too might everyone who attempted to
please all of "his" dead. An attitude of repentance
would be inevitable under such circumstances, as it
would be in a cosmos ruled by a multiplicity of Gods,
or by a God who is of diverse minds.

Won over by Electra's speeches and her dancing,
the crowd, led by the young woman, turns upon Aegisthus,
demanding an explanation, and, when the young woman
begins to follow Electra's example, angrily accuses
him of having lied to them. She has also won over
Orestes. But these two victories rest on different
grounds. Because the Argives' new inspiration remains
within the framework of belief in the active dead,
their faith in her can be shattered by the kind of
demonstration for which she has called rhetorically.
Because his does not, it cannot.

With the failure of Aegisthus' control, Jupiter takes a hand in restoring order. Stretching out his arms (tacitly confirming Electra's act), he pronounces a spell that causes the cavern rock to roll noisily across the stage. Everyone is surprised, not least of all Aegisthus, who does not immediately reassert his own authority. The high priest rebukes the people for heeding sacrilege, and the crowd falls over itself, disclaiming its part in the preceding events, and threatening Electra. (The old woman seizes the occasion to suggest, characteristically, that the young woman be stripped naked and disfigured with whipping.) Aegisthus, now recovered, orders them to their places, but the crowd only grants him its silence. Sensing that his authority has not been completely restored, he orders them to their homes, to accommodate their dead, and banishes Electra from the city, under penalty of death at the hands of whoever might encounter her the next day. She has the one-day reprieve, however, because "[t]he laws of the city forbid me from punishing on this holiday" (p. 67:38-68:1). This self-imposed disability seems to be an attempt by the city to impart a necessary distinction to--to "sanctify"--its most important day. There is a more particular logic to this prohibition too, for the wielding of death as a punishment (or of lesser punishments which are capital punishment-surrogates) seems peculiarly discordant with this day's exalting of the dead as superior to the living. For the second time, law, especially sacred law, supports those who will overthrow the regime. The requirements of public order contain the seeds of its destruction.

After Aegisthus and the Argives leave, Jupiter attempts, in tutorial fashion, to draw a moral conclusion from Electra's fate. But Orestes cuts him short, claiming Electra as "my sister," and orders him away (p. 68:14). Jupiter complies, with casual resignation, followed silently by the tutor. Significantly, Jupiter, in his moralizing, refers to Electra as "[t]hat woman." He concedes the untruth of his first characterization of her as "a child" (pp. 68:13; 38:19). Electra has come of age.

Orestes' Conversion

In the ensuing conversation between Orestes and Electra, which leads up to Orestes' conversion, Electra more fully reveals her imagination and her sense of family destiny, and Orestes displays his longing for

63

situation. Because this dialogue is fraught with vacil-
lations, it is significant that Jupiter overhears only
its latter half. Like the human characters, the God
acts on incomplete information. In the human sphere,
the fortuitous conditions even divine intervention.

Electra still does not know Orestes' identity. It
is still "Philebus" who urges her to flee with him to
Corinth. She acknowledges her danger, but refuses to
flee. She would not know what to do in Corinth; she
is too fundamentally Argive. But she has been changed
by their encounter. Previously she had had only the
"modestly" vengeful desire to see Clytemnestra and
Aegisthus dead. But he had made her forget her hate,
and had inspired her with political ambition to "cure
the people." She had sought to effect this cure
"through words." But because the people "love their
evil," this attempt failed. She concludes, "It is by
violence that one must cure them, for one can conquer
evil only with another evil" (p. 69:29-30, 32-34).
Orestes has already become a part of the Argive situation through his influence on Electra, an influence
that still continues since she now contemplates further
"curative" action. Interestingly, her account of the
preceding public events makes no mention of the mira-
cle--her effort failed because of the Argives' attitude.
In this she anticipates a teaching soon to be made explicit, the dispensability of divine guidance.

She intends to escape Aegisthus' decree by taking
sanctuary in the temple of Apollo, and there to await
her brother, whom she "knows" not to be dead (p. 70:6).
For the third time, ancestral or sacred law will be
used against the rulers. Orestes must come because
"(h)e is of our race, . . . he has crime and ill for-
tune in his blood, like me" (p. 70:8-10). To Electra,
Orestes must be a destiny, and she endows him imagina-
tively with only such qualities as a destiny requires.
He must resemble his father, a tall, fiery eyed
irascible soldier, attracted to where he can do, and
do himself, the most harm. Most important, he must
have no significant will of his own. Electra must stay
because "I have a good head on my shoulders," in order
to show him whom to strike (p. 70:21). Further, he
could not escape the Atrides' destiny, even if he
wished to, even if his background disinclined him to
commit a crime. Electra's argument from the Atride
destiny is inseparable from this fantastic construction. Orestes' later use of a similar argument therefore must not be taken at face value, since he clearly

64

recognizes its non-conclusiveness here. It is, however, his later statement, and not Electra's description, that Jupiter hears.

Orestes now reveals his identity, intending through the destruction of the imaginary Orestes to permit her flight with him. The revelation exposes the fallibility of her long-held anticipation, and places the attractive stranger Philebus into a forbidden realm of consanguinity. The disparity between the youthful Orestes before her, a virgin to all battle (p. 71:13-15), and her fabricated firebrand leaves her only with the thought of Orestes' and her common weakness. But when he again urges their flight, she refuses, recurring to her Atride destiny. Perhaps she is too deeply rooted in Argos to consider fleeing, even at the cost of sure death. Or perhaps Orestes has become somehow less desirable as a travelling companion. Where earlier she had merely told "Philebus" that she did not wish to flee, she now refuses to flee "(w)ith you" (pp. 69:4-5; 71:23). Or perhaps he is too painful a reminder of the falseness of her imaginative construction and the closed attitude toward the future of which it is symptomatic. In any event, the retained argument from family destiny is likely only half-hearted, although Orestes seems not to realize it.

Jupiter now reappears, hiding in order to overhear their conversation. The first thing he hears is Orestes' protestation, "Electra, I am Orestes, . . . your brother, I too am an Atride, and your place is at my side" (p. 71:28-29). Jupiter has entered at what appears to be the same point on which he left (cf. p. 68: 14-15). What he sees is an Orestes looking for any excuse to remain in Argos; what he has missed is an Orestes determined to leave, and to take Electra with him. He sees an Electra who refuses to acknowledge Orestes, who continues to address him as "Philebus" because "Orestes is dead" (p. 71:31); he has not seen Electra's initial acceptance of him a moment earlier. Both have reversed their stances just before, or at the moment of, the God's entry. Left to their own devices, their uncertainties about themselves and each other might conceivably produce yet another reversal. The range of human possibilities includes a resolution more favorable to the non-omniscient God than even the one that he attempts to bring about.

Jupiter witnesses three attempts by Orestes to justify his remaining in Argos. He first asserts a

duty to stand by his sister, beginning with the appeal
to their common ancestry. Electra answers this appeal,
which he has already substantially weakened, by asking,
"(W)ho are you to call yourself one of us? Have you
passed your life under the shadow of a murder?" (p. 71:
13-15). Atridehood is no longer fundamentally a matter
of blood lineage, but of how one has lived. And the
decisive crime is no longer a destined future, but
apparently an event in the past, Agamemnon's murder.
To support this argument, she constructs a tranquil,
contented childhood for Orestes, which she contrasts
with her own existence as a servant when she was already
six years old. This construction is in its crucial
respect as faulty as her earlier one. By Orestes' own
testimony, he passed his childhood conscious of being
an exile, in his own way under the shadow of Agamemnon's murder (cf. p. 42:15-19). The standard of Atridehood which Electra proposes permits of entry into that
status. Since he soon belies the happy notion of his
childhood which she here hypothesizes, she will again
have to shift ground. For Orestes, the ancestral relationship is incidental to the fraternal one. He makes
no further mention of it, stating instead the chief
thrust of the current appeal, his wish not to leave
Electra alone and without her former hope. To this
end he suggests his own serviceability in the capacity
which Electra had envisioned for her "irritated mercenary." She rejects him fundamentally on character
grounds. He is a "noble soul," whereas she needs "an
accomplice"; he is too lacking in hate (p. 72:14, 7,
8, 20). Perhaps too he is not sufficiently lacking
in mind.

At mention of his hatelessness, Orestes' attention
shifts from Electra to himself. In expanding on his
own wish for situation, he even loses sight of Electra's.
Orestes becomes the hopeless one, and Argos his only
possible means of salvation. Having never had the
opportunity to "give himself," he has neither hate nor
love (p. 72:23). Nor has he any of the comforts of
either the childhood Electra has painted for him or his
earlier description of Corinth, neither pretty girls
nor happy city to console him. Argos is his only
chance to gain "my memories, my ground, my place in the
midst of men." He resolves not to leave, notwithstanding Electra's complaint that "your innocence will
make my enterprise fail," because he wants to be "a
man among men," a slave who "is in his city, like a
leaf in foliage, like a tree in the forest" (p. 73:
7-8, 12, 19, 22-24). Electra asserts the impossibility

66

of his adopting such a horizon ready-made, as Jupiter
had argued and Orestes himself had acknowledged earlier:
"Were you to live among us for a hundred years, you
would never be anything but a stranger" (p. 73: 28-29).
But so desperate is Orestes for such a horizon that he
even asks about donating himself for military service
or through his wealth--and this to the city which has
just banished Electra! No event so emphatically indicates how the convergence of Orestes' and Electra's
paths is fundamentally a matter of mere coincidence.
In any case, Electra answers, seemingly conclusively,
that the city has its own supply of "captains (and)
pious souls to do good" (p. 73:36-37).

The dialogue with Electra has left Orestes uncertain about familial duty, his attachment to her, the
character of his sociality, and the possibility of
satisfying it. His prayer to Zeus is thus an anguished
plea for clarity of vision, for the knowledge of good
and evil. But concretely, he knows that he wants to
stay with Electra, and that this entails engagement in
Argos. His prayer is thus also an exercise in bad
faith. He addresses Zeus as "king of heaven," and
frames his appeal accordingly, asking, "(M)ust a king's
son, driven out of his native city, truly resign himself in a saintly way to exile, and vacate the premises,
his head lowered like a setter?" (p. 74:6, 10-12). His
self-depiction as the rightful heir to the throne seems
tempered to fit his new audience, who would presumably
be receptive to claims of royal succession. He had not
made this argument to Electra just before, while
seeking out positions of service to the city. Perhaps
the fact that Argos would not want him either as a
soldier or as philanthropist forces him to scrape the
top of the barrel, to think of service as its ruler.
But his plea to Zeus is not one of desire to serve,
but of hereditary right. This right Orestes has already acknowledged to be subordinate to certain prerequisites of ruling which he lacks (cf. p. 43:35-36).

But if Orestes' object in praying is to articulate
a confusion, he must develop some problem to pit
against this new formulation. The problem he develops,
almost despite himself, consists of the means necessary
to make good a claim to the throne: "And yet . . . yet
you have forbidden the shedding of blood . . . Ah! who
speaks of shedding blood, I no longer know what I am
saying . . ." (p. 47:13-15). Why does he shy away from
this consequence? A few moments earlier, he had almost
dared Electra to order him to strike down her enemies,

as she would have ordered her imaginary Orestes. But
now Orestes speaks of a project that would be distinctly
his own, for which he would be responsible. Moreover,
the imaginary Orestes would mindlessly be attracted to
wherever he "could do the greatest harm." Orestes'
first plea to Zeus is that "I have never wished for
anything but the Good" (pp. 70:16-17; 74:8). The
particular consequence which he has adduced is, however, a necessary part of any Argive venture. This
much remains: If he would will the end, he must also
will the necessary means. For the time being, however,
he has exposed a conflict between two presumed divine
wills. In order to obscure that conflict, and to weight
the case even more in the desired direction, he concludes the prayer with an extreme formulation of one
of his alternatives: "Zeus, I implore you: if resignation and abject humility are the laws which you impose
on me, manifest your will to me by some sign" (p. 74:
15-18). As Electra did earlier, Orestes attempts to
stack the phenomenal deck in his favor. His plea for
a sign is a thinly-disguised plea for confirmation of
a predetermined conclusion through divine silence.

Jupiter, for his part, is eager to oblige, and
provides the requested miracle. In a travesty of the
burning bush of Exodus, he causes light to shine from
the rock. He is high exemplar of the principle of
order; Orestes' characterization of his laws is perfectly accurate. We may, however, doubt the prudence
of this blatant answer. Had Jupiter not given the
sign, what would likely have followed? Orestes would
be left to ascertain and follow the Good as well as he
could through human reason. He would have had to
attempt to reconcile rightful political succession with
the precept against the shedding of blood; to recon-
sider the prerequisites of ruling, what makes a political succession truly rightful, or to search for rational distinctions among different kinds of bloodshed;
and to reflect on tyranny and tyrranicide. Alternatively, he might have reflected that "resignation and
abject humility" are characterizations of divine will
unbecoming a God who must be good; and so come to view
his own choices more moderately. Divine silence might
have led him to political philosophy or to rational
theology. The author has elsewhere stated emphatically
that in the real world there are no signs which can
tell us what to do.[3] By having Jupiter intrude here,
he lends to the attitude of piety and to the doctrinal
position for which Jupiter is the eventual spokesman a
"clarity" which in fact they never have. The

precondition for Orestes' didactic usefulness for
the play's viewers is a gross simplification of the
meaning of piety and the demands of adherence to a
Platonic-Christian principle of the Good. The present
deux ex machina is thus not only Jupiter's attempt to
determine Orestes' judgment; it is also Sartre's
attempt, through Jupiter, to posit among his audience
a fixed point within the moral horizon.

Electra, nearly in hysterics, urges Orestes to
obey the divine sign, to go away. But Orestes, who
doubtless feels cheated by the God's reply, after some
moments' reflection, rejects it:

> Then . . . that's the Good? . . . To
> slink away quietly. Completely quietly.
> Always to say, "Excuse me" and "Thank
> you" . . . that's it? . . . The Good.
> Their Good (p. 74:28-30).

Jupiter has apparently accomplished what he sought
unsuccessfully to do earlier. Orestes has accepted
his answer as definitive for "the Gods" (p. 74:24;
cf. p. 38:8-11). "Their Good" disjoins God from man.
To a typical Argive, accustomed to a life of resignation and humility, this statement of divine will
would be a confirmation of long-established habits.
But Orestes has never said "Excuse me" or "Thank you."
His first utterance in the play is an innocently rude
"Hey!" (p. 31:1). The sign places not only his immediate intention but his entire past into question. But
by the same token Orestes' way of life calls into question the sign's authority. He has asked the divine to
confirm its already-assumed dispensability to human
enterprise. Having already interpreted the God's
silence, he is no less free now to interpret the God's
answer. He had asked for a clarification of his own
wish for the Good. As a statement of divine law,
Jupiter's sign may be definitive; but as a statement of
Orestes' true will, it can only be a hypothetical recommendation to his judgment. Confronting the glowing
rock, Orestes must ask himself, "Is resignation and
abject humility, then, what I have really always wished
for?" (If we are correct in characterizing his prayer
as bad faith, he might add, "although I denied it to
myself even while suggesting it aloud.") Between him
and his own intention there can be no outside arbiter.
Orestes concludes as he must: What Zeus wills is not
what I will. Theirs is not the Good I seek.

This disjunction between Orestes and the Gods is
no less a disjunction between him and all other men,
or among all men simply. Each must be the final arbiter of the consistency between his fundamental wish
for the Good (if this is his fundamental wish--if, indeed, this is still a valid description of a fundamental human project) and the "laws" imposed upon him,
ostensibly in fulfillment of this wish. More, each
must, it seems, be his own original legislator. For,
responding to Electra's frightened reminder that he
has asked for the Gods' orders, Orestes says:

> Orders? . . . Ah yes . . . You mean that
> light around this big pebble? That light's
> not for me; and nobody can any longer give
> me order now (p. 75:1-4).

We may wonder whether this radically individual assertion leaves room for politics of any description.

The first consequence of Orestes' rejection of
the Gods' Good, and of order which is given by others,
is a state of confusion. The "other way" whose
existence he proclaims to Electra has as yet no defined content. He feels isolated in an "immense void,"
and senses the death of something which he cannot
identify (pp. 74:36; 75:9, 12). But this emptiness
is only temporary and transitional. A human being,
it seems, cannot long remain in this open, vertigi-
nous condition. Orestes turns his attention again to
the "other way, . . . my way" (p. 75:12, 14-15).[32]
That way, he declares, leads to Argos. He does not
say why this, rather than, say, writing a guidebook to
Greece, is peculiarly his way (cf. p. 41:10-13). The
path of engagement in Argos was, of course, the direction which he was taking even while pronouncing his
prayer. But if this is truly a moment of radical conversion, if he has truly stared into the abyss and
experienced himself as ethical anguish; then this
former project too, no less than his pious quest for
the Good, must have been called into question. He
does, however, characterize his prospective connection
to Argos in two ways: as descent and as obtaining
weight.[33] Descent contrasts with his earlier attempts
to live "up" to a role, be it as an Atride with a family destiny, a servant to the city, or a dispossessed
prince. Because he is not of the city, he must make
the city his through an original act of appropriation.
His project must be concretized in particular deeds.

He must "take on the ballast of a heinous crime which
will make me sink straight down, to the bottom of
Argos" (p. 75:24-25). The maritime imagery suggests
that Orestes' choice of Argos proceeds from the mere
fact of its proximity, just as a ship in need of extra
weight must draw it from the surrounding waters.
Orestes, it seems, chooses Argos because Argos is
there.

After bidding farewell to his youth, Orestes
fleshes out his commitment by explicating the necessary
means to his end. In order to make Argos his, he must
liberate it politically, "open the belly of those
bigoted houses" like an ax (p. 76:3-4; cf. p. 45:3-12).
In order to open the city, he must "steal" the Argives'
remorse. And in order to make their remorse stealable,
he must dispose of the king and queen. He aims at
removing the weight of remorse from Argos, but not at
giving it some other weight. That is, he makes no
mention of establishing his own rule. He would remove
their remorse, but not do expiation himself. Coming
as a thief in the night, Orestes uses Christ-like language to describe an anti-Christ-like enterprise. His
farewell to youth emphasized the displacing of his
former hope by resolution (p. 75:28-32). His enterprise, while beneficent, is apparently not undertaken
in a spirit of charity, but for the sake of self-sub-
stantiation. And he reveals the kind of faith which it
entails by calling upon the Gods to bear witness "that
I did not wish to shed (the royal couple's) blood"
(p. 76:35-36). This invocation contrasts markedly with
his prayer. He invokes the Gods for a very limited
purpose, and not to ask for approval or disapproval of
a course of action. He invokes all the Gods indifferently to perform this relatively passive function,
not a particular God needing a particular appeal. And
he calls their attention to his will concerning a particular deed, rather than to an amorphous wish for the
Good.

During this elaboration, Electra alternately continues to urge Orestes to leave and expresses puzzlement over the strange new things he is saying. She is
finally won over by his statement of resolution to
kill the king and queen, marking her conquest by addressing him as "Orestes" for the first time. But it
is doubtful that she comprehends the larger project
of which the royal assassination is a part. To her
question, "(H)ow would you be able to load yourself
with our evils?" he had replied, "You only ask to rid

71

yourselves of them. The king and queen alone maintain
them forcefully upon your hearts" (p. 76:30-33).
Electra seems then to become preoccupied with the
thought of killing the king and queen. But her question remains unanswered. Orestes has told her only of
the unloading of the evils from Argos which must precede or complement their being loaded upon him. The
transmutation of the Argives' evil into a self-substantiating good is not made explicit. That she might not
be alert to the full character of the envisioned act
she suggests by resurrecting the emotions and setting
of her dreams and by again invoking family destiny as
the envisioned deed's context (p. 77:7-13, 20-22).

The winning statement itself is Orestes' order
that she lead him to the royal bed. By giving an order
Orestes assumes the prime moving role in their enterprise, which Electra confirms by referring the future
act to "your decision," and by musing that "it is you
who are going to shed (all that blood)" (p. 77:11-12,
17-18). While technically correct, these characterizations too readily lend themselves to Electra's later
attempt to evade responsibility for the killings. By
mentioning the royal bed, Orestes evokes Electra's
erotic fantasy of a dual bedroom slaying of the couple
whose sexual activities so fascinate her. Her thoughts
are tied to the realizing of a particular death scene
of which she has dreamt and which she now regards as
destined (p. 77:14-15; cf. pp. 46:4-7; 69:9-16). Her
own falling away from the enterprise is presaged in the
extreme contingency of these links, which to her are so
necessary.

For Orestes, however, the die is cast. As he
takes Electra in his arms, the tableau ends with
Jupiter, in a travesty of the action which Orestes has
eschewed, quietly creeping away in order surreptitiously to thwart Orestes' plan.

IV. Act II, Second Tableau

The Festival of the Dead Revisited

The second tableau takes place in the royal
throne room, which is apparently not very large (cf. p.
80:3-4). It could easily be dominated by the king upon his throne, or by the "terrible and bloody" statue
of Jupiter which stands nearby (p. 78:s.d.). Still,
the soldiers in the second scene give no sign of
acknowledging this statue's presence. Like Aegisthus'

72

oath to Jupiter, it is there for public consumption.
When men are in private, publicly awesome things can
become negligible. The tableau begins at dusk, and
the greater part of it takes place at night (p. 78:s.d.;
cf. p. 80:28). There is a general cooling off of the
setting and the action. There are no crowds, no haran-
gues, and no hysteria here. Rather, we witness friendly
conversation, private confession, soliloquy, and a dialogue that exhibits the hardness, and the bluff, of a
poker game. Even the killing of Aegisthus is done with
cold calculation (p. 85:32-33). It is only with
Electra's breakdown at the end that the atmosphere again
becomes heated.

Electra and Orestes enter the room clandestinely,
but are immediately forced to hide behind the throne by
the approach of a couple of soldiers. Hidden there,
they overhear the dialogue and monologue of the next
three scenes.

The soldiers' conversation is comic relief, but
the scene also serves the serious purpose of showing
how the festival of the dead registers upon the minds
of commoners (p. 80:23-24). Their revelations modify
the impression of abject terror previously given by the
Argives' public behavior. Their first remarks are about
the oppressiveness of the flies, and only incidentally
about the dead as the cause of the flies' peculiar
frenzy. The flies are merely flies rather than divinely
sent symbols of guilt. And it is only by their smell
that the dead can affect them (pp. 78:8-9; 80:5). The
hold of the official oppression is easily lost in more
immediate discomforts.

Electra peeks out at them momentarily, causing a
slight startling noise; but one of them dismisses it as
the sound of Agamemnon upon the throne. In a travesty
of scholastic disputation, they argue over whether the
dead have weight, coming to the provisional conclusion
that while dead commoners may weigh nothing, a dead
king must surely retain a few pounds of his earthly
portliness. The first soldier observes that if he
were a dead king, with only one day to spend on earth,
he would spend it on his throne, "recalling happy
memories of the past, without harming anyone" (p. 79:
12-13). But if Agamemnon is on the throne, busily
reminiscing, he is not busy haunting Aegisthus or
Clytemnestra. Removed from the earlier mass hysteria,
the dead are transformed from extensions of the living
person's guilt to reflections of his sense of simple

pleasure, and are thus somewhat disarmed. So far this disarming only applies to dead royalty, but he later extends it to common soldiers like himself (p. 80:22-24).

The second soldier doubts the likelihood of the dead's benignity, but his comrade cuts short this discussion by slapping him on the face in order to kill some flies that have perched there. When he announces proudly that he has killed seven at one blow, a whole swarm, the other asks, "Of dead?" (p. 79:19). The same soldier who was sure of the dead's non-weight is open to the thought that they can be "killed" by a physical act. A second disputation follows, on the advantage or disadvantage that would result from the flies' being stillborn, during which the second soldier concedes arguendo that the dead are not really bothersome (p. 79:23-24). The first argues that, given the number of flies that die each day, if there were ghost flies as well as human dead, the air would be so full of them that the living would constantly be eating and breathing flies. This scholastic undermines his own previous argument by attributing corporeal quality to little ghostly flies as well as to fat ghostly kings. The argument should also apply to what falls between them, ordinary-sized human dead, which from the vast span of years past should also number in the millions. He forgets not only the previous distinction, but also the basis for, and limitation upon, the dead's existence--the living's memories. The commoners' conception of the dead is, to be sure, quite confused. But that very confusion underscores their belief's frailty as belief.

A further line of discussion is foreclosed by another sudden noise. This time they search behind the throne. As they go behind it, Orestes and Electra circle around in front, ducking back behind as the soldiers re-emerge from the other side. Apart from its slapstick aspect, this little pantomime verifies that Orestes and Electra, hidden behind the throne, can hear what is said in the chamber. The soldiers recur to the theory that Agamemnon is the source of these noises, and, put on edge at being watched by their old king, straighten to attention. The first soldier's final remark includes the wish to be in the barracks, playing cards in the company of dead former comrades-in-arms. Depending upon the attitude of the living, the company of the dead can be not only untroublesome, but even pleasantly nostalgic.

Aegisthus and Clytemnestra enter, with servants carrying lamps. Night has fallen; any light to be shed from now on will be of human origin. The soldiers and servants, on Aegisthus' order, leave him and Clytemnestra alone. Just as the past scene provided a private look at a couple of common citizens, the next three scenes provide such a view of the rulers.

Aegisthus has been brooding over the afternoon's events. "If I had not struck them with terror," he complains, "they would have thrown off their remorse in the twinkling of an eye" (p. 81:2-4). He is painfully aware of the fragility of his rule by remorse. Interestingly, he, like Electra earlier, disregards the miracle as a factor in the proceedings. Divine intervention is a dispensable term in everyone's account. Clytemnestra reassures him of his ability to "freeze their courage," and he wistfully agrees that he is "only too clever at that play-acting" (p. 81:6-8). He also regrets having had to punish Electra. Clytemnestra, who likely has taken personal umbrage at Electra's perversion of her promise to appear at the ceremony, assures him that he need have no regret on her account. "It pleased you to do it," she tells him, "and I find all that you do good." Characteristically, she pretends outwardly to submit to another's will, while insinuating herself into that will. She also changes Aegisthus' "having had to punish Electra" as a political necessity into an act of private pleasure (p. 81:8-11). Aegisthus, who knows his wife's ways, assures her that his regret is not for her sake. She presses the question, reminding him that he has not loved Electra in the past. We might expect this overheard attempt by Clytemnestra to steel her husband's opinion to harden Electra's hatred toward her. But this very hate might militate against Clytemnestra's death. For were she to live on in a position of subservience after Aegisthus' assassination, Electra could perpetually torment her with this "betrayal of her own flesh and blood" (cf. p. 81:9).

Without explicitly denying the suggestion of a new findness for Electra, Aegisthus shifts the focus back to politics. He is weary of having played the role of public bogey-man for fifteen years. His black garments have finally "taken the color out of my soul" (p. 81: 18). Clytemnestra tries to console him by adverting to her own situation; but he does not let her begin a mournful boast, declaring that he envies her her remorse, which gives her life a furnishing that his own lacks. Too clear-sighted to have remorse himself, his

attitude parallels Orestes' earlier longing for a horizon which he would know to be defective. Again Clytemnestra attempts to comfort him, this time approaching
him as a loving wife. But he rebukes her pointedly for
having no shame to behave thus in the dead king's sight.
Reminded that the rising of the dead from the earth is
merely one of the fables which he himself invented for
the people, he wearily agrees, and more calmly asks to
be left alone to gather his thoughts. Aegisthus' kind
of ruling eventuates in the ruler's entanglement in his
own fabrications. But this vignette also provides a
commentary on the couple's private life. Aegisthus'
rejection of his wife's proffered affections belies the
imagined erotic scenes which have fed Electra's resentment, and might be expected to temper her vengefulness.

## The Discourse on Politics

Alone, Aegisthus soliloquizes on the effect that
ruling has had upon him. Making explicit what has already been suggested, he declares that, for all his
terrible appearance, he is "an empty shell: a beast
has eaten me from within without my noticing it." No
longer capable of genuine joy or sorrow, he describes
himself, in terms reminiscent of his earlier description of a dead soul, and of Orestes' "immense void" at
the moment of his conversion, as "the desert, the
boundless nothingness of sand beneath the lucid nothingness of the sky." Ruling is, in a word, a mortifying
activity (p. 82:8-9, 11-13; cf. pp. 62:24-25; 75:9-10).
Its alienation exceeds that of being ruled, even of
being ruled as the Argives are, because it is necessarily more demanding. Aegisthus has no private life.
Unlike Agamemnon, he takes no solace in the erotic.
Unlike his subjects, he has neither friends nor simple
pleasures (cf. pp. 35:9; 52:3-4; 79:5-7; 85:14-15; 80:
21-22; 87:13-14).

There is, however, a certain stature to his suffering which makes the verbal similarity between this
self-description and Orestes' in his moment of anguish
more than coincidental. Aegisthus is not the mere
buffoon that Orestes makes him out to be (p. 102:14-15).
Rather, he makes a rogue of himself in order to accom-
plish a project that is perhaps as serious as Orestes'
own. For while Orestes seeks to liberate men in order
to constitute himself as "guilt-stealer," Aegisthus
seeks to enslave them in order to constitute himself as
"order-establisher." In our remarks on Orestes' conversion, we questioned this choice of a project of

liberation. Aegisthus, by revealing the other side of
the coin, the defects of a project of ruling (or, as
Jupiter soon calls it, "reigning"), indicates the
grounds for preferring Orestes' project, as one more
becoming a hero.

The rhetorical context of this soliloquy is
Aegisthus' question to the statue of Jupiter, "Is this,
Jupiter, the king whom you needed for Argos?" He does
not question the appropriateness of his terror- and
guilt-inducing actions to the task of ruling, but only
his adequacy to that task. Jupiter enters, remarking,
"Complain: you are a king like all kings" (p. 82:4-5,
15). The statement is ambiguous. Aegisthus' similarity to "all kings" lies at least in the fact of his
complaining. But it may also refer to the substance of
his complaint, that ruling has drained him of any being
of his own. In this case, Jupiter's first words to
Aegisthus obscure what he will soon be required to emphasize, that Aegisthus is, from a Jovian perspective,
a better king than most (pp. 84:25-26; 85:7). Jupiter,
true to form, begins his discourse with a half-truth.

Aegisthus at first does not recognize the God. In
order to effect recognition, he momentarily assumes the
terrible appearance which he has had in Aegisthus'
dreams. Aegisthus conceives of the divine ruler in
terms of thunder, lightning, and terror. But Jupiter,
by his more smiling general deportment and by his curiosity at the extreme ugliness of his statue, points to
other aspects of ruling. In order to rule as Jupiter
does, one must be able to threaten, to cajole, to
deceive, and to crawl, as well as to terrify outright.
Jupiter is alternately a monument of frightfulness and
an oily con man. He attains a kind of dignity only after
Orestes has defeated him. He has come to warn Aegisthus of Orestes; he spends most of the scene urging
Aegisthus to act upon the warning, that is, to preserve
himself. Aegisthus needs urging to that elementary
task. An "empty shell" is not apt actively to resist
the rock about to crush it. Aegisthus must be reminded
that he is more than a shell or the desert. In a kind
of inverted cat-and-mouse game, Jupiter makes a number
of appeals, all ultimately failures. In doing so, the
God reveals himself not only to Aegisthus, but also to
the hidden Orestes.

Observing the statue, Jupiter muses that the
people cannot love him very much. To Aegisthus' remark,
that they fear him, he gives approval, disclaiming any

77

need for love. Then, in a coy about-face, he asks
Aegisthus if he loves him. Implicitly, he is also asking whether he fears him. If Aegisthus loves him, he
can be urged through simple piety. If he fears him, he
can be intimidated. Aegisthus' reply--"What do you want
from me? Haven't I paid enough?" (p. 83:7)--implicitly
denies love, and, in its boldness, casts doubt on his
fear. Yet why has he "paid" so much? Aware of the face
that he has worn in Aegisthus' dreams, and of the general character of kings, Jupiter brandishes both carrot
and stick. He sternly answers the payment question,
"Never enough!" (p. 83:8), but to Aegisthus' further
complaint, that the task is killing him, reassures him
that, with his good health and royal fat, he is constituted to live another twenty years. The prospect does
not please Aegisthus; he wants to die. But to the
query, whether he would submit to an assassin's sword,
he answers that he does not know. Assassination involves the prospect of excruciating pain and, more to
the point, relinquishing power to another person. To
submit to another's power is an affront to Aegisthus'
kingly pride. Still, it would end his royal misery.
In order to tilt this uncertainty in the desired
direction, Jupiter threatens him with eternal kingship
in Tartarus if he lets himself be killed. This is
surely an empty threat, given the drift of Jupiter's
later remark on human mortality as an absolute end
(p. 87:4-7). Aegisthus is possibly alert to this consideration, given his earlier description of a dead
soul (p. 62:24-29). If so, then he is alert to Jupiter's attempted deception. In any event, he shows
interest only in the factual suggestion that someone
is seeking to kill him. He guesses that it is Electra;
Jupiter adds, also Orestes.

Aegisthus accepts this news with resignation, as
"in the order (of things)" (p. 83:30). But Orestes'
being alive implies that his command of fifteen years
ago, that the child be killed, was disobeyed. That he
is not angered at this treasonous disobedience suggests
that the news does not greatly surprise him. And this
lack of surprise in turn suggests that he has long
lived with the conscious possibility of disobedience
to his most fundamental political command, the one
intended to secure the regime from its most likely
pretender. Ruling, then, has within it this second
fundamental flaw: Despite all of the ruler's arduous
and alienating efforts, he must depend upon the will
of others. Disobedience, a chance divergence of wills,
even a misunderstanding, may turn his projects into

78

mere "gestures."[34] Aegisthus acknowledges implicitly
what Jupiter soon states aloud, that human freedom may
jeopardize any political dispensation. But this is no
less a risk for Orestes' political project than for
Aegisthus'.

Jupiter mocks Aegisthus' "What can I do about it?"
(p. 83:31, 32), telling him to order the immediate
arrest and imprisonment of the young foreigner Philebus
and Electra. So concerned is he over Orestes that he
is willing to have Aegisthus violate two of the city's
ancient laws, the requirement of hospitality to strangers and the holiday amnesty law (cf. pp. 53:5-6; 67:
38-68:1). Since he does not add such words as "wherever they may be," he stops short of endorsing violation of the third ancient law, sanctuary at the temple
of Apollo. Possibly Jupiter is limited by his fellow
God's sphere (cf. pp. 69:37-70:1; 100:10-13). But his
general rebuke of Aegisthus is clear. In addition to
voicing a false notion of fate, he is too scrupulous
about respecting customary restraints when the regime
is endangered. For the time being, however, the explicit argument is not that Aegisthus should save the
regime, but that he should save himself. He refuses to
summon his guards, stating as his reason merely that he
is weary. But his eyes reveal more than weariness to
Jupiter. They show a will to resist the God. With his
own intimidating gaze, Jupiter ridicules him and predicts that he will end up obeying him. For Jupiter
does not leave Olympus without a motive. He wishes to
warn Aegisthus of the crime because it pleases him to
prevent it.

This wish to warn him puzzles Aegisthus. Indeed,
it is strange that Jupiter would seek to prevent the
killing through Aegisthus' agency rather than more
directly, unless he either lacked the necessary power
or had some ulterior motive for proceeding in this way.
Jupiter attempts to divert Aegisthus' attention from
these possibilities by depicting his warning as a personal favor. Aegisthus remains understandably skepti-
cal. He has not requested continued life; and the
activity which it entails, continued rule, has just
been wielded as a threatened punishment. Moreover,
why didn't Jupiter warn Agamemnon, who wanted to live?
Jupiter answers that Aegisthus is dearer to him than
Agamemnon was. But this dearness is not personal, for,
responding to the accusation that Orestes is really his
favorite, since he is being protected from himself,
Jupiter confesses that he loves nobody. Aegisthus is

dearer than Agamemnon because of his policies. Earlier, Jupiter had called Aegisthus "a ruffian" and Agamemnon "a good man," but suggested that Aegisthus was the better king (p. 35:5, 9-13). Like the threat of a moment ago, this pretense of personal favor rings hollow. When Aegisthus accuses him of injustice for treating him differently from Orestes, the discourse moves to the plane of rulership as such.

Aegisthus conceives of Orestes' contemplated crime as essentially the same as his own, the murder of an old king and the installation of himself as the new king. Thus, Orestes is being rescued from the alienation and possible futilities of ruling. Aegisthus' accusation of injustice is one of treating equals, murderer-kings, unequally. Jupiter responds, "All crimes do not displease me equally" (p. 85:7). He offers an alternative standard of justice, that of treating unequals, crimes, unequally. Aegisthus' view is too democratic. But it is in their serviceability to Jupiter's purposes that the contemplated crimes are unequal.

The God himself committed the first "crime" by "creating mortal men":

> After that, what could you do, you others,
> the assassins? Give death to your victims?
> Go on; they already carried it within them;
> at the very most you hastened its blooming
> a bit (p. 85:9-13).

Why is this act a crime rather than merely a mistake? Whose law did it transgress? Possibly Jupiter is engaging in hyperbole. But possibly too this act was a crime against Godhood. Godhood implies perfection, and death corruption. The creation of something corrupt itself casts doubt upon the creator's perfection. Now, mortality characterizes not only man but other living, and in a sense also non-living, things. Since everything that comes into being passes away, all becoming indicts the Being-that-is. In non-theological language, becoming betokens the imperfection of nature. But perhaps there are discernible in these becomings constant patterns, laws of nature, which are eternally. Nature can perhaps be "saved" as an expression of Godly perfection.

It is rather human mortality which constitutes Jupiter's crime, because it makes the task of certain men, the assassins, futile. Taken literally, this

80

explanation is paradoxical. Far from confounding assassination, mortality is its very precondition. But
if death is certain, the mode of dying is not. Assassination is not merely a hastening of the inevitable,
but the infliction of pain and indignity. Even the
ludicrous natural death "of apoplexy upon a beautiful
slave girl's breast" (p. 85:15), which would have been
Agamemnon's fate had Aegisthus not killed him, may in
these respects have been rationally preferable to his
actual demise. But the necessity of death also brings
into being the possibilities of staking one's life and
of dying heroically. Heroes are the peculiar bain of
the assassins to whom Jupiter refers--not just murderers, but murderers who are kings, like Aegisthus
(cf. p. 84:34-35). It is not killers for whom Jupiter
is solicitous, but rulers whose killings are acts of
political founding and perpetuation. A full awareness
of their mortality frees men from their earthly rulers.
But insofar as the official crimes of rulers serve
Jupiter's purposes of universal order, the heroic attitude which confounds rulers also confounds these purposes. Heroes such as Orestes are even more a threat
to the God than they are to rulers such as Aegisthus,
since the opposition of this particular hero to this
particular ruler is a matter of contingency; but the
God is implicated in all ruling as such.

Conceivably, Jupiter could repair his "crime" by
expunging his creation. But short of this total remedy,
his efforts are problematic. For in order to subdue
men, he must either attack them as bodies by entering
into the natural chain of causation, or beguile them
through magic. But the former subjects the God to the
contingencies of corporeal beings. This corporeal
Jupiter, for instance, is not omniscient. He only
knows what he can gather by being in one place at a
time. In the present scene, he is apparently unaware
of Orestes' presence behind the throne. Magic, on the
other hand, may be intimidating, but men are still
fundamentally free to reject its claimed significance,
as Orestes has done. Jupiter's magical displays tend,
moreover, to be trivial. Possibly a major miracle
would require an unacceptable disruption of a natural
order in which he, or the other Gods, have too much at
stake. Understandably, Jupiter does not mention his
limitations to Aegisthus. The human possibilities
which make Orestes dangerous could also pertain to
Aegisthus as a human being. Despite his promise to
speak to him frankly, Jupiter continues to attempt
to manipulate him.

For his part, Aegisthus is absorbed in personal resentment at Jupiter's revelation that had he not been assassinated Agamemnon would have died three months later anyway, but that the crime which he has been expiating for fifteen years "served me." Jupiter responds, "It is because you expiate it that it serves me; I love crimes that pay" (p. 85:16, 19-20). He describes Aegisthus' crime as a passionate, unthinking act of rage and fear, followed by the wish not to recognize it. And from this attitude has accrued profits for Jupiter. "For one man dead, twenty thousand others plunged into repentance . . . I didn't strike a bad bargain"(p. 85:27-29). In this account Jupiter exaggerates the importance of Aegisthus' own remorse. He had earlier doubted that Aegisthus repented at all, but discounted its importance since "repentance is measured by the pound" (p. 37:24-26). Aegisthus claims to "see what all these discourses are hiding: Orestes will have no remorse" (p. 85:30-31). He does not indicate whether he sees the more weighty consequence, that Orestes will do no expiation, that the city will be freed from repentance. Jupiter continues along a personal line, trying to provoke Aegisthus' sense of individual pride, and not at all developing this political consequence. Orestes is proceeding with remorseless, cold calculation. "He will kill you like a chicken, the sweet young man, and will go away with red hands and a pure conscience; I should be humiliated over it in your place" (pp. 85:38-86:2). By conjecturing himself into Aegisthus' place, Jupiter situates himself discursively out of that place. He denies their equal kingly standing which he had asserted a moment ago in order to avoid conveying his own present vulnerability. Aegisthus refuses this appeal to pride. His resentment of Jupiter is stronger. If anything, it has been cemented by the God's present revelations and rhetorical stance.

Jupiter's argumentative ploys have proven to be double-edged. As a matter of dialectical necessity, he must now be more candid. Changing his tone as he had not done before, he addresses himself to Aegisthus' "king's conscience; . . . for you love to reign" (p. 86:5-6; cf. p. 85:8). He asserts a natural bond between them: "I have made you in my image: a king is a God on earth, noble and sinister like a God" (p. 86: 8-10). His use of the term "sinister" startles Aegisthus, who had described his own internal barrenness in this way (p. 82:13). Is the God, who has just proclaimed the king's empty exercises to be part of a

grand design, himself empty? Aegisthus is conscious
of his own emptiness as a lack of emotion. He is
"neither sad nor gay" (p. 82:11). Looking at Jupiter,
he beholds the same absences. Jupiter now names the
foundation of their common emotionlessness. They both
make order reign, each in his respective realm, and
they both guard the same "grievous secret," that men
are free (p. 86:17; cf. p. 38:11). The promotion of
order and the keeping of this secret require the exclusion of such luxuries as sorrow and joy in the ruler.
They require that he set himself apart from men. The
implications of the grievous secret for earthly rule
are clear to Aegisthus. If men knew it, "they would
set fire to the four corners of my palace. For fifteen
years I've been play-acting to mask their power from
them" (p. 86:20-22).

But while this apprehension may indicate the practical necessity for him to maintain his masquerade now,
it does not explain his having undertaken it in the
first place. It is these kings' other activity which
lies at the base of their secret-keeping. They "make
order reign." Aegisthus reigns not chiefly for his own
sake, but for that of order itself, "that it might
reign through me" (p. 87:12-13). And the demands of
this principle, in its own right, are total. He has
therefore not been content to rule men's bodies. His
acts and words have all aimed at composing an image of
himself that "each of my subjects (would) carry within
him," such that "he (would) feel, even in solitude, my
severe look weighing upon his most secret thoughts"
(p. 86:25-29). Order, if it is to prevail, must prevail over thought as well as acts. The consequence of
which he despairs, that he has become his own "first
victim," that, he believes, he is now only "the fear
which others have of me," is the necessary goal of his
project (p. 86:29, 33). But that Aegisthus has not in
fact reached that goal is evidenced by his confession
that his image, which he sees reflected in the "gaping
well of (my subjects') souls . . . revolts me and fas-
cinates me" (p. 86:31-32). He implicitly answers his
own question, "(W)ho am I, if not the fear that others
have of me?" (p. 86:32-33). He is the repugnance and
fascination which beholds that fear. Aegisthus' passive desire for the reign of order is accompanied by
the active desire to know that order reigns. But the
attempt to achieve the latter, the desire to know,
which may be endemic to being human, renders inaccessible the full accomplishment of the former. To know
is to stand apart from the thing known. If order is

to reign, it must reign in the ruler as well as through his realm. But the attempt to verify this reigning contradicts this very order.

Ruling's third defect thus stands revealed for Orestes. To rule, as Aegisthus rules, is to be a pawn in an order not of one's own making. It is to "reign" in order that Jupiter may rule. And if Jupiter is himself empty, if there is no God, it is to lose oneself for the sake of an emptiness, for a foundationless abstraction. Further, the goal of perfect order is in principle impossible for a human being, whose very being, as freedom, is at core an exception to such an order. But what, then, is the status of Orestes' project? If freedom is indeed a stepping back from ordered being, then order of some description or other is a necessary precondition to freedom. Orestes' project, as an attempt to realize the principle of freedom for the Argives, needs to posit some order or other, with reference to which their freedom would become effective. But this order would proceed from Orestes himself. In order to be a liberator, he too must be an order-establisher. As an attempt to substantiate himself, however, neither the posited order nor the project of freedom could suffice. As author of both, he would be beyond both. Orestes cannot be contained by his project; his project must be short of total.

Even Jupiter, in his quasi-human incarnation, may partake of this human ontological quality of detachment from his projected image. At this scene's beginning, he had beheld his image, the statue, with a repugnance and fascination perhaps akin to Aegisthus' (pp. 82: 23-83:3). But as a God, he differs from Aegisthus more than he would have him believe. Almost forgetting himself, he reflects:

> For a hundred thousand years I have been dancing before men. A slow and somber dance. They must look at me: as long as they have their eyes fixed upon me, they forget to look within themselves. If I forgot myself for a single instant, if I let their look turn away . . . (pp. 86:36-87:2).

He leaves the thought unfinished. When Aegisthus presses him to complete it, he responds, "This concerns only me" (p. 87:4). But we may complete the thought within the context of Jupiter's rhetorical insistence upon their similarity: If he let them turn away, they would look within themselves, discover their freedom, and "set fire to the four corners" of the God's "palace," the world. For unlike men, who exist irreducibly in the world, the God's being is essentially borrowed; it depends upon men's belief. Aegisthus is human enough, and resentful enough of Jupiter, to require having this difference concealed from him. Jupiter thus continues to depict the principle of order as their common destiny. And Aegisthus, for his part, accepts this account, confessing that "(i)t is for order that I seduced Clytemnestra, for order that I killed my king" (p. 87:11-12). Must not this overheard confession, which belies Electra's already-shaken fantasies of lust between Aegisthus and her mother, leave some impression on her? Clytemnestra, in the final analysis is merely a pawn in this man's political designs, a description which could also lend itself to her own later relation to Orestes.

In the name of the order they both serve, Jupiter commands Aegisthus, "my creature and my mortal brother," to seize Orestes and Electra. Aegisthus' query, whether they are so dangerous, receives the simple answer, "Orestes knows that he is free" (p. 87:19, 23). The fact thoroughly engages Aegisthus' passion. Orestes must be stopped; he threatens to "contaminate my whole kingdom and ruin my work." He asks, "Almighty God, what are you waiting for to strike him down?" (p. 87:27-29).[34a] Jupiter is forced to make his final revelation. Now avoiding Aegisthus' glance, he wearily announces the Gods' other secret, that they are powerless to do anything more to a man within whose soul freedom has exploded. It belongs only to men "to let him go or to strangle him" (p. 87:36-37). Aegisthus repeats the second of these alternatives. But looking at the hunched-over God, he must now see it as only one of two real alternatives. He states that he will doubtless obey him, but tells him to add nothing and not to remain much longer, "for I won't be able to stand it" (p. 88:2). Jupiter's continued presence could now only deepen his sense of the fragility of all order. The God obligingly leaves without another word.

The Assassination

Despite his assurance of obedience, Aegisthus does not summon his guards immediately upon Jupiter's

85

departure.  He remains alone for a moment, with the
opportunity to reflect on what has transpired.  Like
Electra and Orestes earlier, he has addressed an inquiry to an otherworldly being and has been answered
to his dissatisfaction.  Unlike them, his answer was
given through a human medium, speech, and most explicitly affirms the fullness of his human potential,
which the miracles had sought to obscure.  The abstract wish for the release of death has become the
imminent possibility of being assassinated, to be
weighted against the natural alternative of living
another twenty years.  Relinquishing his life has
been linked not only to his own loss of rule but to
destruction of the regime.  But the regime's continuation has been revealed as fundamentally a matter of
human choice.  Its divine prop removed, Aegisthus is
free, perhaps for the first time in his life, seriously
to contemplate its destruction.  But is there perhaps
a third way open to him?  Aegisthus' death will eventuate in the regime's collapse only if Orestes sustains
his own sense of freedom.  If that sense can be infected with remorse, if Orestes' crime can be converted
into a re-enactment of Aegisthus' crime, then Aegisthus
might be able to embrace his desired death while sal-
vaging his work.

Presumably Orestes and Electra could also reflect,
in that intervening moment, on the matters which they
have overheard.  But Electra's task-minded order to
Orestes as they emerge from behind the throne--"Strike
him!  Don't let him have time to cry out . . ."--sug-
gests that her reflections have been of an instrumental
order (p. 88:4-5).  Orestes immediately departs from
her program.  He gives Aegisthus more than enough time
to cry out, for they engage in two sets of verbal exchanges before he strikes his first blow.  Crying out
for assistance could not save Aegisthus' life at this
point, but it could foil the rest of Orestes' project.
Orestes is apparently willing to take this risk.  He
orders Aegisthus to defend himself.  He would rather
do battle than assassinate outright.  The outcome of
such a battle would not be a foregone conclusion.
While we have no indication whether Aegisthus has ever
engaged in armed combat, we know that Orestes has not
(p. 71:13-15).  He would prefer to be heroic in the
means as well as the end.  Aegisthus is unobliging;
he wants Orestes to assassinate him.  He is weary.
But perhaps he also wishes to deprive the impending
killing of heroic content, and if possible to make it
shameful.  Consenting to be an assassin, Orestes

86

strikes. To him, "(t)he means are of little importance" (p. 88:11). By implication, the end is everything.

Staggering from his wound, Aegisthus clutches
Orestes, looks at him directly, after the fashion of
Jupiter attempting to evoke guilt, and asks, "Is it
true that you have no remorse?" The following dialogue ensues:

> Or. Remorse? Why? I am doing what
> is just.
> Aeg. What is just is what Jupiter wills.
> You were hidden here and you heard him.
> Or. What does Jupiter matter to me?
> Justice is an affair of men, and I don't
> need a God to teach it to me. It is just
> to crush you, filthy rogue, and to ruin
> your empire over the people of Argos, it
> is just to return to them the sentiment of
> their dignity (p. 88:15-24).

Orestes offers a political defense of his action, in
terms of justice, the political virtue. Aegisthus'
reference to the will of Jupiter is tainted by his
current disobedience to that will in not defending
himself. But Orestes eschews this ready rebuke, for
it would concede the primacy of Jupiter's will even
while destroying Jupiter's agent. Orestes' elaboration
of the things that are just makes reference to this
world only. The three just ends seem to be arranged
in an ascending hierarchy. But his list differs from
the hierarchy of ends which he had suggested at the
time of his conversion. Then, the political liberation of Argos was depicted in terms perhaps character-
izable as giving the people a sense of their dignity,
but not so characterized explicitly. But this liberation then had an end outside itself, the acquisition
for Orestes of the right to the city (p. 76:3-8, 12-25).
Does he now perceive an incongruity between the justice of the Argives' sense of dignity and the project
of situating himself among them? The drift of the
overheard discourse has been from concern with the
private to concern with the public, from Aegisthus'
self-preservation to the preservation of the regime as
an expression of the principle of order. Even Aegisthus' failure to preserve himself has entailed an
attempt to save the regime. Orestes' statement confirms the public consequence of his act which Aegisthus
and Jupiter had so dreaded. It too moves from the

private to the public as an expression of the universal. There would perhaps be something petty about turning from the principle of freedom, in the aspect "sentiment of dignity," to a private design. But Orestes' statement itself has a self-substantiating character which is not at all petty. It is a pronouncement on the nature of justice, made in supersession of a contrary pronouncement by the founder and ruler of this regime. Its reference to restoration notwithstanding, it is an act of legislation of the most fundamental order, the beginning of Orestes' self-constitution as founder of a new regime.

His attempt to save the regime having failed, Aegisthus is thrown back to the inescapably private, his own pain. Electra notes with horror the ugliness of a dying man. She had not anticipated seeing her enemies in the actual pain of dying; her dreams had pictured them already dead. The only actual cutting which she had envisioned was the splitting of the lifeless, bloodless statue of Jupiter (pp. 69:9-17; 44:12; 45:1-12). Unlike Orestes, she had not embraced the means with the desired end. Orestes orders her to be silent in order that Aegisthus' last sight might be that of their joy. He wishes to stifle the possibility of remorse, but also to savor the moment in a calculated cruelty. To Electra, however, this cruelty is gratuitous. When Aegisthus next curses them both for it, he lays part of the groundwork for her later resentment toward Orestes, for the suffering man is cursing her for her brother's cruelty. Continuing in this vein, Orestes expresses impatience at the duration of Aegisthus' dying--an especially contemptuous gesture given his earlier expressed wish to die--, and strikes him again. Aegisthus' dying words--"Watch out for the flies, Orestes . . . All is not finished."--seem to be a final attempt to evoke regret in Orestes through fear of the divine; for the flies, as the Furies, are minor deities in the service of Jupiter. Without understanding this aspect of the statement, Orestes, in a final flourish, kicks the corpse and declares, "For him, all is finished in any case" (p. 89:3-4, 6-7).

Turning to Electra, he tells her to guide him to the queen's room. He regards Clytemnestra, as he had at his moment of conversion, in her political capacity. But Electra hesitates, observing, "She can no longer harm us . . ." (p. 89:10). The sight of someone dying in agony has impressed her deeply. She is shaken by

88

the thought of such a death being wrought upon her mother, who is so like herself (cf. p. 70:25-26). From a private perspective, her observation on Clytemnestra's harmlessness may be quite correct. Deprived of Aegisthus, she could easily be reduced to a position of subservience, substituting one remorse for another, or superadding it to the other. As the humiliated queen mother, and as someone who has shown no inclination to rule directly, she would be unlikely to threaten the deposition of an Orestian regime. But as a remorseful presence, she could constantly infect that regime, both by herself and through Electra, with the very spirit which Orestes seeks to overthrow by the assassinations. Electra has let her political concern--what it means to be proud of one's city--be drowned in the personal (cf. p. 47:24-25). Both Orestes and Electra have become partial persons. Electra's partiality enervates her; Orestes' is a necessary condition of his task. Fear or pity at this moment would be inimical to political liberation. No longer either the sweet young man or Electra's fantastic instrument, he goes out to complete that task alone.

Electra's deterioration begins with her witnessing Aegisthus' painful dying, which she had not anticipated in her fantasies. The departure of events from her imaginings was signalled more subtly by her order to Orestes at the start of the assassination scene, which had to take account of Clytemnestra's absence (cf. p. 88:4 with p. 70:22-23). Her single "Strike!" has exhausted the role which she had set for herself. She is now superfluous; her very being is in question. Her soliloquy, spoken during Clytemnestra's killing, exhibits her peculiar confusions and failings of the moment. Her attention shifts continually from Clytemnestra to the dead Aegisthus to her own wishes. But she considers these wishes as a state of mind, viewed from without. She attempts to picture the imminent killing, but cannot do so. Instead, she finds that she must reassure herself of her own intentions, that "I wanted it! I want it, I must still want it" (p. 89: 18-19). She regards her will as a thing, predetermined by its previous states. She seeks the false comfort of passivity. But what she wanted was something much neater, much more "essential" than what occurs. Orestes would be merely an executioner; her single order to strike would have been the sufficient essential order; Aegisthus would end up with a sword through his heart, the seat of life, and would thus be most essentially dead; his body would seem to sleep, for a corpse has no need to look active (pp. 79:20-23; 89:22-23). Her dreams had partaken of the spirit of Aegisthus' rule, the wish for order. The actual assassination is parcel to human reality, fraught with freedom, disordered and ambiguous, excessive and deficient. Orestes has a will of his own; a second episode is necessary to dispose of Clytemnestra; and the corpse is not just a dead thing, but a frozen advertisement of Aegisthus' last agonized moment of life.[33] She even fancies that its open eyes, departing from "corpsehood," are looking at her, and she throws a cloak over its face. Finally, the finality of this death entails the finitude of her project. "He is dead--and my hate died with him" (p. 89:25-26). Formerly, Electra was her hate. Her enemies' deaths make a continuation of that hate idle, and so require her to redefine herself in terms of another project. If she would retain that hate, she has a stake in Clytemnestra's remaining alive. Thus, she wonders just what it was that she wanted, and expresses apprehension over Clytemnestra's awaited cries.

When she hears those cries, her immediate reaction is to blame Orestes for having struck "our mother." The maternal relationship which formerly was only incidental has now become focal (pp. 89:31-90:1; cf. p. 46: 28-36). This emphasis might have been mitigated had both assassinations occurred together. Then the victims might have been "the paramours." Clytemnestra, she quickly assumes, is dead, not merely wounded. She wishes the facts to be decisively settled. But her self-uncertainty remains. Because she is not enjoying this moment as she had imagined she would, she wonders whether she had been lying to herself for fifteen years. Unwilling to admit this possibility, she attempts repeatedly to convince herself that she does want the present situation and that she is enjoying it. She tears the cloak from Aegisthus' face, steels herself to Clytemnestra's continued cries, and, when they stop, balances the killing of "our mother" with the afterthought that "my father is avenged" (p. 90:13). To Orestes, however, who enters, bloody sword in hand, she appears afraid. Insisting that she is not afraid but drunk with joy, she presses him for details of the killing. To compensate for her experience of Aegisthus' death, she wishes now to embrace the means with a passion. But Orestes refuses to speak of it, explaining that "there are some memories that one doesn't share. Know only that she is dead" (p. 90:22-23). He has gained the object of his first expressed longing, some

90

memory of his own, of an act performed within a situation. To describe this act would apparently compromise its uniqueness and give it a borrowed character. But by concealing the details he prevents Electra from sharing in his project. She does, however, elicit one detail from him: Like Aegisthus, Clytemnestra died cursing them. Electra draws temporary solace from this datum. It restores her share in the act, and sustains her former hate in a way that a final show of motherly forgiveness might not. But this comfort can only be provisional. Cursing would be the normal reaction under the circumstances. It can provide no lasting vindication of the supposition that Clytemnestra had always hated her.

Orestes' and Electra's ways have begun dramatically to part. Even while embracing, they speak past each other. Orestes is taken with his freedom, which he now identifies with his act. That act will weigh him down forever, and he will proudly bear its weight (p. 91:24-28). In making this identification, however, Orestes seems to commit the same error as Aegisthus did when he equated himself with the fear that others had of him. They collapse freedom into the appearance or attitude which manifests it. In the language of Being and Nothingness, they treat being-for-itself as being-in-itself. Orestes seems to be guilty of bad faith, even in the course of displaying a positive moral teaching.[36] Electra questions this boasted freedom, asking "Can you prevent our forever being our mother's assassins?" (p. 91:21-22). She misconceives freedom to be omnipotence. But omnipotence would be the destruction of the kind of freedom which Orestes claims, which requires the embracing of a set of contingencies as irrevocably one's own. Even if one later changes his mind, this freedom, as past, cannot be expunged, only built upon.[37] But how to build upon it is a completely open question (cf. p. 91:33-34). Also, just what is the act which Orestes so emphatically calls his own? Undoubtedly it is at least the dual assassination. But his assertion that Electra now "belongs" to him suggests that he may also regard his accomplished act to be the political liberation and the political and personal appropriations which he had projected at the time of his conversion (p. 91:2; cf. pp. 75:18-19; 76:19-25). If so, then Electra's remarks already signal the dubiousness of this claim.

The unclarity of this exchange to Electra has been accompanied by a gradual dimming of her vision. The

air seems to her to grow thick, the room to become
dark. She fetches a torch, the better to see Orestes,
for she must have him before her eyes to be reassured;
but even this fails to ward off the darkness. His
voice too becomes harsh to her. She finally realizes
that the flies are coming between her and her source
of light, and the sound of their buzzing distorting
other sounds. To Orestes, the flies are merely flies
and of no importance. But Electra recognizes them as
the Furies, the goddesses of remorse. As Orestes has
given substance to his freedom, Electra has become
remorseful.

Voices from without indicate that Clytemnestra's
cries have attracted the guards. Orestes orders Electra
to lead him to the Apollonian sanctuary, where he will
rest until morning, and then "speak to my people" (p.
92:25). He believes that he has appropriated the Argives. But whether in fact he has, or can, remains
unsettled.

## V. Act III

### Electra's Inauthenticity

Act 2 has depicted Orestes' overthrow of Aegisthus.
But it has also indicated the crucial link between
Aegisthus' tyranny and the principle of order, of which
Jupiter is the divine advocate. If Orestes' victory is
to be complete, and truly heroic, he must also confront
and overthrow Jupiter. Act 3 presents that confronta-
tion and overthrow. But this victory occurs on grounds
that disjoin the heroic from the Godly as such. The
Act, which takes place under the benign protection of
Apollo, transcends even God in his benignity.

As the Act opens, Orestes and Electra are asleep
at the base of Apollo's statue, their arms wrapped
around its legs. This statue, unlike the Jovian statues,
is designed to provide solace. But it can do so only
temporarily. The protection which Apollo affords from
the Furies extends only to the most immediate vicinity
of the statue itself. One of the Furies anticipates
that "soon thirst and hunger will drive them from this
shelter" (p. 94:13-14). The God's protection could be
lasting only for a being that did not need to eat or
drink, that is, only for the dead or another God. This
limitation of the divine sphere by human need subjects
the divine to human valuation and use. Electra, for
instance, beguiled by Jupiter, abandons Apollo because

92

his divine rival in effect offers her a better bargain.

The Furies surround them, also asleep but in a characteristically unhuman posture, standing up "like water birds" (p. 93:s.d.). Unlike the sleep of Aeschylus' Furies, theirs is not the result of an Apollonian spell, but rather a normal biological process, from which they awaken refreshed.[38] But this refreshment is quite unnatural; one Fury describes herself as having a soul "of copper" (p. 93:11). And their ambiguous status, as minor deities within the world, implicates their physical powers as well as their biological needs (cf. pp. 96:12-18; 97:27-36; 98: 13-18; 109:8-9). Once awake, their remarks reveal them as personifications of guilt--predatory, ambitious, craftsmanly, self-righteous--, but their threats to the pair are blatantly those of physical disfigurement as well as of psychic torment (p. 94:11, 15-17, 29-30). Their chorus, sung as they encircle the sleepers, buzzing like flies, describes remorse in terms both highly physical and impalpable: first, as the viscous, sticky quality of "a tartine," "pus," "green honey" (pp. 94:37; 95:1,3); then, as the anxious feeling of being watched, even in the actual absence of another person; finally, as a kind of presence, a something-else, which robs one of the fullness of his own experiences.

The Furies' speech and their buzzing startle Electra from her sleep, but recognizing them, she concludes, "Then we have really killed them?" In this first half-awake "we" she implicitly admits her role in the assassinations, a role which she spends the remainder of the scene attempting to deny (p. 95:29-30; cf. p. 96:2). This denial begins almost as soon as Orestes awakens. Expressing puzzlement at the absence of "anything written" on his face, she identifies him as the killer no fewer than three times in as many sentences. For his part, Orestes acknowledges having killed them, and expresses his own fearful puzzlement over how much Electra's features have changed, as though "a beast (had) ravaged your face with its claws." Electra again drives her point home by naming "(y)our crime" as the beast (p. 96:2-9). Turning her attention to the Furies, she asks who they are. This question too is parcel to her evasion. If she is guilty of no crime, then there is no reason for her to know them. But she is deceiving herself; she has already recognized them and their significance. Orestes assures her of the Furies' powerlessness. The first Fury dares Orestes to let Electra come among them, "and you will see whether we can do nothing to her." But he disdainfully orders the"bitches" to the kennel (p. 96:15-17).

Concentrating again on Electra's features, he realizes that she has come to resemble Clytemnestra. The thought that the price of his crime has been the vindication of Clytemnestra's prophecy horrifies him (p. 96: 21-23; cf. pp. 49:4; 52:14-25). The first Fury interjects that it is he who horrifies Electra. Electra refuses to speak to this assessment, but her behavior toward him has tended to confirm it. The Fury, attempting further to stir up Electra, asks how she could not hate him:

> She was living tranquilly with her dreams;
> you came, bringing carnage and sacrilege.
> And there she is, sharing your sin, riveted
> to this pedestal, the only piece of earth
> that is left to her (p. 96:29-32).

She suggests to Electra a deceptively inviting half-truthful account of what has happened. Orestes has indeed effected the change from dream to bloody reality, and Electra's domain has contracted to the limited range of the sanctuary. But while her former life did not contain actual bloodshed, she grew up "in the shadow of a murder"(p. 71:34-35). And her desecration of the statue of Jupiter in Act 1 surely was a sacrilege.

Orestes urges Electra not to listen to the Fury. But her attention is already engaged by an account which places the full blame on Orestes. The Fury continues by describing the killing of Clytemnestra in agonizing, obscene detail, dwelling upon the actual infliction of wounds, in a manner geared to excite Electra's morbid curiosity and to discredit Orestes' competence even as an assassin. Orestes does not contradict this account, but urges Electra more strenuously not to question the Fury because "(s)he wants to separate us, she is setting up walls of solitude around you." Whether to overcome a sense of shame at the manner of execution or to spare Electra's squeamishness, he invites her attention to an alternative partial perception of the past events: "(W)e decided on this murder together, and we must bear the consequences together" (p. 97:13-14, 16-17). Is such partial perception an unavoidable component of any shared enterprise? Electra resists the assertion of even this much common ground, distinguishing somewhat

94

uncertainly between dreaming of the crime and wanting it, and more definitely between dreaming of it and committing it. The distinction between dreaming and wanting, suggested by the Fury's characterization of events, introduces a refinement into the psychological determinism which Electra had expressed in her soliloquy over Aegisthus' body, but without fundamentally abandoning the idea of determinism itself. The past seems variously describable and redescribable according to the purpose to which it is put.[39]

Orestes briefly turns from the past to the future, by articulating a project within which this past may become tolerable: When they will emerge from the sanctuary onto "the sunny roads, . . . these daughters of the night will lose their powers: the day's rays will pierce through them like swords." But the first Fury offers an equally plausible future. They will stand between her and the sun, and "you will everywhere carry night above your head" (p. 97:27-29, 33). Her future depends upon the attitude she assumes toward the Furies' actual presence, that is, to the immanent possibility of remorse.

Orestes therefore recurs to the present, to the example of his own attitude. He repeats the thought that the Furies are only as powerful as one lets them be. He suggests that he has lived through everything that Electra has. He will always hear Clytemnestra's moaning and see her immense eyes, and be conscious of Electra's anguish. "But," he concludes, "what does it matter to me: I am free. Beyond anguish and memories. Free. And at one with myself" (p. 98:5-6). He does not seek to expunge unpleasant thoughts from his consciousness. But his formulation provides for more than their mere toleration. If his freedom does indeed make him "at one" with himself, then he does not just accept the consequences of the deed which substantiates his freedom; he subsumes them into his freedom. He admits Clytemnestra's and Electra's sufferings into his being by refusing to admit them as causes for guilt, that is, by rejecting their moral claim. He insulates himself from the Furies' ravages only by a monumental self-assertion which either minimizes the seriousness of the pains inflicted upon others or transforms them into positive goods (cf. p. 91:23-24). Electra is understandably astounded and repulsed by his statement, and declares that he frightens her more than the Furies do. She might have been prepared for some argument that would acknowledge regret over the matricide but would maintain its necessity for some demonstrably greater good. Instead, the good with which she is presented is Orestes' state of soul, which reconciles him even to her own immediate suffering, and which is not at all tinged with regret.[40] There is something truly frightening about this freedom.

The Fury offers her what in context arises as the readiest alternative to Orestes' overcoming of anguish through self-assertion--forgetfulness through self-mortification: "(Y)ou need our cannibalistic love to distract you from the hate you bear toward yourself; you need to suffer in your body in order to forget the sufferings of your soul"(p. 98:15-18). Moral repose is offered at the cost of physical mutilation. She will "forget" rather than transcend the reality of dreadful thoughts. Judging from earlier examples, this offer seems to be a swindle. The mere passage of time tends to bring the fading of memories. And the positive attempt to forget is doomed to failure; there is always a looking-back to see whether the hated thing is really gone (cf. pp. 63:9-13; 52:14-24). For Electra the discourse has attained its proper level. The Furies' offer and their slow dance fascinate her and entice her away from the statue of Apollo (cf. p. 86:36-37). Evading Orestes' attempt to hold her back, she descends the steps, and the Furies fall upon her. Her cry for help provides the occasion for Jupiter's entry onto the scene.

## The Discourse on the Divine

Jupiter's first words to the Furies--"To the kennel!"--replicate Orestes' own, vindicate his judgment, and presage his imminent rise to equality with the God (p. 99:1; cf. p. 96:17). The Furies heed their master's voice, and reluctantly back away from Electra.

Jupiter seeks to assure the continuation of his kind of regime in Argos. The readiest way to do so would be to have Orestes and Electra assume the rulership roles just vacated by Aegisthus and Clytemnestra. But to do this they must be made to behave as Aegisthus and Clytemnestra behaved. To this end he makes use of the array of play-acting techniques which he has already employed on past occasion. Orestes, however, having witnessed the attempt to lure Aegisthus, and overheard Jupiter's admission of man's freedom and the Gods' limitation, is alert to his interlocutor's propensity to bluff. Their initial exchange suggests that

he himself may be dealing similarly with Jupiter.
Jupiter assumes an attitude of pity, and, proclaiming
himself Electra's protector from the Furies, piously
chides the "presumptuous and mad youth" which has done
itself such evil. They continue:

> Or. Leave off this good-natured tone:
> it ill becomes the king of the Gods.
> Jup. And you, leave off this proud
> tone: it is hardly proper for a culprit in
> the process of expiating his crime.
> Or. I am not a culprit, and you could
> not make me expiate what I don't recognize
> as a crime. (p. 99:12-19).

But earlier, he had not disputed Electra's reference
to his "crime," and had even joined in this description
of his act; and he does so again at the end, in his
oration to the Argives. He will not admit to the God
what he readily admits before men (pp. 96:9, 24; 97:16,
21; 110:13, 23-25). This is perhaps fully consistent
with his pronouncement to Aegisthus, that justice is
an affair of men. But the pronouncement also contained
a definition of justice, according to which Orestes'
act would not be a crime; or, if one, one of that
peculiar species of crimes the criminality of which is
customarily obscured by myth, crimes of political
founding (p. 88:20-24).

Jupiter begins his attempt to correct Orestes'
"error" as he had begun his discourse with Aegisthus,
with a spurious appeal to love (cf. p. 83:3-6). He
points to Electra's abasement, and calls Orestes' lack
of regret over it a sign that he does not really love
her. Orestes answers that he loves her more than
himself, but that "her sufferings come from herself;
it is she alone who can deliver herself from them:
she is free" (p. 99:29-31). His love for her must take
account of--indeed, must take its cues from--her freedom to assume her own attitude. The foundation of love
is the recognition of freedom, the according of fundamental human dignity to the beloved.

Orestes combats Jupiter's guilt-ploy by seeing
others as he sees himself. Jupiter's response is to
attack this freedom by making him assume an objective
stance, to see himself as others might see him. He
invites him to look at himself,

> all curled up between the legs of a protecting

God, with these bitches who assail you.
If you dare to claim that you are free,
then it will be necessary to speak highly
of the freedom of the prisoner loaded down
with chains, at the bottom of a dungeon,
and of the crucified slave (p. 100:4-8).

As he had appealed to Aegisthus' kingly pride before,
so Jupiter now appeals to Orestes' presumed heroic
pride (cf. p. 85:38-86:2). As it is unbecoming for a
king to be killed like a chicken, so it is unbecoming
for a hero to boast of something common to prisoners
and slaves. Orestes' answer is a simple "Why not?"
(p. 100:9). Even the enchained prisoner and the crucified slave are free to assume any attitude toward
their chains and crucifixion. But why should one
speak highly of such a freedom? To be sure, it signals
the prisoner's and the slave's moral autonomy. But it
is not at all obvious that such a freedom is in itself
praiseworthy, apart from its use, either to rebel
against or to embrace the chains and the cross. But
Orestes does not say that one must praise this freedom.
Rather, he asks rhetorically why his own claim of freedom would not necessitate such praise. The logical
answer, that praise would not be necessary because
freedom is not intrinsically praiseworthy, points either
to the presence of some other dignifying principle in
Orestes' situation, or to the more general conclusion
that nothing is intrinsically praiseworthy. Understandably, Jupiter does not take up either of these
alternatives. To choose the first would be to emphasize the distinguishing features of Orestes' freedom,
its employment for political liberation and its defiance of divine authority. To choose the second would
be to undermine from the outset one of the objects of
Jupiter's presence, to entice Orestes into a position
of rule, a position which is customarily spoken of
highly. Even to dispute these matters would be to
enter upon Orestes' ground, a concession which Jupiter
cannot afford to make, expecially in Electra's presence.

But Electra's loss is, in this instance, also that
of the play's viewers, who, in the absence of an elaborate answer, are left to flounder in the glib suggestion of Orestes' rhetorical question, One aspect
of that suggestion merits particular attention. To
the extent that human freedom is unassailable through
physical torture, physical torture becomes innocuous
since it cannot reach the crux of man's being. The

teaching which dignifies the prisoner and the slave
also lends legitimacy to the tyrant. It was in order
to, counter this legitimacy that the tyrant's activity
had been revealed as flawed in itself, as both unsatisfying and--insofar as it aims at something impossible,
obliterating the Other's freedom--absurd. But a less
ambitious tyranny, one which contented itself with
constraining or even assailing the Other's body while
recognizing, even advertising, his freedom to assume
any attitude, would, from this teaching's perspective,
be quite acceptable. Are we not justly apprehensive
about a teaching which arms an incomplete Aegisthus, or
an oppressively self-indulgent Agamemnon, with the con-
venient argument that their victims' sufferings "come
from themselves"?

Rather than pursue this line of inquiry, Jupiter
challenges the situational context of Orestes' boldness,
Apollo's protection. Apollo, he declares, "is my very
obedient servant. If I lift a finger, he abandons you."
Orestes in turn challenges Jupiter to "life (your) whole
arm" (p. 100:11-13). But Jupiter declines to do so,
averring that he has come not to punish but to save
them. His failure to make good his threat, coupled
with his earlier invocation of other Gods., calls into
question his supposed divine kingship (pp. 40:4; 54:20;
67:6; 74:20). Beyond the immediate context of an
ancient pantheon, the question is one of contradiction
within the idea of divinity itself. Are God-the-Ruler
and God-the-Protector perhaps equally necessary faces
of divinity? Can the offer of divine protection ever
be finally withdrawn without also severing the hierarchical bond between God and free man? Jupiter
attempts to reconcile this divine division by appro-
priating salvation to himself as ruler of the universe,
as the source of Natural Law itself. Jupiter Chris-
tianizes the play's divine cast. The confrontation between him and Orestes, the man who knows he is free,
effects a Godly, as well as a human, conversion.

The dimension of this transformation of the divine
is indicated by Electra's expression of surprise at
Jupiter's promise of salvation, "Stop making fun, master
of vengeance and of death, for it is not permitted--even
for a God--to give a false hope to those who suffer"
(p. 100:16-18). To be serviceable, a God must be credible, both in offering hope and in tendering threats.
Jupiter transgresses both parts of this rule. The
promise which he here makes to Electra, that she may be
out of the sanctuary, "safe and sound," within a quarter

99

of an hour, if only she gives "a little repentance,"
is fulfilled only by default, by the Furies' independent decision not to pursue the by-then hysterically
repentant Electra after Jupiter has left the scene (p.
100:20, 27; cf. p. 108:5-11). This failure reflects
upon the other promises and threats which he makes to
her and to Orestes. For the time being, though, the
offer of relief from her current torments transforms
Jupiter, in Electra's eyes, into the "good God, ador-
able God" (p. 100:24-25). But Jupiter, as God, is in
fact not bound by the moral rule which Electra enunciates. Perhaps a God who rules men must, while
appearing credible, wield false hopes and threats. Insofar as a man's overthrow of a God entails his assumption of God-like status, this problem is also that of
such a man.

Orestes warns her to be wary of this bribe.
"(T)his nothing (i.e., a little repentance) will weigh
upon your soul like a mountain" (p. 100:28-29). Would
this weight, we are entitled to ask, be greater than
that of chains and crucifixion? Implicit in Orestes'
statement are the thought (which might be unremarkable
were it not so frequently disregarded) that the worst
afflictions are those which reach to the soul, and the
corollary thought that supposed solutions to the ills
of man's estate which reach only to material relief
are only half-solutions at best. Yet it was peace of
soul through bodily torment that the Furies offered,
and the thoughtful agony of freedom that Orestes coun-
ter-tendered. While the first of these is presented
as a flimsy sham, could Electra really be content with
the latter? Orestes' comment invites a calculation of
likely psychological pleasures and pains. Electra's
choice for Jupiter on this ground cannot be simply dismissed, assuming the implicit calculation to be possible. This possibility seems to depend upon a standard of values, according to which different experiences
and sets of concerns may be weighed comparatively.
Both Jupiter and Orestes, in their rivalry to hold
Electra, appear to take such a standard for granted.
Jupiter offers safety from the Furies in exchange for
the "almost nothing" of voluntary repentance (p. 100:
26). In order to induce her to disavow the crime, he
invites her to view herself as the mere victim of
circumstances, a pawn in another's game. In this invitation he follows a pattern already set by Electra herself, and encouraged by the Furies (cf. pp. 77:17-18;
97:21-22; 96:29-32). But Orestes, in opposing this
suggestion, also attempts to fix Electra's intention

on the basis of the past. Is she, he asks, "going to deny fifteen years of hate and of hope?" (p. 100:34-35). He suggests that her past defiance should determine, or decisively influence, her present attitude. We recall that it was in large part to "save" his own past that Orestes rejected the Gods and undertook his commitment to Argos (cf. p. 74:28-31). It appears, then, that the vitalizing issue about which the teaching of free engagement turns in practice is the vindication of one's most strongly held, and especially one's defiantly held, past attitudes.

Jupiter provisionally accepts the content of the past as the crucial factor, at least in Electra's case. Rather than admit her hate and hope as real but erroneous, he attempts to rob these attitudes of their full significance. He sets himself up as the true judge of intentions, as he who "reads within hearts." He revives the distinction between willing and dreaming which Electra had earlier proposed, and therewith reliance upon a psychology of the unconscious (p. 101: 2; cf. p. 97:18-21). Finally, he constructs a plausible picture of Electra's childhood which makes these "dreams" of sorrow, misfortune, and murder the predictable result of growing up alone and of her fascination with "the atrocious destiny of your race" (p. 101:14-15). Electra responds to this construction, moving from incredulity, through "hope" that he is not mistaken in what he says, to "see(ing) clearly into myself" (p. 101:3, 10-11, 21).

Orestes rebuts this attempt to revise Electra's past with an argument derived from his own experience with the prayer in Act 2: "What you willed, who can know it if not you? Will you let another decide it?" (p. 101:23-24). But his appeal is not only, or even perhaps chiefly, intellectual. Perhaps in recognition of the fact that Jupiter is trying to bribe as well as to fool her, or perhaps unavoidably, Orestes also appeals to definite passions. His attempt to evoke these particular attitudes reveals something of the positive ethical accompaniment of a teaching of engagement. She is now, he says, truly "guilty" for letting another make this decision of her past will for her. He continues:

> Why distort a past which can no longer defend itself? Why deny that irritated Electra which you were, that young goddess of hate whom I loved so much? And don't

you see that this cruel God is playing
with you? (p. 101:23-28).

He exhorts her to observe a kind of battlefield honor
toward the past which he himself, as Jupiter soon
points out, did not observe toward his human opponents.
He urges her to be consistent, but the consistency is
in terms of her appearance to Orestes. We have noted,
however, the partiality of that appearance. His appeal
not to let herself be played with invokes a defiance-
born sense of pride. His emphasis upon his own love
for Electra, as she seemed to him, points, however, to
his own stake in convincing her, and casts upon all
these appeals the suspicion that he may himself be
attempting to manipulate her, albeit not cruelly, for
the sake of his desire to retain her company. To defy
Jupiter is, under the circumstances, to comply with
Orestes.

Jupiter continues the bribery attempt by raising
the ante. He offers to install them both upon the Argive throne if they repudiate their crime. By making
this offer, he implies that Orestes would not have the
throne otherwise, that his dynastic claim as Agamemnon's
son would not suffice to install him. Jupiter obscures
the force of tradition; he speaks from the perspective
of rulership as such. Orestes is to be the successor
of Aegisthus, Jupiter's model king, rather than of
Agamemnon. Likewise, Electra is to follow in the foot-
steps of Clytemnestra because the public example of the
repentant queen is useful to Jupiter's purposes, and
also because Orestes obviously desires her continued
company. If she can be bribed with half the rulership,
perhaps Orestes can be bribed through her to assume the
other, the greater, half. But there is an obvious difference in the original relationships between Orestes
and Electra on the one hand and Aegisthus and Clytemnestra on the other. Is Jupiter willing, perhaps
eager, to disregard yet another, the most basic, of
traditional laws, the injunction against incest, in
order to obtain, and possibly through subsequent guilt
to secure, his kind of regime in Argos? However this
might be, Orestes resists this grand bribe. His resistance is occasioned by disgust at the thought of
assuming Aegisthus' public role, of "slip(ping) into
the britches of the buffoon whom I have killed" (p.
102:14-15). Ironically, Jupiter may have re-enforced
this resistance by emphasizing the ease with which the
transition from Aegisthus to an Aegisthian Orestes
could be effected. Orestes would dress in black, since

he is in mourning for his mother; his subjects, who
are accustomed to dressing in black, would not have to
disturb their fixed habits. As Jupiter himself remarked
in Act 1, however, Orestes is "eager and strong" and has
"better (things) to do than to reign over a half-dead
city, a corpse of a city tormented by flies" (p. 39:5,
6-8). The bribe of ruling over a pre-existing city of
this description is not grand enough for Orestes.

Jupiter therefore returns to the task of deflating
Orestes' pride by ridiculing his accomplishment. He
"struck a man who didn't defend himself, and an old
woman who asked for mercy; but he who would hear you
speak without knowing you could believe that you saved
your native city, while fighting alone against thirty"
(p. 102:16-20). Jupiter's ridicule reveals his apprehension: The Argives, who do not know Orestes, just
might believe this if they were to hear him speak.
They have, after all, demonstrated some responsiveness
to liberating rhetoric, delivered self-confidently by
another of Agamemnon's children. If the killing of
Aegisthus signals a change of regime, then this possible
belief which Jupiter mentions, apart from its exaggerated embellishments, may be true. "Perhaps in
fact," Orestes answers, "I have saved my native city"
(p. 102:21). More satisfying to his pride than to be
king is to be his city's savior and the founder of a
new regime. But a new regime, even more than a mere
change of rulers, requires public acceptance. Jupiter
points out that "all the men of Argos . . . are waiting
for their savior with stones, pitchforks, and cudgels
to prove their gratitude to him. You are as alone as
a leper." Orestes merely answers, "Yes" (p. 102:23-
27). His being alone only makes his accomplishment
greater.

Having tried insinuation, threat, bribe, and ridicule, Jupiter finally turns to philosophic argument.
Invoking his status as Orestes' creator and the creator
of all things, he displays the star-spangled firmament,
and discourses, in a magnified voice, on the Good, that
which Orestes had formerly declared to be the only thing
for which he ever wished(p. 74:8). The Good, which
Jupiter at one point identifies with himself, is the
principle of order which pervades nature. Operating
"according to justice," he (it) has regulated the
course of the planets, so that they turn without ever
colliding. The province of divine justice is the
orderly preservation of the natural things. Through
him, living creatures perpetuate themselves after their

103

kind, the tides rise and fall at their proper time, and plants grow. The Good is in the parts, qualities, and structures of all natural things. The human body itself "betrays you, for it conforms to my prescriptions." As the laws of physics, the Good pervades all actions, and even "permits the success of your evil enterprise," through "the clarity of the candles, the hardness of your sword, the force of your arm." The very Evil which Orestes claims is, he suggests, but "a reflection of being, . . . a false image whose very existence" is conditioned by the Good. He exhorts Orestes to re-enter the universe, in which he is but "a mite," to re-enter nature, to "cast (your sin) from you like a decayed and stinking tooth." In order to re-enforce this exhortation, he warns him to "beware lest the sea recede before you, lest the springs dry up along your path, lest the stones and rocks roll out of your route, and lest the earth crumble to dust beneath your steps" (pp. 103:11; 102:38; 103:16, 19-30).

As with his speech in Act 1, the parts of this speech are discordant with each other and with their implications. The justice which keeps the eternal bodies from colliding manifestly does not prevent collisions among the lesser beings. The species which perpetuate themselves prey upon each other.[41] The other side of the growth of living creatures is their decay. And one may at least question whether the survival of the species can adequately console the self-consciously mortal individual. The human body too has an aspect other than its conformity to laws of physics, namely conformity to human will. The fact that physical laws permitted Orestes' act indicates that the natural order, in its physical aspect, lends itself indifferently to all human enterprises, regardless of moral purpose. Orestes, moreover, unlike Electra's imaginary warrior, does not seek to do evil as such, but makes his project a self-sustaining good (p. 91: 23-24; cf. p. 70:16-17). The image of the rotting tooth in effect points up the incipient divergence between human ends and nature, if not a turmoil within nature itself. And in the end, it is doubtful that Jupiter would make good the threatened conspiracy of natural forces. To do so would require disturbance of the chain of being, an act of divine injustice.

This speech states a corruption of Christian theology. Jupiter explains the universe in terms of a single principle, the Good, which he personifies. Other Gods are dispensed with, although he presents

104

several aspects of himself--the creator, the pervasive
spirit of the whole, the way of errant man's return to
nature. But his natural law doctrine, for all its
Christian allusion is disturbingly modern. The pervasive manifestations of the Good, the principle of
order, are all sub-rational. Notably absent is an
account of man as rational animal.[42] The cosmology to
which Orestes opposes himself, while pretending to be
Thomistic, is more nearly Newtonian. Jupiter attempts
to impose the Good upon the human realm from the hea-
vens, rather than to lead Orestes to it through human
necessity. This deliberate abstraction from the human
as such is apparent in his reference to the mite--"you
are a mite in the universe" (p. 103:25)--, which is a
travesty on a well-known selection from Pascal's
Pensées, concerning "man's disproportion."[43] Pascal
invites the reader to consider both the infinitely
large and the infinitesimally small in nature. Man
without God is lost between these incomprehensible
extremes. Compared with the all he is as nothing;
compared with the mite he is as all. Jupiter emphasizes only half of Pascal's formula, the half which
minimizes man's place within nature. Pascal makes two
further points relevant to Jupiter's speech. First,
the utter incomprehensibility of either of these extremes leaves man adrift in the universe, a condition
which he can remedy only by submitting to God. This
conclusion agrees with Jupiter's argument. But
secondly, Pascal argues the utter irreducibility of
human spirit to matter. Man's submission to God must
be an act of free commitment; it cannot be, as Jupiter
tries to make it appear, a necessity following from
man's place within nature as a corporeal being. But
to admit man's freedom, even if for the purpose of
pointing that freedom toward God, is to admit the validity of the ground for Orestes' act. This is a position which Jupiter must avoid at all costs.

But Orestes permits him to avoid it no longer.
He defiantly accepts Jupiter's challenge:

> Let (the earth) crumble! Let the rocks
> condemn me, and let the plants wilt at my
> passage: all your universe will not suf-
> fice to blame me. You are the king of the
> Gods, Jupiter, the king of rocks and of
> the stars, the king of the waves of the
> sea. But you are not the king of men
> (p. 104:20).

In terms that brook no compromise, Orestes affirms that man is a kingdom within a kingdom. His answer departs from the terms of Jupiter's speech in two important respects. He omits mention of Jupiter's kingship over animals, although he does not deny it, and he concedes what Jupiter has not explicitly claimed, his kingship over the Gods. The amibguous status of animals indicates something about human freedom. Animals are conscious and may have immediate purposes, but they also have determinate natures, and they lack the sentiment of dignity and the consciousness of death as a personal possibility. From what we have seen of Jupiter, this description might also fit the Gods. Further, by conceding Jupiter's kingship of the stars, Orestes suggests the dispensability of intermediate Gods, including the very one that may have sent him to Argos and whose sanctuary he now temporarily enjoys. He implicitly accepts Jupiter's Christianization of the pagan pantheon. But by making Jupiter king of the Gods, or the only God, he makes his own victory more complete.

The walls of the temple close again, a crushed Jupiter reappears, and a brief catechism ensues. Jupiter created Orestes, but he created him free. Even if he gave him freedom in order to serve the God, it has turned against him and there is nothing either of them can do about it. When Jupiter calls this slavery to freedom an excuse, Orestes answers, "I am neither the master nor the slave, Jupiter. I _am_ my freedom! Scarcely had you created me than I ceased to belong to you" (p. 104:18-19). At this Electra interjects a plea to Orestes, "(b)y our father," not to join blasphemy with crime (p. 104:20). Her plea is a barometer, as Jupiter points out, of her unsalvageability through Orestes' new and shocking reasons. Jupiter no longer attempts to refute or to deceive Orestes. Their remaining conversation, while emotional, is civil. Orestes has become Jupiter's equal. More, perhaps, for he appears to instruct him in what it means to be a man, and even what it means to be a God. In tendering this instruction, and in pronouncing the foregoing doctrine of freedom, however, Orestes becomes more than Orestes; he becomes the playwright's mouthpiece. His words, he announces, are as strange to his ears as they are to Electra's, so that he can "scarcely understand myself"; they are "too large for my mouth, they tear it open" (pp. 104:27; 106:23-24).

Orestes' status vis-à-vis the playwright is of

particular issue here because it is in the remainder of this scene that he articulates a teaching that seems to draw the play's meaning into a few short but memorable sentences: "(E)very man must invent his way" and "human life begins on the other side of despair" (pp. 105: 29; 106:17-18). These statements are presented both as elaboration on the meaning of man's freedom and as the basis for and content of Orestes' political dispensation. But it was Jupiter who first announced, as "the grievous secret of Gods and kings," that man is free (p. 86:17-18). It seems strange that Jupiter would need instruction on the meaning of his own secret. But in fact it is the play's viewers who are the intended recipients of this instruction. The general content of this teaching is democratic and individualistic. Orestes presents himself as exemplary for all men. But this content is markedly discrepant with what he later says to the Argives; or, if not discrepant, that final oration at least presents it in a manner quite different from these concise but moving phrases. If that difference is at all explicable in terms of what transpires between Jupiter's departure and the oration, then this intervening material merits especially close attention. And if the present language is not the play's last word on the concrete meaning of freedom in the world, then we are left to evaluate the belief of those viewers of the play who would take it as final.

Indications of this disjunction between Orestes and the author continue in his account of what he calls Jupiter's abandonment of him the previous day, an account which, like Electra's and Aegisthus' accounts of the festival events, makes no explicit reference to divine intervention (cf. pp. 69:29-32; 81:2-4). But neither does he claim to have himself been the moving spirit in his conversion. Rather, he says that freedom "swooped down upon me and chilled me" (p. 105: 4-5).[44] What he describes is a kind of Passion, the especial victim of which was his youth. Can someone as young as Orestes is supposed to be spontaneously give birth to the reflective self-awareness of separation from nature which is presented as the precondition for his peculiar engagement? Or, practically speaking, is some kind of mid-wife needed to extract this thought from him? Is the dramatist to the play's young viewers what this autonomous freedom, or the miracle-producing Jupiter, was to Orestes? If Orestes' remarks do indeed indicate some kind of <u>deus ex machina</u>, the relevant <u>deus</u> is at any rate not one of the Gods

107

of the named pantheon. Once overcome by his freedom,
Orestes reports, he sensed himself as an ageless, soli-
tary being, apart from nature, "like someone who has
lost his shadow" (p. 105:7). The loss of a shadow suggests the abolition of a certain relation between an
object in the world and a source of light, such as the
sun. Orestes' simile gives a peculiarly Apollonian
content to the principle which he soon states more
generally: "What is there in common between you and
me? We slide past each other without touching, like
two ships. You are a God and I am free" (p. 105:35-
106:1).

Jupiter tries a final appeal to Orestes as a social being. He contrasts the repose of grazing among
the God's flock with the unhealthful solitude of being
an exile from nature. Orestes sternly accepts the
designation "exile," because "(o)utside of nature,
against nature, without excuse, without other recourse
than myself, . . . I am condemned to have no other law
than my own . . . .For I am a man, Jupiter, and every
man must invent his way" (p. 105:16, 23-29). But exile
implies a home from which one is excluded. We recall
that Orestes' earliest reported knowledge was that of
being exiled (p. 42:15). By emphasizing the newness
of Orestes' exile from nature, Jupiter implies the
insufficiency of his old exile from communities of men.
But because he has always been some kind of exile, the
social image of grazing with the flock was never quite
apt either. Orestes' experience has been a development
from the intellectual's necessary political alienation,
an attitude unusual for most men most of the time, to a
fuller and deeper metaphysical alienation. He suggests
that "in the course of this long night" he had sought
remorse, as one seeks sleep, but that he can now no
longer have remorse, nor can he sleep (p. 106:3-4).[45]
He has obtained neither an Argive character nor a nature.

What he has attained, however, are solitude and
anguish similar to a God's (p. 106:1-2). What is a
God's anguish? The facet of divinity that Jupiter has
most strongly emphasized in this scene is that of creator. Godly anguish would in this respect be the anguish of the creator in his relation to the created,
given the latter's freedom, virtually from the moment
of creation, to "invent his way" (p. 104:19). This
would be Orestes' anguish if he were also a creator.
But what does Orestes create? He may answer this question implicitly in addressing Jupiter's seemingly more
down-to-earth inquiry concerning his plans. He calls

the Argives "my men," and states the necessity of
opening their eyes (p. 106:8-9). Whence this necessity?
Two answers seem indicated. On the one hand, Orestes
calls his despair "their lot," and states that despair
is the precondition for human life (p. 106:15). It
would thus be necessary to open their eyes because it is
necessary, as a duty, to make them human, or fully human.
But such a duty, formulable as the moral imperative
"make human life possible for others," surely implies an
a priori standard, "a Good and Evil in heaven." This
is precisely what Orestes' freedom has led him to see
does not exist (p. 105:8-9). This would, moreover, be
a necessity which applied to all men as such. But
Orestes identifies his despair as a peculiar gift to
this people. We are thus led to another alternative,
that despair, the access to human life, is the Argives'
lot only because Orestes, as their would-be creator,
makes it so. Jupiter's brief practical question, "What
will they do with it?" receives the similarly brief
answer, "What they will: they are free, and human life
begins on the other side of despair" (p. 106:16-18).
But in order to do anything with it, or to will anything
about it, that despair must be intelligible to them.
Orestes appears sanguine at this point that this will
be the case. But the fate of Electra's much simpler
attempt at enlightenment in Act 2 suggests a problem.
Even that skillful attempt depended crucially upon a
mythic appeal, the invocation of Agememnon, which very
much affected its success (cf. p. 65:30).

However questionable Orestes' expressed intention
might be in the context of Argive political reality,
Jupiter does not question it. Perhaps Orestes, as a
self-consciously free man, is fundamentally inscrutable
to the God. Instead, he returns his attention to
Electra, admonishing her that his reign is not yet
ended, and that she see to it whether she be with him
or against him. Although she has witnessed this entire
exchange, Electra lacks Orestes' essential insight.
She remains within the realm of belief. Her fate thus
presents in microcosm one of the possibilities still
open to Argives, and thus too a final lesson in Orestes'
political education.

## Orestes' Political Dispensation

That education comes fast upon Jupiter's departure.
Electra rises, and despite Orestes' impassioned pleas
not to leave him alone, she rejects his company. She
wishes "to the Gods" that she had never met him. She

accuses him of robbing her of the modicum of calm and the few dreams which were all she had, thus implicitly accepting Jupiter's fabrication of her past, and of betraying his obligation as "the head of our family" to protect her instead of "plung(ing) me into blood" (p. 107:6, 12-13; cf. p. 100:31-101:20). She abstracts from those facts of the immediate past which made bloodshed necessary even for the very protection of which she speaks. And when Orestes offers his protection by inviting her to depart with him, sharing the weight of his crime, patiently to seek themselves, she insists upon a more precise destination. She is unwilling to face an open future. By her appeals to piety and to family, by her longing for protection and for a determined future, she signals that she still belongs to Jupiter. As the Furies again approach her, her hysterical call upon Jupiter to protect her from them, from Orestes, from herself, and her pledge to "consecrate my entire life to expiation," confirm this belonging and Orestes' failure to win her through words alone (p. 108:4-5). Just as Electra had earlier concluded on the need for violence to free the Argives from a violent oppression, so now Orestes is left to reflect on the need for an appeal beyond the merely human to liberate human beings from the God's reign (cf. p. 69:3-4).

The Furies permit Electra to run away--she can generate her own remorse. Orestes' "tough" soul presents more of a challenge, and they buzz around him menacingly as he reflects on his solitude (p. 108:11). His fragmented remarks reveal the train of his thoughts: He is alone. Until death he will be alone. "And then . . ." And then, nothing (p. 108:18). To be alone is his life-long destiny. The first Fury anticipates his collapse under the strain of this thought. But he instead remarks, "Poor Electra!" (p. 108:25). His own fate is, it seems, still preferable to Electra's. He signals, in this final reference to Electra, his personal reconciliation to her fate as the situational precondition for the future exercise of his freedom. Henceforth, her failure, like his crime, will be part of the world with respect to which he must act. He will not wish for it not to have occurred. Embracing freedom entails openness to the most painful of prospects and deprivations. It requires a special kind of toughness of soul.[46]

The tutor now reappears, bringing Orestes food, with the intention of remaining in the temple until

night and then fleeing, and news that the Argives are
besieging the temple. When the Furies block his way,
he comically dismisses them as superstitions, and expresses nostalgia for the Attic country "where my
reason was right" (p. 109:7).[47] Through his peculiar
kind of closedness he reminds Orestes that the world
at large continues as always. Orestes warns him not
to approach, lest the Furies tear him apart. Since
Orestes had earlier asserted the Furies' inefficacy
against those who fail to take them seriously, this
warning, which speaks to the tutor's materialism, suggests that this reminder has not been lost on him (cf.
pp. 96:12-13; 97:35-36). In any event, the tutor does
not test the issue, but, true to his materialism, offers
them meats and fruits to calm them, treating them merely
as large flies or other wild animals. Questioned by
Orestes, he confirms the Argives' presence before the
temple, comparing them to the Furies in their ugliness
and eagerness to harm Orestes. In the tutor's eyes,
the supervening fact of hostility blurs any distinction
between man and beast. But this report also conveys
the vital information that the Argives do not indeed
regard the tyrannicide as an evident favor. They may
even at bottom have liked Aegisthus' reign. More than
the late royal couple ties them to their ills, and more
than the assassination is needed to free them. After
a moment's thought, Orestes orders the tutor to open
the temple door. After twice resisting the order, on
the third command he complies.

The mob bursts into the temple, but Orestes at
first disregards them, so absorbed is he by the bril-
liant sunlight which now floods the temple's interior.
One part of nature at least seems to smile upon him.
One part of the Furies' threat is refuted. Apollo is
apparently not, as Jupiter had claimed, his "very
obedient servant" (pp. 100:11; 97:30-31). The opera-
tions of nature are indifferent to divine threats. The
mob's appearance confirms the tutor's description. They
call for Orestes' death, for his stoning, for his dis-
memberment, blinding, and cannibalization. Orestes
beholds in an instant how extraordinarily base men can
be. His remarks must take account of this baseness,
even while attempting to inspire them to extraordinary
heights.

Orestes' final speech to the Argives is, therefore,
the political expression of the preceding day's lessons.
It contains three elements: self-revelation, abdication, and myth. He addresses the mob as "my very loyal

111

subjects," replicating his earlier sarcastic reference
to them as "the very loyal subjects of King Agamemnon"
(pp. 110:8-9; 59:11-12). Orestes knows his addressees'
limitations. And yet, when he announces himself as
"Orestes, your king, the son of Agamemnon, " they
immediately fall silent (p. 110:9). Even after a fifteen year hiatus, the principle of legitimate political
succession carries some weight. The Argives' quick
abandonment of their overt hostility toward Orestes
modifies Jupiter's description of them as "awaiting
their savior" with murderous intent (p. 102:23-24).
That description was true only provisionally. Thus,
in rapid succession, two of the adversary deities' dire
predictions have fallen. Orestes has no reason, apart
from his will, to cease opposing them.

But although the Argives fall silent, they do not
proclaim Orestes as their king. Such a proclamation
might be pointless, since he has just proclaimed his
own kingship. But it illustrates what Orestes himself
proceeds to emphasize, the temperamental difference
between them, which leaves the Argives in an important
respect still close to Aegisthus. They fear Orestes
because he, unlike "the other murderer," has "the
courage of his acts." When Aegisthus had appeared before them, with "red gloves up to the elbow," they
could read in his eyes that he was one of them. They
therefore did not fear him, but welcomed him as their
king. He was one of the Argives because both he and
they could not "support" their crimes (p. 110:13, 17,
14, 18). Orestes, on the other hand, openly claims
his crime as his own possession, his reason for living
and his pride, and asserts that the Argives can neither
punish him nor pity him. While giving an account of
himself in terms of his deed, he thus points both to
his own continuing foreignness and to a kind of patho-
logy in the absence of fear on the part of subjects
toward their rulers.

Thus far, Orestes' account is hardly surprising.
It encapsulates part of the ethical teaching which has
been present throughout the play. But he next proceeds
to make some remarkable claims, which, while politically
edifying, seem to fly in the face of much that has gone
before. He calls the Argives "my men," says that he
loves them, and claims emphatically that it was for
their sake that he killed, again obscuring his project's
more final personal end (p. 110:26). And he declares
that he "had come to claim my kingdom and you have
repulsed me" (p. 110:28). But it is not evident that

they have repulsed Orestes, whose identity has only just been revealed to them. Orestes seems to extrapolate from Electra's rejection of him, and to interpret the Argives' present silence by reading rejection beneath its surface acquiescence in his succession. But this Christ-like self-description forms the mythic-historic ground for the refounding of Argos. He invents a history within which the citizens exercise a sovereign power to repulse even a lawful king.

He claims, however, that he is now one of them, for "we are tied together by blood, and I deserve to be your king" (p. 110:30-31). Earlier he had declared himself to be "doubly united" with Electra, "for we are of the same blood and we have shed blood" (p. 91: 4-5). Why should the present sanguinary claim be any more convincing? Perhaps it can become convincing to the Argives only if they, unlike Electra, will not be called upon to share his project, to rise to heroic stature. Thus, he does not announce to the Argives the universal formula of individual creativity which he had stated to Jupiter. Rather he addresses them collectively, and speaks of their future as a collective fate, while distinguishing himself from them. Nor does he mention his gift of despair. Instead, he emphasizes his removal from them of various burdens, taking upon himself their sins and their remorse, their nocturnal anguishes, Aegisthus' crime, their dead, and their flies. The meaning of this theft of repentances is hardly clearer now than when Orestes first announced it as his project to Electra. Its meaning is made especially doubtful by his inclusion of Aegisthus' crime, that is, the murder of Agamemnon, among his appropriations. He complements his fabrication of a past with a mystification of the present.

Looking to the future, he tells them not to fear, and declares that he will not take the Argive throne, for "a God offered it to me and I have said no" (p. 111:4-5). By referring to "a God," rather than Jupiter in particular, he sets before the people an anti-theological teaching of the broadest scope: One can say No to a God, any God, in one's own name, without relying upon another God's patronage. In fact, Orestes may, by his abdication, be saying No to more than one God, depending upon what it was that he heard at Delphi. He offers as an explanation of his refusal of the throne his wish "to be a king without land and without subjects" (p. 111:5-6). He wishes to be a king without a kingdom. We are again reminded of Spinoza's formula.

Man may be in principle an enclave within the kingdom
of nature, but is Argos, or any existing city, fully
within the realm of man? If not, can liberated Argos
now become a city of men in the full sense? Orestes'
first indication is that it can. Bidding "his men"
farewell, he tells them to attempt to live, for "all
is new here, all is to begin" (p. 111:6-7). His abdication, he would have it appear, creates a truly revolutionary situation, a political clean slate. But in
his final words he proceeds to give that slate its
first marks. He presents a myth that resembles the
first part of the famous story of the Pied Piper of
Hamelin. The flutist in this myth rids the city of
Scyros of its plague of rats. Drawing the parallel to
himself and Argos' flies, he concludes the myth by
having the flutist disappear with the rats forever. At
this, he leaves, with the Furies in hot pursuit, and
the play ends.

Three aspects of this myth seem noteworthy: First,
it is about a human hero. The story makes no reference
to Gods. But if Gods have become dispensable to Argos,
legends apparently have not. At least the legend of
the savior has a place. It does not seem at all far-
fetched to imagine the Argives, under the influence of
this dispensation, replacing the statues of Jupiter
with ones of Orestes. It is in any case difficult to
imagine that they would not somehow commemorate this
enigmatic figure who appeared from nowhere, overthrew
their government and its patron God, and then in quick
succession claimed and disclaimed the throne. However
they may choose to orient their lives and institutions,
it will almost certainly have to be with reference to
Orestes. But it will not be with reference to Orestes
himself, but to an image of him which he constitutes
by this very speech. Orestes has situated himself in
Argos emphatically but only in a highly equivocal sense.
He himself remains outside and "above" the city (cf. p.
75:16-17). Despite his egalitarian pronouncements,
Orestes remains in the end radically distinguished from
the Argives. Secondly, the flutist story ends with his
ridding Scyros of its rats. But we know that Hamelin's
citizens refuse to pay the Piper, and consequently
suffer the spiriting away of their children. Orestes'
elliptical story implicitly conveys the threat: Behave
unworthily of this new, heroic dispensation, and you
will see your youth lured from you! Finally, the myth's
hero is musical, a quality of which Orestes, until this
moment, has given no indication. But if Orestes has
no muse, surely the dramatist has. We are in the end

114

left to wonder what in The Flies' teaching is true and
what is myth, what is meant to enlighten and what to
threaten and to edify.

Especially in conjunction with the second point,
we may wonder what the unworthy behavior of the play's
audience might be which could eventuate in the loss of
their young. In the play's immediate historical context, one answer readily occurs. Failure to act upon
the play's propagandistic teaching, to recognize the
Vichy regime's despicability and its underlying political and theological principles, and, casting off the
false pretense of guilt, to oppose them and the Occupation, will result in a "lost generation" of Frenchmen.[48] But there may be another danger to the nation's
youth, implicit in the tension between Orestes'
earlier pronouncements on human necessity and his current action. Those pronouncements, we noted, present
a democratic ethical teaching. His final act, on
the contrary, emphasizes his and the Argives' dis-
similarity and inequality. But if, as seemed to be
the case, Orestes' choice of a project of political
liberation, rather than a possible project of political enslavement, was made under the influence of
an erroneous belief in the easy universalizability
of his own experience with the abyss; then removal
of that belief opens up for him, and for those who
may be inspired by his example, the temptation to
enslave and tyrannize. Orestes ultimately rejects
this temptation because he is too high-minded, because
the example of Aegisthus warns him of the ignobility
of tyrannizing. But short of being able to rely upon
such high-mindedness, it is to the interest of communities like Argos that the philosopher-dramatist
obscure the tyrannic potentials of his young intellectual liberator-followers by fostering the belief
among them that the encounter with existential anguish
yields an egalitarian insight. The price of ignoring
the dramatist-philosopher's egalitarian mythic dispensation may well be the loss of the next generation
to the existential hero of the Right. The political
salvation of modernity, and the particular liberation
of a country oppressed by a bastardized fascism, may
thus require a project that must flirt with the prospect of fascism at its peak.

But if Orestes' final speech answers the Argives'
political needs, we may still ask what it is that
Orestes has gained from his Argive venture. He is at
the end even more alone than he was at the beginning.

He has exchanged the tutor's company for the Furies'.
Philosophy in the tutor's sense is still unviable.
He will not have the pleasures of Electra's company,
nor the social rewards of living within the city's
horizon. And while he has his act, which he says he
will bear proudly, the meaning of such pride becomes
increasingly problematic the further he goes from
Argos, the place for which the act itself has meaning.
Perhaps this is why he does not say that he will proclaim his crime to other men but "to the sun" (p. 110:
24). But if the sun is in this case a surrogate for
God, then this gesture too has lost its meaning consequent upon his disjunction of the human realm from
the Godly. Or must Orestes reconstitute the Gods in
order to sustain his pride, just as Jupiter's gaze
had sustained the Argives' guilt? To revise Voltaire's
observation, if there were no God, man would have to
invent Him in order to defy Him. Alternatively, perhaps the sun image is merely emphatic, and Orestes'
pride consists in his self-sufficiency, in the knowledge of his absolute freedom from all a priori values.
But in this case, it is difficult to see what his political act has gained him that he did not already possess before. It seems to be a needless and personally
unprofitable detour. Orestes' optimistic departure
would either be another instance of false consciousness
or a publicly edifying posture.

Perhaps this is why the Furies, rather than obedi-
ently filing out behind him, analogous to the rats in
the flutist myth, hurl themselves after him, shrieking,
apparently full of vigor (p. 111:21-22). Deprived, at
least for the present, of Argos, they may merely be
venting an impotent rage against Orestes; impotent, that
is, if they are indeed powerless against the unrepen-
tant, or if Orestes' resolution will stand firm. But
their hot pursuit of him may also signal, if not actual
repentance on his part, the existence of something
problematic and regrettable in his situation. Even the
supreme political accomplishment may be personally unsatisfying to the existential hero. We are reminded
of a teaching concerning the disjunction of politics
and philosophy which forms part of a tradition at least
as old as Plato's Republic. But unlike the sanguine
Socrates, for Orestes the philosophic life is impossible.[49]

## VI. Summary and Transition

We return to Kaufmann's thesis--that in The Flies
Sartre transmits Nietzsche's philosophy, that Orestes
is a revised Zarathustra--, but, unlike Kaufmann, we
regard this as self-conscious and deliberate.[50] More
specifically, radical political change and the advent
of the post-Christian era[51] require the alienated,
philosophic, and resolutely committed Great Individual.
But Sartre, more immersed than Nietzsche in the spirit
and the realities of a democratic age, more clearly
sees, or at least acknowledges, that this heroic favor
must be popularly accepted. Thus, the project of
political-religious liberation and refounding also
requires a propagandistic appeal to egalitarianism
alongside the mythic appeal to heroism.

What are the prospects for such a dispensation?
In the end, this question may depend less on "Orestes"
himself than on the capacity of alienated souls of
the next generation, like the young boy mentioned in
Act 1 (p. 37:9-12), to act on his inspirational teaching. Orestes himself seems fated either to continual
recapitulation of his deed or (what may amount to the[52]
same thing) to some new mode of philosophizing.
What appears certain, however, is his incompatibility
with Argos on anything but an extra-ordinary, momentary, and adventitious basis.

So matters stood in 1943. The intellectual hero
leads political society toward radical change while
himself remaining essentially on the outside. Though
necessary for true revolution, he is necessarily only
an accidental revolutionary. It is from this point
that our survey of Sartre's subsequent career departs,
and to this point that it will recurrently refer.

117

# NOTES

[1] Cumming, pp. 233, 234.

[2] For the text of _Bariona_, see Contat and Rybalka, vol. 2, pp. 72-136.

[3] For a brief account of these events, see Sartre's article "Forgers of Myths: The Young Playwrights in France," _Theatre Arts_ 30 (June 1946): 324.

[4] Beauvoir, _Prime of Life_, p. 585.

[5] Contat and Rybalka, vol. 1, pp. 87-89.

[6] Parenthetical citations in this chapter are from the volume _Les Mouches: Drame en trois actes_, ed. F. C. St. Aubyn and Robert G. Marshall (New York: Harper and Row, 1963). Such citations include page and line numbers, separated by a colon. The abbreviation "s.d." refers to the stage directions which may precede the numbered lines on a given page. The interrogatory notes provided by the editors of this volume have been quite helpful to my plot description, though not necessarily to my interpretation. All translations from this volume are my own. I am grateful to Alfred A. Knopf, Inc., who holds exclusive copyright on all English-language publication from _The Flies_ in the United States, for granting me permission, in the interest of literalness, to translate directly from the French.

[7] Throughout this chapter, I follow Sartre's peculiar usage of capitalizing the words "God and "Gods," even though they supposedly refer to pagan deities. The only exceptions are specific references to an idol (pp. 31:s.d.; 38:6; 46:18). What the meaning of "Gods," a plurality of supreme beings, might be remains a question. Does this perhaps indicate the co-existence of a number of contradictory principles competing for rule over the universe, or rather over the chaos that we fashion into a universe by invoking one or another of them? Cf. Max Weber, "Science as a Vocation," in _From Max Weber: Essays in Sociology_, trans. and ed. by H. H. Gerth and C. Wright Mills (New York: Oxford University Press, 1958), pp. 147-48. On Jupiter's kingship of the Gods, see infra, p. 99.

[8] It seems, however, to have been lost on Stuart

Gilbert, translator of the standard English edition of
The Flies, in No Exit and Three Other Plays (New York:
Alfred A. Knopf, Inc., 1955). Gilbert changes Jupiter
to Zeus, despite Sartre's clear indication, by way of
Orestes' prayer to Zeus in Act 2, that the name "Jupiter" is deliberately chosen. Even Walter Kaufmann,
who is usually more careful concerning translation,
refers to Sartre's "bring(ing) Zeus onstage." Tragedy
and Philosophy (Garden City, New York: Doubleday and
Company, Inc., 1968), p. 259. For further observations
on difficulties stemming from faulty translations, see
infra, p. 126.
  Were the German censors unusually obtuse in letting The Flies be performed? Or did they judge, correctly, that the collaborationist literary critics
could be depended upon to stifle public interest in the
play without needlessly creating a cause célèbre? Or
did they perhaps even see something congenial in its
teaching? See infra, pp. 35-36, 115.

⁹Contat and Rybalka, vol. 1, pp. 14, 199-200,
21, 29, 535-36.

¹⁰Beauvoir, Prime of Life, p. 649.

¹¹Jean-Paul Sartre, Qu'est-ce que la littérature?
(Paris: Gallimard, 1948).

¹²Kaufmann, Tragedy and Philosophy, pp. 258-63.
The eight works of Nietzsche which Kaufmann cites are
Thus Spoke Zarathustra, Ecce Homo, Twilight of the
Idols, The Will to Power, Genealogy of Morals,
Nietzsche contra Wagner, The Gay Science, and Beyond
Good and Evil. But some of these references are merely
tangential. The two which are clearly relevant are
Zarathustra and Ecce Homo. Section 295 of Beyond Good
and Evil, which contains the Pied Piper image, is also
important to The Flies, but Nietzsche reproduces the
relevant passage from this section in Ecce Homo, part
3, section 6.

¹³Kaufmann, Tragedy and Philosophy, p. 262. But
cf. p. 263, where Kaufmann finds an important Nietzschean expression in No Exit.

¹⁴Ibid., p. 263.

¹⁵Being and Nothingness, p. 87. Sartre refers the
concept of ressentiment to Max Scheler. But Scheler,
for his part, is unstinting in acknowledging his own

indebtedness to Nietzsche. Max Scheler, Ressentiment, ed. Lewis A. Coser, trans. William W. Holdheim (New York: Crowell-Collier Publishing Company, Free Press of Glencoe, 1961), pp. 39, 43-45.

[16] Being and Nothingness, pp. 4, 692.

[17] Cf. Nietzsche, Thus Spoke Zarathustra, Part 1, chap. 17.

[18] What lies behind that joyousness is, of course, a separate question. Cf. ibid., Part 2, chaps. 6, 18.

[19] Kaufmann, Tragedy and Philosophy, p. 260. Cf. Nietzsche, Thus Spoke Zarathustra, Part 1, chap. 12.

[20] Orestes mentions some Spartan friends at p. 44: 9, but these friends may be no more than casual acquaintances. There is no suggestion at the play's end that he will look to them for solace. Cf. p. 108:18.

[21] Cf. Aeschylus Libation-Bearers 23-211.

[22] See Being and Nothingness, pp. 340-400, esp. pp. 347-52, 385-86.

[23] Possibly in allusion to Christianity, sets of three appear repeatedly throughout the play. I take note of some of these as they occur.

[24] While the discussion of death in Being and Nothingness invites the inference that it is not as central a notion to Sartre's philosophy as it is, say, to Heidegger's, The Flies may redress somewhat the misconception that he seeks to slight its importance to the self-constitution of the human being. See Being and Nothingness, pp. 680-700; Marjorie Grene, "Authenticity: An Existential Virtue," Ethics 62 (July 1952): 266. Cf. "The Wall"; and the following: "The choice that each of us made of himself was authentic, because it was made in the presence of death, since it could always be expressed in the form, 'Rather death than --.'" Cumming, p. 233.

[25] It is probable that Electra's age is about twenty-one, and that her reference to Orestes as "my elder brother" (p. 77:20) is merely figurative. Cf. pp. 52:9-10; 72:6; 107:12.

[26] The formula "sans famille, sans patrie, sans

religion, sane métier" is a travesty of the Vichy motto "famille, patrie, travaille." Orestes is from the start the antithesis of the homme vichyssois, but merely to be this is insufficient.

[27]Cf. Nietzsche, Ecce Homo, Part 2, sec. 10: "At an absurdly early age, at seven, I already knew that no human word would ever reach me . . ."

[28]Cf. Orestes' self-introduction, "Je m'appelle Philèbe," with her more externally oriented "on m'appelle Electre" (p. 45:19, 20).

[29]Cf. Homer Odyssey 2. 267ff.; cf. 22. 205-210.

[30]A barometer of this temporary humility is the reversal of their use of the "tu" and "vous" forms of address. Cf. p. 61:37-62:2 with pp. 60:2; 63:32-33; 68:10-15. But cf. p. 68:17.

[31]L'Existentialisme est un humanisme, p. 47.

[32]Cf. Nietzsche, Thus Spoke Zarathustra, Part 3, chap. 11.

[33]Cf. ibid., Prologue, sec. 1. But while Zarathustra needs to descend among men in order to dispense his own superabundance, Orestes must do so in order to fill his own emptiness. Does Sartre's reversal of Nietzsche's imagery perhaps see beneath the surface of Nietzsche's rhetoric?

[34]For a discussion of the project-gesture distinction in The Flies, see Keith Gore, Sartre: La Nausée and Les Mouches (London: Edward Arnold Ltd., 1970), pp. 44-67.

[34a]Perhaps anticipating Jupiter's answer, Aegisthus shifts to the familiar "tu" form of address in asking this question.

[35]There is a hidden irony here: Insofar as the action of the play is the author's imaginative creation, these "contingencies" become "essential," the characters' freedom becomes necessity, their disorders order, and the excesses and deficiencies perfectly measured. Cf. "Forgers of Myths," p. 332.

[36]Cf. Being and Nothingness, pp. 100-12.

[37]Cf. ibid., pp. **637**-47.

[38]Cf. Aeschylus Eumenides 67-70.

[39]Cf. Being and Nothingness, p. 640.

[40]Cf. Nietzsche, Thus Spoke Zarathustra, Part 1, chap. 17; and Ecce Homo, Part 2, sec. 10.

[41]Jupiter mentions the reproduction of plants and animals, but the growth only of plants (p. 103:3-5, 6-8). Cf. supra, p. 43.

[42]Cf. St. Thomas Aquinas Summa Theologica, II. 94. 2.

[43]Pascal, Pensées, sec. 72 (Brunschvicg ed.).

[44]An alternative reading would be, "(F)reedom melted upon me (a fondu sur moi) and chilled me."

[45]Cf. Being and Nothingness, p. 113.

[46]Cf. Nietzsche, Thus Spoke Zarathustra, Part 1, chap. 17.

[47]". . . où c'était ma raison qui avait raison."

[48]Cf. supra, p. 3.

[49]Cf. supra, pp. 46-47; cf. Plato Republic 519B-520A.

[50]See supra, pp. 36-38.

[51]Cf. William Barrett, Irrational Man: A Study in Existential Philosophy (Garden City, New York: Double-day & Company, Inc., 1962), chap. 8.

[52]Cf. Nietzsche, On the Genealogy of Morals, Third Essay, sec. 12.

## 4. THE "HUMANIST" GAMBIT

> And in the market place one convinces with
> gestures.  But reasons make the mob mis-
> trustful.  And if truth was victorious for
> once, then ask yourself with good mistrust:
> "What strong error fought for it?"

Nietzsche *Zarathustra* 4. 13. 9.

### I

The end of World War II brought a crystallization
of the French political scene and also Sartre's sudden rise to fame.  These two developments converged as
the nation looked, in part, to its intellectual
leaders for guidance in the nascent post-war era.  The
essay "Existentialism Is a Humanism,"[1] one of Sartre's
most popular works, is an early product of this con-
fluence of events.

It is virtually a matter of universal judgment
among Sartre's critics, and perhaps Sartre's own
judgment as well,[2] that this essay is one of his worst
pieces; and it is not difficult to sense the grounds
for negative criticism.  It contains blatant contradictions, both internally and with the presumably more
authoritative philosophy of Being and Nothingness.  In
particular, it presents an ethical doctrine, super-
ficially similar to Kant's, which finds no place in
that larger work.  It is, in its own right, poorly
argued, the illustrative examples often being inappo-
site to the points which they are supposed to prove.
It contains certain slight but glaring inaccuracies,
suggestive of editorial carelessness.  Throughout, and
perhaps at the root of all these faults, it seems
tainted by a scarcely concealed desire on its author's
part to popularize, even to vulgarize, a philosophic
doctrine.

These faults have taken their toll.  Karl Jaspers'
and Martin Heidegger's public denials that they are
Existentialists seem to have been largely occasioned
by Sartre's attempt in this essay to define Existentialism.  Walter Kaufmann, in the very course of
reprinting it in his popular anthology of Existentialist writings, feels constrained to apologize for
its popularity as "unfortunate because it is after all
only an occasional lecture which . . . bears the stamp

123

of the moment." And Sartre himself, defending it from the criticism of Georg Lukács in 1949, characterized it as only a transitional work.[3]

All this notwithstanding, it may be worth our while to give this essay a modicum of serious attention. It did, even if unfortunately, thrust Sartre into the center of controversy, thus making its presentation one of the pivotal events in his career. However ill advised its initial presentation may have been, Sartre did not suppress the work, but edited it for written publication. The text which we have thus represents not only his hasty first thoughts but also his presumably more sober second.[4] Experience with other "poorly written" works teaches us that "obvious errors" are sometimes more apparent than real, especially if they can be reconciled with some supervening rhetorical design. Even assuming the reality of these errors, it may be a source of fruitful reflection to wonder what circumstances might justifiably tempt a serious and intelligent person like Sartre to deport himself in this clumsy and heavy-handed way.

II

In the essay's background are certain biographical data which are helpful in understanding its peculiar rhetoric. Simone de Beauvoir reports the following incident of a conversation which took place among Jean Grenier, Sartre, and herself early in 1943:

> They chatted for a while, and then Grenier turned to me. "What about you, madame," he inquired. "Are you an existentialist?" I can still recall my embarrassment at this question. I had read Kierkegaard, and the term "existential philosophy" had been in circulation for some time apropos of Heidegger; but I didn't understand the meaning of the word "existentialist," which Gabriel Marcel had recently coined. Besides, Grenier's question clashed with my modesty and my pride alike. I was not of sufficient importance, objectively considered, to merit any such label; as for my ideas, I was convinced that they reflected the truth rather than some entrenched doctrinal position.[5]

As late as mid-1945, she and Sartre resisted this designation:

> During a discussion organized during the summer by the Cerf publishing house--in other words, by the Dominicans--Sartre had refused to allow Gabriel Marcel to apply this adjective to him: "My philosophy is a philosophy of existence; I don't even know what existentialism is."

"But," she continues, "our protests were in vain. In the end, we took the epithet that everyone used for us and used it for our own purposes."[6]

The first product of this decision was a short article in Action, a left-wing journal of limited circulation, in which Sartre dispensed with his former protestation.[7] But it is the "Humanism" essay, first delivered as a public lecture on October 28, 1945, that marks his debut as an Existentialist before the general public. This switch, however, was more than an instance of rolling with the punch of public opinion; it was also a coup. For under Marcel's guidance, philosophy of existence looked to become a doctrine so compatible with religious orthodoxy that discussion of it could be sponsored by the Dominicans.[8] It is against the backdrop of the efforts of this latter-day Kierkegaard that Sartre's accomplishment must be gauged. Virtually overnight, he appropriated Existentialism to himself, rescued it from the clutches of the Church, and gave it a peculiarly secular direction. The essay whose announced purpose is a defense of Existentialism from its detractors[9] is equally an offensive against its founder.

Simone de Beauvoir's remarks on its and its author's reception are equally revealing. She reports that Sartre, suddenly a famous figure, and his doctrine of atheist Existentialism were subjected to "a rising flood of calumnies" from the Right. This, however, left them "unaffected," for Sartre "had torn himself away from his class, so the animosity it displayed toward him was natural." But, she continues, "(t)he animosity of the Communists . . . struck him as an injustice." For he was, through his criticisms of orthodox Marxism, "seeking exchanges" with the Communists at a time when "intellectually a dialogue . . . was possible."[10] This datum leads us to wonder in particular what the relationship might be between the

"Humanism" essay's public teaching and Sartre's dialectical interest vis-à-vis the Communists, and what
the character was of the "exchanges" which he sought.

### III

Part of the essay's bad repute, especially among
English-speaking critics, is due to certain errors of
detail which seem to evidence slipshod preparation.
But examination of the relevant passages leads us, if
not to acquit Sartre, then at least somewhat to
appreciate the referred-to rhetorical projects.
Kaufmann points to two such apparent errors: Sartre's
supposed reference to Karl Jaspers as a "professed
Catholic"; and his assertion that it was an angel who
commanded Abraham to sacrifice his son, whereas in
both the Bible and in Kierkegaard it is God Himself
who does so.[11]

The error concerning Jaspers may be less attri-
butable to Sartre himself than to his translators.
The original reads:

> What renders things complicated is that there
> are two species of Existentialists: the
> first, who are Christians, and among whom I
> shall rank Jaspers and Gabriel Marcel, of
> Catholic confession; and, on the other side,
> the atheist Existentialists among whom it is
> necessary to rank Heidegger, and also the
> French Existentialists and myself.[12]

The antecedent of the adjectival phrase "de confession
catholique" is ambiguous; the phrase could refer to
both Jaspers and Marcel, or to Marcel alone. The
latter reading is argued for by its truth; by the
earlier characterization of both Jaspers and Marcel as
"Christians," which would make the alternative reading
somewhat redundant; and by the clause's peculiar
rhetorical thrust: Even a "confessed" Catholic like
Marcel calls himself an Existentialist! While Sartre
proceeds immediately thereafter to identify the ground
that all these Existentialists share--they all believe
that "existence precedes essence"[13]--, he makes no
positive use of the possibility of religious belief
in his subsequent development of this theme. In his
closing remarks he confidently, and categorically,
states that "Existentialism is nothing else than an
attempt to draw all the consequences of a coherent
atheist position," a position of God's irrelevance to

man, which he contrasts, also categorically, with the
position of "the Christians."[14]

The mistake in the Abraham story seems more clear-
cut. But how important a mistake is it really? In
the context of the immediate argument, that it is we
who decide the authority of our authorities, it seems
to make little difference whether the command comes
from God or an angel. But there is a hint of irony
here. For just before making this mistake[15] Sartre
states rhetorically, "You know the story."[15] Is it
not precisely his audience's ignorance of, or unconcern
for, Scriptural accuracy upon which he banks and at
which he aims? Our suspicion of a calculated carelessness in this minor instance is bolstered by a later
anecdote--that of the young man choosing between the
Resistance and his mother--which argues primarily,
but in a confused and self-contradictory way, the point
about deciding our own authorities, and secondarily,
but clearly and emphatically, that one cannot trust
priests to give impartial advice.[16] In any event,
the substitution of the angel for God in the Abraham
story leaves only one instance among his examples of a
person claiming, albeit somewhat tentatively, direct
word from God, that of someone identified as "a madwoman."[17]

It would be difficult to deny the charge that
Sartre vulgarizes. During a discussion following a
second, more private, presentation of the "Humanism"
lecture, one of the questions addressed to him concerned an apparent "weakening" of his viewpoint in the
Action article. In his response, Sartre not only
admitted the possibility of such a watering down, but
also confessed his choice to vulgarize, both in the
article in question and in the lecture. He went on
to justify this practice on three grounds: First, it
is essentially the same as the kind of simplification
in which the philosophy teacher must indulge in class
in order to make a thought understood, a practice
which "is not so bad."[18] Secondly, the theory of
engagement itself substantively requires that it "be
lived in order to be truly sincere"; that is, that one
practice what he preaches, even, it would seem, if
practice means concretely to preach something slightly
different from the pure theory. The pertinent appli-
cation of this principle is that one answer questions
in the terms in which they are posed, in the present
instance on "the political or moral plane" rather than

"a strictly philosophic plane."[19]  Hence, his asso-
ciation of Existentialism with humanism, "because the
problem poses itself thus."  And thirdly, vulgarization is preferable to the alternative of relying on
chance to make effective a doctrine which "wants to be
an action."

Sartre added a caveat to this last reason:  The
vulgarization must not "deform" the doctrine.  But it
is not self-evident what constitutes a deformity in
this context.  The degree of alteration necessary to
make a doctrine "have an action" in the world at large
may be considerably greater than that which would be
proper to make a thought accessible in a philosophy
class.  If the measure of permissible distortion is
proportionate to the former end, then Sartre may give
himself a fairly wide berth indeed.[20]  He is not, for
instance, above flattering his audience; for while he
here disjoins the political or moral plane from the
strictly philosophic, in the lecture he had suggested
that it was upon the latter that he was addressing the
problem.[21]  Again, while he here speaks of grappling
with the problem as it poses itself, he anticipates in
the essay that "(m)any people are going to be surprised
at what is said here about humanism."[22]  An astute
teacher must, it seems, take a hand in framing the
questions that "pose themselves."  And even the appearance of the fortuitous may have to be calculated.

IV

The essay's peculiar structure also deserves a
word of attention.  Sartre begins by mentioning four
common reproaches against Existentialism.  He then
gives a short preliminary response to these reproaches,
in which he broaches the theme of humanism, but he
refrains from responding fully because of a prior need
to define his terms.  In the lengthy section that
follows, which occupies approximately half the essay,
he defines Existentialism and discourses on three
concepts central to it:  anguish, forlornness (or abandonment), and despair.  He then returns to the anti-
Existentialist reproaches, answering them more exten-
sively.  In brief closing remarks he explicitly returns
to the humanist theme.  The issue of humanism, then,
while providing the rhetorical context for his remarks,
is for the most part left to inference.

Rhetorically, this peculiar order enables him,

first, to refocus attention away from the objections
to Existentialism and toward Existentialism itself;
and secondly, to shift his emphasis in the responses
as between the objecting camps. Of the four objections stated at the outset, Sartre associates two with
Christians, one with the Communists, and one with both
camps. There is thus an initial appearance of evenhandedness. He even calls one of the Catholic reproaches, that Existentialism emphasizes the ignoble
and ugly, "the basic charge against us."[23] But in fact
he spends the least time answering this charge, and his
answer consists not of a substantive refutation, but
of impugning the motives of its propounders, the
advocates of "the wisdom of the ages" (la sagesse des
nations).[24] By the time he comes to his extended
responses, the pretense of evenhandedness has been
effectively dropped, the Christian position has been
repeatedly ridiculed, and he feels at ease to devote
his more serious responsive energies to a comparatively
gentle chiding and educating of the remaining side, the
Marxists. The essay's structure thus contributes to
a reorientation of its audience's attention from a
discredited remnant of Christianity, by way of Existentialism, to a coherent radicalism.

The discrediting of Christianity begins almost
immediately, in the presentation of the anti-Existen-
tialist reproaches. Both Christians and Communists
accuse Existentialism of losing human solidarity in a
morass of subjectivity. But while the Communists do
so on the basis of the serious philosophic objection
that the Cartesian cogito leads to solipsism, no cor-
respondingly serious reason is given for the Christians.
Instead, the Christians object that the suppression of
divine eternal commandments leaves our acts in a state
of strict gratuity, and leaves us unable to condemn
the viewpoints and acts of others. Where the Communists are concerned about the status of a possibly
constructive human solidarity, the Christians are
depicted as interested only in condemnation. It is
they, moreover, who propound the low view of man
embodied in the sagesse des nations. Even so self-
assertive a structure as a Christian trade union is[25]
apparently likely to be a vehicle of resignation.
In the context of this repeated sniping at the Christian camp, as merely negative, as uninspiring, as
tinged with self-serving delusions of otherworldly
guidance; the anti-Thomist formula for Existentialism--
"existence precedes essence"[26]--makes rhetorical

sense, even if it is substantively questionable in
its own right.

V

The core of Existentialism's positive teaching
lies in the two associated concepts of anguish and
forlornness, on the uneasy relationship of which I
shall remark presently. Anguish, as here presented,
is the sentiment of total and profound responsibility
we feel at legislating, through our acts, for all mankind. Each of us is responsible for all men, and our
every act, even those which seem to be strictly private, engages all mankind. This, because every act
posits implicitly an image of man as we estimate he
ought to be, and because nothing can be good for any
one which is not good for all. Thus, we ought always
to ask ourselves, in performing any act, "What if
everyone acted that way?" We should comport ourselves
as though everyone were watching us and were using our
conduct as the rule for his own. Further, one escapes [29]
this thought only through a kind of bad faith. [27] The
operative premise of this highly questionable doctrine
seems to be that all men are fundamentally alike, equal,
and emulative. For if others were not especially
inclined to take our behavior as a model for their own,
our idiosyncratic acts would be, in this respect, innocuous; and the conjecture, even the fact, that
others were watching us would be, in this respect,
completely insignificant. (That others were watching
us might still, of course, be relevant in other
respects, for instance, insofar as it might require
us to be discreet, even devious, in order to prevent
them from embarrassing us or thwarting our idiosyncratic ends.) Sartre thus seems surreptitiously to
import a conception of human nature into his account,
despite his express assertion to the contrary. [28] This
doctrine's practical thrust is to direct men toward
thinking collectively, toward doing only those acts
whose maxims are universalizable, in a word, toward
the ethics of Kant.

Forlornness, on the other hand, is the necessity
of drawing the full consequences from God's non-
existence. With the fall of God there also falls the
possibility of finding an intelligible realm of a
priori values, such as honesty (Sartre's chosen
example). Therefore, all is permitted. Further,
there is no determinism, either of values or orders

130

which will legitimate our conduct; or of the passions, which in fact gain their efficacy only because we consent to them. (The denial of a determinism of the passions is not, of course, a denial of the existence of human passions altogether.) Consequently, man is alone, condemned to be free; man must invent man, in the face of a virgin future. In particular, the Christian and Kantian moralities are too vague to help us make concrete choices, since the real world presents situations in which competing claims are made for our favor, situations which are too complex to be truly resolved through universàl rules. This concept emphasizes each man's uniqueness and directs us to think creatively.[29]

The elaboration of the concept of despair and the greater part of the extended responses to the initial objections seem to be directed to the Marxists, with the objects in mind of demythologizing radicalism of philosophy of history and providing it with a sound philosophic base in phenomenology. Because man is free, there can be no historical inevitability. The Revolution is necessarily a gamble, to be undertaken with resolve rather than complacent optimism. The focus of revolutionary fervor is thus redirected from the future to the present; it is in the lived moment that the Revolution finds its justification. But by the same token, the future is rescued from the indignity of epigonism. The post-Revolutionary generation will have the same freedom, and a comparable moral choice, as the Revolutionary. In what sense one speaks of "the Revolution" under these conditions remains a question. Sartre does, however, explicitly replace the notion of progress with that of amelioration.[30]

As for his remarks on subjectivity and the Cartesian cogito, they seem to be an earnest, though perhaps terminologically inaccurate, attempt to redress the problem of solipsism which had been laid at Descartes' doorstep, and which the dominant branch of Marxism had sought to overcome through a philosophically naive materialism. Far from leading to solipsism the Cartesian cogito, properly understood through phenomenology, is the very foundation for intersubjectivity, and therewith meaningful collective action. This, because the existential cogito contains the consciousness of the Other's existence as a direct intuition, as the very precondition of self-consciousness in the world. Besides granting philosophic

certainty, this doctrine alone confers upon men an
elementary measure of dignity, since it is as a freedom that we are conscious of the Other.[31] This doctrine of freedom, then, forms the capstone of the
"Humanism" essay's positive teaching. Because the
Other's freedom is ontologically a part of my own
consciousness, my freedom depends upon that of the
Other. Each engagement takes as equal and necessary
ends my own freedom and that of others. I thus must
will freedom as the foundation of all values. And
the meaning of the acts of men of good faith is the
quest for freedom as such. This will, presumably,
be the goal of a coherent and disillusioned leftism.[32]

## VI

Despite Sartre's emphatic assertion that there is
no human nature, that man is only what he makes himself be, he seems at various places to invoke a cluster
of human qualities which imply just such a nature. We
have already noted that his denial of a determinism
of the passions does not preclude the existence of
universal human passions as such, and that the concept
of anguish points to the premise that human beings
are emulative. We should further note his assertion
that those who would deny the universal significance
of their acts as models for all humanity must be ill
at ease with themselves because they do so only through
a kind of bad faith, that is, a self-deception. This
suggests not only a fundamental human inclination
toward common modes of behavior but also the presence
of common, emulative "humanity" as an innate idea.
Finally, in describing the fundamental "human condition," a concept which he offers as a substitute for
human nature, Sartre enumerates the following compo-
nents: the necessity for man to be in the world, to
be at work there, to be in the midst of others there,
and to be mortal there.[33] But the necessity to work,
unlike the other conditions, points beyond man's situation to an end or ends outside itself. We work in
order to obtain some end, such as self-preservation.
Does Sartre, then, unknowingly rely upon Hobbesian,
or even medieval, a priori values--self-preservation
and the innate idea of humanity--, even in the course
of denying a priori values? Is he merely scratching
the surface of human freedom while in fact thriving
on the residual "fat" of older philosophies? Is he,
in a word, merely a confused, unself-conscious
naturalist?

132

But perhaps we should not leap to this conclusion without searching for an alternative account of these passages. We note, for instance, that the context of the account of the "human condition" is an argument against materialist philosophies, made in the interest of saving a sense of human dignity. It is surely conceivable that Sartre, like other philosophers, feels compelled, while recognizing the extent of human "bondage," to emphasize freedom, as the antidote to actual or incipient widespread moral enervation or complacency.

But a still more radical alternative is available. Perhaps these naturalistic suggestions, which seem to undermine a doctrine of radical freedom, must be viewed through the corrective lens of freedom. For example, the formula "to be at work" differs from "to work" by a crucial nuance. Assuming our radical freedom to choose any end, to choose self-destruction, say, rather than self-preservation, we would still have to "work at" that end in order to give it effect. "Being at work" might then merely express the necessity of confronting resistance, even if only the resistance involved in being corporeal, in the course of pursuing any end whatever. Again, the ensemble of attitudes associated with "anguish"--the tendency toward emulation, the idea of common humanity, the bad conscience one feels at denying this idea--might in the end be only a product of freedom through the agency of will: I feel anguish only because I will myself to feel anguish, or, less reflectively, because I choose myself spontaneously as anguished.[34]

But these accounts call into question either the validity or the veracity of practically all of the "Humanism" essay's announced doctrines. Let us therefore re-examine these doctrines.

## VII

Sartre's doctrine of freedom is, to put it mildly, somewhat loosely argued. The Other's freedom, which is an ontological component of my own consciousness, is nothing more than my apprehension of the Other as a consciousness, who, as consciousness, is beyond my control. This concept of freedom may express a certain trivial ontological truth, but it says nothing in itself about people's mutual rights and obligations. Because the Other is _given_ as a freedom, it is impossible _not_ to premise his freedom in undertaking _any_ act toward him. Even an attempt to enslave him or to tyrannize over him is in this sense compatible with, because it presupposes, this freedom.

Secondly, Sartre's transition from freedom as the universal premise to freedom as the universal end is altogether too glib. It seems to rest upon the reflection that because every other end requires an act of creation, and because every act of creation presupposes freedom, freedom is the only candidate for universal value capable of surviving the contingency of creation. (One might just as well speak of the universal "value" of corporeality or location in time and space, because these too are presupposed in our acts toward others. But Sartre might perhaps readily agree that these concepts are implicit in "freedom.") On the other hand, exactly because man is a contingent, situated being, it is unclear what the meaning would be of an act specifically done for the sake of consciousness-freedom. Rather, it seems that every concrete act must also posit some other particular end, and that good faith--in the sense given here--is, therefore, impossible. But Sartre may in fact provide such another end by his choice of the ambiguous term "freedom," which, unlike the drier term "consciousness," imports from the realm of politics all the overtones of a popular slogan. In particular, political freedom, because it admits of degrees, may be the goal of projects of political liberation, however understood. But consciousness-freedom is integral. We may make others more enlightened, but not, in this sense, more free. (Why, then, does Sartre not, for instance, urge enlightenment as the universal end? Perhaps this would sound too particular, too academic, to be a useful rallying cry. But perhaps too Sartre does not in fact seek universal enlightenment.)

There is one sense in which consciousness-freedom may indeed be the universal end, understanding "end" not as goal but as the terminal condition of any project. Freedom in this sense is what we are left with after every (futile) attempt to become any thing; it is Being-for-itself's contamination of the project of constituting itself as Being-in-itself; it is that by virtue of which man is a useless passion. This understanding of "end" may explain an apparent slip in one of the essay's earlier statements. Sartre had explained the asserted precedence of existence over essence as a matter of temporal sequence: Man exists

before he makes himself be any particular thing. But
he had then referred to man's being only what he wills
himself to be "after this thrust <u>toward</u> <u>existence</u>,"
where we might have expected him to say "toward
essence."[35] Is man's every flight toward essence,
then, in the end merely a flight of existence toward
itself? In this case the Existentialist definition
should perhaps read "existence precludes essence."
On the other hand, man does have an essence, in fact
many essences, insofar as he is Being-for-others, a
being-in-the-midst-of-the-world, an object. In this
respect, a man is not what he makes himself be so much
as he is at the mercy of others, who may convert and
subvert his every project. (Sartre, then, avoids
universal enlightenment at least insofar as he sup-
presses these pessimistic facets of existential philosophy.)

There would seem to be two ways to overcome the
power of others to subvert the essence which anyone
chooses for himself. One way would be to have everyone will himself and others toward the same essence.
The other would be for a man to overwhelm others by
constituting himself so powerfully and pervasively
that others could not practically undo what he had done.
The concept of anguish seems to promote the first of
these alternatives and to discourage the second. On
closer inspection, however, Sartre's discussion of
anguish resurrects the latter possibility as the ultimate ground of the former.

On its face, the official account of existential
anguish corresponds to very little in the realm of
everyday experience. It is extremely difficult to
think of any act which we do simply as human beings
and which would be an appropriate model for all human
beings as such. Rather, we undertake our acts as
workers and employers, males and females, parents and
children, citizens and foreigners, rulers and ruled,
and in innumerable other particular capacities. The
moral rule which would blur these distinctions by
absorbing them into a common being of humanity has the
task of identifying the locus of that humanity. But if
that same rule is conjoined with the teaching that
there is no essence of man, or that man is to-be-made,
then either that locus is lost completely, or (what
may amount to the same thing) "humanity" is subjected
to an infinity of re-definitions according to our particular ends. Sartre's positing of freedom as the
universal and may be an attempt to circumvent these

difficulties by locating humanity in a non-essence,
in a kind of openness to becoming.  But this, as just
noted, leads to social chaos.  Further, if consciousness is the hallmark of humanity, then such beings as
the dog and the horse would have to be called human.[36]

Practically, however, social chaos might be
avoidable if everyone were as a matter of fact to con-
cur in a substantive conception of humanity and to be
engaged in common, or at least non-conflicting, concrete projects.  But such a state of belief and practice, if it is ever to be, must be brought about by
acting upon men as they are, in their various parti-
cularities, guiding them, by word and deed, toward the
desired condition.  It requires a project of political
legislation, which, if it is to avoid re-introducing
the chaos of infinite "humanities" through an infinity
of legislators, must preclude other comparable legisla-
tive projects by obscuring its own radical status.
It requires, in brief, promulgation of a Founding lie.
That the doctrine of anguish may indeed involve such
a project requires a close examination of Sartre's
discussion of this concept, which is possibly the
queerest part of the essay.

## VIII

The term "anguish," we recall, also occurs in
Being and Nothingness, but there its meaning is closer
to what Sartre here calls "forlornness": "the mode of
being of freedom as consciousness of being"; "my
consciousness of being my own future in the mode of
not-being"; "the reflective apprehension of freedom by
itself"; the experience of the openness of one's horizons, especially one's ethical horizons, in the consciousness that "my freedom is the unique foundation
of values and that nothing, absolutely nothing,
justifies me in adopting this or that particular value,
this or that particular scale of values."[37]  Granting
an author's general prerogative to redefine his terms,
there is something suspect about this particular substitution, involving as it does a concept thought to
be absolutely central to existential philosophy.  It
seems to be a singularly dishonest gesture.[38]  Substantively, the "humanistic" anguish of exemplary
actions appears to conflict with the notion of forlornness.  If there are really no a priori values, if
all is indeed permitted as a consequence of God's non-
existence; then either the ground for this universalist formula disappears, or, if it is to survive,

it must be drawn from forlornness itself, that is, it must be created.

Curiously, the examples which ostensibly support the universalist notion carry this undertone of creativity. Sartre gives five examples in relation to anguish: the worker who joins a Christian trade union, someone who marries, the story of Abraham, the madwoman having auditory hallucinations, and the military leader. Only the first two are explicitly related to the principle of universality, and these occur before the definition of anguish has itself been enunciated. The first of these is, however, stated completely hypothetically:

> If I am a working man and choose to join a Christian trade union rather than be a Communist, and if, by being a member I want to show that the best thing for man is resignation, that the kingdom of man is not of this world, I am not only involving my own case: I want to be resigned for everyone. As a result, my action has involved all humanity.[39]

The universal meaning of this act seems itself to be a matter of this worker's conscious choice. The second example is more categorical. The choice to marry or not is willy-nilly a choice for or against monogamy as a way of life for all mankind. This is, however, not Sartre's last word on this example. He recurs to it in his extended responses toward the end, where his concern is to distinguish existential choice from mere caprice. While he again asserts that man engages all humanity by his choice, his emphasis now is less on the truth of this doctrine than on its contribution to the actor's sense of responsibility.[40]

After his first elaboration of the marriage example, Sartre offers his definition of "anguish," which is again in its own terms hypothetical:

> (T)he man who involves himself and who realizes that he is not only the person he chooses to be, but also a lawmaker who is at the same time choosing all mankind as well as himself, cannot escape the feeling of his total and deep responsibility.[41]

But he answers this hypothetical character by claiming

137

that those who are not anxious are merely disguising
and fleeing from their anguish, that one escapes the
disquieting thought "What if everyone acted that way?"
only by a kind of bad faith.  Sartre has it appear
that what follows is the necessity for universalizable
acts, for he states:

> A man who lies and makes excuses for him-
> self by saying, "not everybody does that,"
> is someone with an uneasy conscience, be-
> cause the act of lying implies that a uni-
> versal value is conferred upon the lie.[42]

He then proceeds to his version of the Abraham story,
which contains, if not a lie, then at least the aforementioned inaccuracy.  Abraham's problem, moreover,
is not to perform an exemplary act, but to justify a
special act which is a test of his particular faith,
and which requires him to depart from a universal
moral norm.  The issue is not morality as law but absolute obedience to divine edict, and his problem is
not whether his faith is to be exemplary but the more
urgent problem of whether it is well placed.[43]

In this context, Sartre brings up the example of
the madwoman, who seems to be a foil to Abraham.  Her
voices come to her in today's supposedly demytholo-
gized world.  We might thus expect Abraham's problem
to be obviated:  With God's departure from the scene
there is no dispensation from universal moral norms.
But Sartre, in a sequence of rhetorical questions,
rather suggests the ultimate displacement of God, not
by some impersonal moral law, but by some human
teacher:

> And what proved to her, in effect, that it
> was God?  If an angel comes to me, what
> proves that it is an angel?  And if I hear
> voices, what proves that they come from
> heaven and not from hell, or from a sub-
> conscious, or from a pathologic state?  Who
> proves that they are addressed to me?  Who
> proves that I am really appointed to impose
> my conception of man and my choice upon human-
> ity?[44]

His answer, that "it is always for me to decide that
this is the angel's voice;. . . it is I who will
choose to say that (this act) is good rather than
bad," points to the concept of forlornness.[45]

But upon what basis shall I say that this act is good? Sartre again asserts the obligation of doing exemplary acts. But he again calls this obligation into question by stating that "every man ought to say to himself, 'Am I really the kind of man who has the right to act in such a way that humanity might guide itself by my actions?'"[46] If this is a serious question, then it could conceivably be answered No. In this case we are left with several questions: How do I reach such an answer? Who, if anyone, has such a right? What should my stance be toward such a person? By shifting the question from one of obligation to one of rights, Sartre moves it into the realm of volition. From the perspective of forlornness, absent any a priori standard for rights as well as for obligation, we seem to be in a radicalized version for the Hobbesian State of Nature (radicalized because Sartrean forlornness removes even Hobbes' implicit necessity for self-preservation)--each has the right to all, hence to choose himself as anything in relation to others. In terms of the question at hand, I have the right to be he whose acts may rule humanity if I so choose myself, and can make good my choice. Conversely, those who regulate themselves by my acts do not choose themselves as possessors of such a right, even though their acts may coincide with those of many others. The vacillation between obligation and rights suggests a two-tiered concept of anguish, one relating to followers, the other to leaders. (By a quirk of French vocabulary, the question which Sartre poses for each man could also be rendered, "Do I follow him who has the right to act in such a way that humanity might regulate itself by my acts?")[47]

Declaring that he is here speaking of "a simple sort of anguish, that anybody who has had responsibilities is familiar with," Sartre presents his fifth example, that of the military leader, who "takes the responsibility for an attack and sends a certain number of men to death."[48] This final example presents an act in its very nature undemocratic, an act of leadership; the anguish of which consists not in being exemplary but in choosing "alone" to order uniform exemplary behavior by others; and the responsibility of which is not that of submitting to a universal formula, but rather the responsibility of concrete responsibilities. Others are indeed engaged by this act, but as followers, instrumentally. Such an act involves an anguish which "(a)ll leaders know."[49] Presumably, this description includes leaders of philosophic movements and of public opinion.[50]  Indeed, it may in the end refer especially to them since even the military leader's anguish occurs in the course of executing orders which proceed from above.[51] The true leader's anguish would be that of the one who, completely forlorn, originates his own orders.

## IX

What are the consequences of this division between the anguish of leaders and that of followers?  One consequence seems to be that very few people will truly experience forlornness.  For what the leader sees as his radical freedom, consequent upon the absence of God and of any a priori values, the follower, under the aegis of his democratic a priori value, experiences only as a vague, albeit perhaps emphatic, atheism.  Under these conditions, "forlornness," like "freedom," would for the many become essentially a slogan.

The success of the anguish-dispensation would also bear upon the meaning of "despair."  For if the many are diverted from realizing the radical freedom of full forlornness, then some measure of predictability is introduced into human affairs.  To be sure, that predictability cannot be perfect, since men are incipiently radically free, and so there will always be room for despair.  But practically, this despair can lead in either of two directions.  We can recognize the freedom of others to undo whatever we do as signifying the ultimate futility of public acts, and therefore withdraw into private activities which will be out of their reach, ultimately into the most private activity, contemplation.  Or we can attempt to overwhelm others, as I have suggested, by simply giving them more than they are likely to want to, or to be easily able to, undo.  A political Founder, for instance, who despairs of establishing a regime which will last forever, may nonetheless take heart at the prospect of shaping men's lives for the next several generations.

Sartre seems to guide his auditors between these alternatives.  Manifestly, he is at pains to defend Existentialism from the charge of quietism, but the defense is hardly air-tight.  Thus, he asserts that man is "nothing else than the ensemble of his acts," suggesting the necessity for a kind of rabid activism; but he defines this ensemble of acts so broadly as in principle to admit an essentially contemplative life

within its ambit.[52] Again, the general formula for
anguish seems designed in part to impugn contemplation,
both as an evasion of one's social responsibilities and
as a selfish indulgence in a way of life which, because
it requires mental faculties and a degree of physical
security not available to everyone, may be in its
nature un-universalizable. But to one who has seen
the other side of anguish, the forlorn anguish of
leaders, such considerations could not be decisive.
In the present essay, Sartre speaks in the voice of one
whose normal way of life is that of "technician[33]and
philosopher," a highly particular way of life. On
the other hand, the counsel of despair does seem geared
to moderate the Left's blind faith in the future, and,
as we have seen, to turn revolutionary attention to
the present. The condition for doing so, however, is
the enunciation, perhaps even promulgation, of a doctrine which looks to acceptance in the future as well
as the present by virtue of its claim to trans-historic
validity. Sartre's own despair with respect to the
Left is that of a Founder.

In line with this interpretation we can understand, as attempts to legislate, certain passages which
might otherwise seem groundless: The assertion that
each man is responsible for all mankind is itself an
attempt to promote such a sense of responsibility.
The self-evident truth that we are all fundamentally
alike becomes "self-evident" only through being publicly proclaimed. We ought to act as though everyone were watching us because henceforth we will watch
each other more. We will not have to choose to treat
anyone unjustly because that explicit option is obscured through the formulation of our choice as a
commitment to universal freedom. We need not seek
others' advice because, we are hereby advised, to do
so is already to have made up our mind. Bad faith,
while not morally blamable, is an "error" of incohe-
rence, and thus suspect. Further, its practitioners,[54]
it is hereby stipulated, are "cowards" and "bastards".

X

How can we account for these peculiarities? Perhaps Sartre is just too hopelessly confused to make a
coherent argument. But perhaps he is not. The passages upon which we have focused suggest an attempt
partially, but only partially, to obscure, in public
teaching, the extent of his reliance on materialist

naturalism on the one hand, and the nihilistic and undemocratic dimension of existential philosophy on the other.  These two enterprises would be consistent insofar as materialism has a provisional validity respecting those who remain unaware of the truly radical character of their freedom.

What would be the basis for such an attempt? Some clue may lie in certain distinctions which Sartre makes.  We have already noticed one such distinction, that between Christian and atheist Existentialists, which he makes toward the beginning.  The tendency of his subsequent argument is, as we have seen, to discredit the former of these alternatives as incoherent. This early distinction separates him and Heidegger from Jaspers and Marcel.  He later suggests, much less openly, his own parting of company from Heidegger by referring to "forlornness" as "a term Heidegger was fond of."[55]  While the concept is also central to Sartre, he seems to be much less enamored of the term, and, I have suggested, even goes out of his way to use another term to describe examples which in fact point to this concept.  Toward the end of the essay, when the theme of humanism re-surfaces, Sartre raises another distinction.  There are, he tells us, two kinds of humanism:  Existentialist humanism; and another kind, which Existentialist humanism opposes, which exalts in the image of the Great Man, and which leads to fascism.  This humanism, he says, is absurd, because "only the dog or the horse would be able to make such an overall judgment about man" as this doctrine does.[56] That is, to expand on Sartre's imagery, the precondition for the non-absurdity of this kind of humanism would be the existence of a judging being who could stand apart from the humanity upon which he passes judgment; and there is no such being.

It seems strange that so important a distinction as this, a distinction the practical consequence of which is no less than the avoidance of fascism, should be left unmentioned until this penultimate passage, and then only raised as a kind of afterthought.  It seems stranger still that Sartre should place Existentialism so foursquare against a doctrine of the Great Individual when that very image was so central to the inspirational teaching of The Flies.  Perhaps the two-and-a-half year interval between these works had opened his eyes to some crucial new truth.  I have indicated my reasons for disbelieving that the

"Humanism" essay's quasi-Kantian formula for anguish
was such a truth.

But truths come in different shapes and sizes.
The end of the war had brought the collapse of the
intellectual Right (such as it was) and the discrediting
of things Germanic. While "Existentialist" faddism
flourished,[57] serious existential philosophy, product
of "the Nazi Heidegger," was in bad odor, especially
among the Left. Despite Sartre's feeble effort to
defend Heidegger as "a philosopher well before he was
a Nazi,"[58] it may well have appeared to him that some
stronger remedy was necessary to preserve this philosophy's public respectability, and to disguise its
truly explosive potential, without going Marcel's
route of religious revival. In this light, the "Humanism" essay emerges as a calculated attempt to steer
between the shoals of superstition and atrocity.

This project, however, seems to require the fostering of fanaticism. For how else should we regard
the teaching of a form of self-reliance which eschews
the seeking of advice as a matter of principle? How
else the promotion of immoderate characterizations
of rival positions which are of questionable fairness?
A project so conceived and so executed must, whatever
may or must be said for it, raise the most serious
doubts about its prudence, its honesty, and its aesthetic appeal as a construction.[59]

But if the anguish-myth and the freedom-myth are
aimed at a credulous public, at whom are the subtle-
ties which reveal these teachings as myth directed?
It might be consistent to suggest that an author who
would regard the writing of an abstruse philosophic
treatise essentially as a kind of self-expression would
similarly regard these ironies.[60] In this case the
inner movement of the "Humanism" essay would be a
reflection of Sartre the man, and would be directed to
nobody in particular. But it is also possible, especially in the light of Simone de Beauvoir's remark
about "exchanges" with the Communists, to discern a
more communicative design. Despite his uncompromising
stand on strictly philosophic questions, which he
fleshed out the following year in a pointed critique
of the theory of dialectical materialism, Sartre's
political receptivity to the Left is evident in these
pages. In the post-war milieu the radical Left may
well have appeared to be the only locus of vitality, as

against the moribund bourgeoisie. Sartre knew from personal experience that the Communist leadership's political astuteness included an appreciation for politic lies. If that leadership could itself be led to a philosophic rededication of political radicalism along Sartrean lines, the way might be paved for a vital politics, based on existential premises but hedged against those premises' worst possibilities.

Such a prospect presupposed that the Left's leaders could be lured from slavish attachment to the Moscow party line, a possibility that the Communists' wartime role in the Resistance might have encouraged. But the subsequent failure of even the most intelligent Communist of his time to rise to Sartre's bait signalled the failure of this hope.[61] Thereafter, Sartre would either have to go his own way or collapse into ideology. True to form, he did both.

NOTES

[1]Hereinafter called the "Humanism" essay. Quotes are generally from the Bernard Frechtman translation, copyright by The Philosophical Library, Inc., as it appears in George Novack (ed.), Existentialism versus Marxism: Conflicting Views on Humanism (New York: Dell Publishing Co., 1966). I have translated certain key passages directly from the original French edition, L'Existentialisme est un humanisme (Paris: Editions Nagel, 1946). This volume also contains the text of a discussion in which Sartre participated sometime after delivery of the "Humanism" lecture. I regret the awkwardness of this dual system of citation, which has been necessitated by Nagel's unexplained and ungenerous refusal to permit extensive direct quotation from the original. For one possible explanation of this refusal, see Contat and Rybalka, vol. 1, pp. 189-90.

[2]Contat and Rybalka call it "the only work Sartre has largely rejected" (vol. 1, p. 133). But they cite no positive evidence of such rejection. Rather, they seem to infer it from Sartre's subsequent non-reliance on the essay; his reference to it as "only an oeuvre de passage" (p. 221); and his eventual abandonment of the treatise on ethics, to which the essay was presumably the transition. None of this is, of course, decisive. Equally compatible with these facts is the inference that Sartre, seeing the failure of the

rhetorical project constituted by the essay's public teaching, preferred to let sleeping dogs lie. See also Robert V. Stone's editorial note in Jeanson, p. 22 n 4.

[3]Alasdair Macintyre, "Existentialism," in Mary Warnock (ed.), Sartre: A Collection of Critical Essays (Garden City, New York: Doubleday & Company, Inc., 1971), p. 2; Martin Heidegger, "Letter on Humanism," trans. Edgar Lohner, in William Barrett and Henry D. Aiken (eds.), Philosophy in the Twentieth Century, vol. 3: Contemporary European Thought (New York: Harper and Row, 1962), pp. 192-224, esp. pp. 202, 205, 209, 220, 222, 224; Walter Kaufmann (ed.), Existentialism from Dostoevsky to Sartre (Cleveland: The World Publishing Co., Meridian Books, 1956), p. 45; "Jean-Paul Sartre reproche à Georges Lukács de ne pas être marxiste," Combat, 20 January 1949, p. 1.

[4]Contat and Rybalka, vol. 1, pp. 132-33.

[5]Simone de Beauvoir, Prime of Life, p. 659.

[6]Idem, Force of Circumstance, p. 38.

[7]See Contat and Rybalka, vol. 2, pp. 155-60.

[8]For Marcel's use of existential phenomenology to sustain traditional religious categories, see, e.g., Gabriel Marcel, "On the Ontological Mystery," in Barrett and Aiken, pp. 286-308.

[9]"Existentialism Is a Humanism," p. 70.

[10]Force of Circumstance, pp. 43, 45.

[11]Gen. 22:1-2. Kierkegaard is emphatic on the point that Abraham must stand in an immediate relation to God. See Soren Kierkegaard, Fear and Trembling, trans. Walter Lowrie (Princeton: Princeton University Press, 1954), p. 34.

[12]"L'Existentialisme est un humanisme," pp. 16-17.

[13]"Existentialism Is a Humanism," p. 72.

[14]Ibid., p. 84.

[15]Ibid., p. 76.

[16] Ibid., pp. 80-81. The contradiction consists in Sartre's claim that when we choose an advisor we already basically know what advice we shall receive; and in the fact that the young man, having gone to Sartre for advice, was told by him that he was free and should choose for himself. On its face, it seems unlikely that anyone would seek out someone else just in order to get this piece of non-advice. It is, of course, possible that he sought Sartre out in order to be reassured of his moral autonomy. But this reassurance then becomes part of a self-serving calculation, and its status as truth becomes distinctly secondary. Sartre in fact later indicated that his answer was geared to the young man's particular desire and that he "knew" what his questioner would do in the end, implying that he might have given a different answer to someone else. ("L'Existentialisme est un humanisme," p. 141).

[17] "Existentialism Is a Humanism," p. 76. One may well wonder why a self-proclaimed atheist not beset by the danger of religious persecution should play cute games of this sort. Is it perhaps an unfortunate fact of our time, but not only of our time, that a public speaker can ingratiate himself with one political group only through such ridicule of another? Cf. Leo Strauss, What is Political Philosophy? (New York: The Free Press, 1959), pp. 225-26.

[18] "L'Existentialisme est un humanisme," p. 101.

[19] Ibid., p. 102.

[20] Sartre reiterated this thought in his reply to Lukács: "Nous estimons que tous les moyens sont bons pour réaliser une fin, à condition qu'ils ne détruisent pas cette fin." Combat, 20 January 1949, p. 4.

[21] "Existintialism Is a Humanism," p. 72.

[22] Ibid., p. 71.

[23] Ibid.

[24] Ibid., pp. 71-72.

[25] Ibid., p. 75.

[26] Ibid., p. 72.

[27]Ibid., pp. 74-76.

[28]Ibid., p. 74.

[29]Ibid., pp. 77-78.

[30]"L'Existentialisme est un humanisme," p. 79.

[31]Ibid., pp. 65, 66.

[32]Ibid., pp. 83, 84, 82.

[33]Ibid., p. 68.

[34]Cf. "Existentialism Is a Humanism," p. 74.

[35]Ibid., p. 74. Emphasis supplied.

[36]Cf. ibid., p. 83.

[37]Being and Nothingness, pp. 65, 68, 78, 76.

[38]Cf. "Existentialism Is a Humanism," p. 78.

[39]Ibid., p. 75. Emphasis supplied.

[40]"L'Existentialisme est un humanisme," pp. 73-75. It is passingly curious that, unless Sartre uses terms especially loosely here, the alternatives which he states for this marriage example--"either he will remain chaste, or he will marry without having children, or he will marry and will have children" (p. 75)--do not include an apt description of his then-famous relationship with Simone de Beauvoir. Cf. Simone de Beauvoir, Force of Circumstance, p. 46.

[41]"Existentialism Is a Humanism," p. 75. Emphasis supplied.

[42]Ibid., p. 76.

[43]Kierkegaard, in his account, goes to great length to emphasize the non-universalist character of Abraham's act, as a "teleological suspension of the ethical." Fear and Trembling, Problem 1 ( pp. 64-77).

[44]"L'Existentialisme est un humanisme," pp. 30-31. Emphasis supplied.

[45]"Existentialism Is a Humanism," p. 76.

[46]Ibid.

[47]". . . suis-je bien celui qui a le droit d'agir de telle sorte que l'humanité se règle sur mes actes?" "L'Existentialisme est un humanisme," p. 31.

[48]"Existentialism Is a Humanism," pp. 76-77.

[49]Ibid., p. 77.

[50]Cf. Sartre's curious disjunction of himself and "the French existentialists" (ibid., p. 72).

[51]Ibid., p. 77.

[52]"Existentialism Is a Humanism," p. 83; "L'Existentialisme est un humanisme," p. 58.

[53]"L'Existentialisme est un humanisme," p. 16.

[54]"Existentialism Is a Humanism," pp. 74-75, 76, 79-80, 80-81; "L'Existentialisme est un humanisme," pp. 24-26, 29, 31, 42-43, 46, 81-82, 84-85, 86-88.

[55]"Existentialism Is a Humanism," p. 77.

[56]Ibid., p. 83.

[57]Cf. ibid., pp. 71, 72.

[58]"A More Precise Characterization of Existentialism" (1944), in Contat and Rybalka, vol. 2, p. 156.

[59]Cf. "L'Existentialisme est un humanisme," p. 76.

[60]Cf. supra, pp. 23, 25.

[61]See Georg Lukács, "Existentialism or Marxism?" in Novack, pp. 134-53.

# 5. SARTRE'S MARXIST ODYSSEY, 1946-1961

> We cannot assume that the times in which
> we live are not catastrophic, merely
> because it is we who live in them.
>
> Robert Bolt, State of
> Revolution

> Neither shalt thou go up by steps unto
> mine altar, that thy nakedness be not
> discovered thereon.
>
> Exodus 20:26

> (T)he genuine are always rare, espe-
> cially genuine actors.
>
> Nietzsche Zarathustra 3.
> 5. 2.

## I. Overview

The dominant issue during most of Sartre's post-
war career was his relation to Marxism. Under the
political circumstances prevailing in France at this
time, this perforce meant his relationship with the
French Communist Party.[1] It was a checkered relationship, alternately involving mutual praise and recrimi-
nation, waxing and waning enthusiasm, with each new
turn justified by heady dialectical analysis. That
Sartre chose to frame his case in this way, that by
1956 he could appear to be but one step away from
joining the CP, and that in his most explicit pronouncement on the relation of Existentialism to Marxism he
seemingly demoted the former to the status of "ideology" within the latter's more comprehensive "philosophic" framework, all contribute to the conclusion
that Sartre had fundamentally abandoned his earlier
philosophic identity and become a Marxist. Orthodox
Marxists, however, recognizing that there was something queer about his brand of Marxism, resisted wel-
coming Sartre into their ranks.[2] An overview of the
events in Sartre's life during the decade and a half
following the war suggests a thesis both more modest
and more ambitious than that of Sartre-the-Marxist-
convert-and-ideologue.

The "Humanism" essay was followed in 1946 by a

149

two-part article, "Materialism and Revolution," in which Sartre criticized, on practical as well as theoretical grounds, the "Marxist scholasticism" of the prevailing Stalinist line.  This article, Simone de Beauvoir tells us, was part of Sartre's quest for "exchanges" with the CP.[3]  The exchange which Sartre received consisted of virulent denunciations in the official Communist organs, which labelled Existentialism "public enemy number one"; and a set of comically sinister encounters with the French Communist leadership, which, if they aimed at anything, seemed geared to emphasize Sartre's inefficacy as a leader of young Leftists.[4]  This prompted him, in 1948, to accept the invitation of a group of independent Leftist intellectuals to help lead the Democratic Revolutionary Assembly, a nascent political organization designed to provide a forum for Communists discontented with their own party's insularity, Socialists seeking a new home from their apparently moribund party, and left-leaning bourgeois elements.  The RDR, while not a political party, apparently entertained the ambition of becoming the dominant Leftist influence on French politics, perhaps analogously to the way in which the Gaullist Popular French Assembly sought to pre-empt the French Right.  It pointedly criticized the CP for subordinating the interests of French workers to Soviet foreign policy.  Its positive political vision, which hardly seems radical from the vantage point of the 1980's, included the reorganization of the French economy under a national Plan, independence for the colonies, and the formation of a basically socialist European economic community, politically independent of, and able to mediate between, the US and the USSR.[5]  By mid-1949, however, it became apparent to Sartre that the workers were not about to abandon the CP, and that the RDR would not go far as a political movement.  Personal differences with the other RDR leaders precipitated his break with the organization in October of that year.

There followed two and a half years of political hibernation, during which he abandoned the project of writing an Ethics, immersed himself in the works of Marx, and "drift(ed) in uncertainty."[6]  He emerged in 1952 as a virulent pro-Communist.  His long article "The Communists and Peace," the first two parts of which appeared that year, constitutes a kind of mea culpa, as he turned his polemical guns upon the anti-Communists of the Left and the Right, appearing to

defend the USSR as a peace-loving country and the CP
as the necessary and exact expression of the French
working class.[7] Over the next four years, he concerned himself almost exclusively with practical politics, employing his considerable polemical skills in
solidly pro-Communist stands on a number of issues.
In 1954 he visited the Soviet Union, where he was
treated royally, as a special guest of the Politbureau.
By early 1956 he could even criticize, for undisci-
pline, one of the French CP's leaders who had harried
him in 1947 and who had turned renegade over the
Party's closedness. For all appearances, Sartre was,
in the phrase of his former colleague Merleau-Ponty,
an "ultra-bolshevik."[8] Parcel to Sartre's affinity
to the Communists in these years may have been the
belief, fortified by Khrushchev's speech at the
Twentieth Party Congress, that Communism was moving in
the direction of greater openness. The suppression
of the Hungarian revolt, however, proved to be another
turning point. Sartre, along with many other Leftists,
including some Communists, condemned the move, and[9]
thereafter returned to a more independent Leftism.
While still professing his own subordination to Marx,
he thereafter sought inspiration from sources other
than Moscow--at various times, from Cuba, China, and
the New Left Youth--and formulated a social theory
which is distinctly his own.[10]

This sequence of events could indeed indicate a
mere ideologue, living through a series of self-
deceptions.[11] But they could equally be those of a
political tactician, astutely and ruthlessly trimming
his sails to ideological currents. We can be confi-
dent that there was never any love lost between Sartre
and the Communists. They had spread the slander that
his boyhood friend, Paul Nizan, himself a long-time
Communist, who had quietly criticized the 1939 Hitler-
Stalin pact and who was killed at the front in 1940,
was a police spy; and they had attempted to isolate
Sartre himself during the Resistance years by fostering
the rumor that he was a secret collaborator. His
dealings with them were always as hard-nosed as those
of Politbureau members with each other. He was
always careful, even in agreeing with the Communists,
to distinguish himself from them, so that even his
most vehement support proceeded from a standpoint of
independent and superior judgment.[12] If Sartre was
an ultra-bolshevik, it was, as likely as not, in order
to appropriate bolshevism. In 1960, the same year as

the publication of his "Marxist" <u>Critique of Dialec-</u>
<u>tical Reason</u>, he recounted the events of the Nizan
affair in a foreword to one of Nizan's novels, in
which he described the men whom he had formerly called
"our Communist friends" as "a bunch of moral cripples,"
"sub-men unaware of their sub-humanity," and "the
enemy."[13] While there is no more reason to deny
Sartre's later political sympathy with the New Left
than his former political sympathy with the Old Left,
this chronology does suggest that one take somewhat
guardedly his more recent expressions of affinity with
Castro, Mao, or the students of May 1968.[14]

Lest this chronology seem to bespeak merely a
dispute among personalities, it would be helpful to
state at the outset certain substantive peculiarities
of Sartre's Marxism. His position on the inevitability of revolution was always equivocal at best, and
he never ventured to predict the withering away of
the State. While owning Marxism to be the authoritative philosophic system for our time, he explicitly
denied any claim it might have to absolute, trans-
historic validity. Rather, its chief theoretical
value is said to be its usefulness in understanding,
describing, and criticizing capitalist society in
terms of class conflict. This decisive usefulness
notwithstanding, Sartre defined social structures
through categories which are distinctly his own; cata-
gories which one could as readily use to understand,
describe, and criticize so-called "socialist" societies. Moreover, by emphasizing psychological, historical, and political "mediations," his analysis
deliberately departs from the orthodox Marxist emphasis on economic determination. He justifies particular
actions or social structures, not essentially because
they promote the classless society, but because they
invoke certain existential virtues. There is even a
suggestion of the kind of free political judgment, at
the peak of certain social structures, that traditional political theory attributes to the Founders of
regimes. Though the context and the practitioners be
changed, he preserves what he can of Orestes' heroism.

## II. "Materialism and Revolution"

Sartre's clearest theoretical statement on Marxism is the early critical article "Materialism and
Revolution."[15] Its basic criticisms, none of which he
substantially repudiated, focus on three areas:

materialist metaphysics, the nature of the dialectic, and the cult-like character of Marxist materialism as a practiced doctrine.

Despite the materialists' attack on metaphysics in general, in the name of a kind of positivism, Marxist materialism is itself metaphysical since it claims a certainty on some issues--the non-existence of God, the universal rationality of the real--which no positivism could provide. The universal materialist metaphysics to which it thus lays claim is, however, absurd because it destroys the ideational value of materialism itself by absorbing it into a system of material causation. In order to rescue itself, therefore, materialist metaphysics must implicitly appeal to idealism in the form of certain subjective cri- teria of thought: consistency, clarity, distinctness, permanence.

This difficulty might be resolvable through a coherent dialectical account which subsumes this sub- jective element. But Marxist materialism, unlike Hegel's dialectic for instance, has thus far offered no such account. Instead, it makes a set of false appeals to Science, that is, to the natural sciences, as the model for the dialectical understanding of man. But nature, as studied by modern science, is mechanis- tic, not dialectical—matter is characterized not by the totality to which the dialectic appeals, but by inertia. Even the theory of evolution describes, not a process of synthetic production, but of the elimi- nation of species. In making this critique, Sartre implicitly insists upon the radical separation of man, the subjective being for whom a properly constructed dialectical account would be appropriate, from nature, which receives its due from non-dialectical natural science.[16]

Finally, he finds odious the fanatical devotion demanded by Marxist materialism, which requires its adherents totally to submit their judgment to a truth which is, by its own terms, historical, and thus only provisional, and for the sake of an end which is it- self problematic. The problem, however, consists only in the premised inevitability of the Revolution and of the ensuing classless society; Sartre does not question their desirability. On the basis of this concession, he urges materialism's rehabilitation. For he regards it as no mere coincidence that, from the time of Epicurus, materialist doctrines have been positively related to the revolutionary attitude. Thus, he concludes, materialism is a politically useful myth. But since a long range undertaking needs the truth, the philosopher's task is to construct an alternative framework which will contain materialism's partial truths within a comprehensive description of man, while not sacrificing the myth's usefulness to the revolution.[17]

## III. The RDR Episode

Sartre's activity in the RDR may have been an attempt to redress at least the practical complaint of Communist cultism, and possibly also the mentioned lack of a comprehensive theory which could properly incorporate Marxian materialism. In his 1948 public discussions with David Rousset and Gérard Rosenthal, two other RDR leaders, one of the points made repeatedly and emphatically was the need for a corrective to the CP's hierarchical closedness and mystifications. The RDR was to be a forum for left-wing elements, which, patterning itself on the model of pre-war syndicalism, would place the highest premium on the value of democratic deliberation and on the formulation of openly-stated reasons for its policy decisions. It aimed at a political system in which free debate, diversity, and opposition were not only tolerated, but regarded as essential.[18] One wonders whether this political liberalism did not ultimately supersede Marxism in the RDR design, for Sartre, describing the RDR's basic principles, calls democracy a means of emancipation and the final end, while referring to the revolution which liquidates the capitalist social structure only as a means. However this may be, he calls upon Marxism to become, in the short run, an ."open philosophy."[19]

On the theoretical front, he begins the kind of phenomenological account of revolutionary psychology that he was to develop in subsequent writings. But the terms in which he frames this thumbnail account equally point back to the ethical project of the "Humanism" essay. By proceeding from concrete needs to abstract formulations, he says, we of the RDR not only avoid the Communist vice of mystification, but also place ourselves on the way to an infallible understanding of universal justice, for "all need surpasses itself toward a humanism." Thus, my hunger implies the universal value of being-fed.[20]

While it is difficult to tell, from this fragmentary account, how far Sartre wished to take this point, it deserves some passing comment. Sartre uses as his point of reference an experience, hunger, which is both concrete and universal. In this, he avoids the indeterminacy of the "Humanism" essay's positing of freedom as the sole universal end. He also revives the notion of a determinate human nature--man is the hungering being--, implicitly abandoning the common sense-defying insistence$_2$that we freely give our passions their efficacy. But if the example indicates a conception of human nature, or of the character of the humanism which grows from it, it still does not take us very far. That all men should eat may suggest something about the proper organization of a distributive economy, but it hardly presents a goal of humanity which is anything more than bestial. To call this a humanism is to debase the term "human." But to speak of other, more idiosyncratic,needs is to gear the idea of humanity to a non-universal conception. And to broach the need which some men might have for distinction as such is to contradict this universalism outright. But we saw the question of the distinguished man to be central to both The Flies and the "Humanism" essay. We must thus regard this account of the generation of principles of universal justice as self-consciously partial. As a public teaching, it is consistent with the "Humanism" essay's rhetorical thrust. And its emphasis on basic need anticipates the increasingly plebeian direction which Sartre's teaching was to take.

## IV. "The Communists and Peace"

Four years later, in "The Communists and Peace," Sartre busied himself at conspicuously retracting the polemical position of "Materialism and Revolution" and the RDR discussion. For all that, his theoretical defense of adherence to the CP proceeds along the independent lines suggested in these earlier enterprises. For analytical purposes, we may consider three broad aspects of this very important article: its delineation of Sartre's actual situation vis-à-vis the CP, his attacks on the positions of anti-Communists, and his own "Marxist" account of French society.

In a brief preface, Sartre takes particular aim at Georges Altman, anti-Communist editor of Franc-Tireur and a former leader of the RDR, as one of a company of "slimy rats" (<u>rats visqueux</u>) who seek to slip around the crucial political datum of the time, that one cannot both believe in the proletariat's "historic mission" and be against the CP. Rather, the attempt to be selectively revolutionary, to be for Lenin but against Stalin, "doesn't hold up." The call for a "Bold Social Democratic" party to preempt the CP's position is futile because "it takes years before a political group acquires enough influence to be represented in the National Assembly." He ridicules those who condemn the CP for "pulling the chestnuts out of the fire for the USSR." And in the 1954 sequel part, he attempts to demonstrate the inappropriateness and even the moral dubiety of trade union democracy on the old syndicalist model.[22]

All this is in obvious opposition to his own RDR position.[23] Altman is in this respect a partial surrogate for Sartre himself formerly, a fact which he indicates by calling himself a "slimy rat."[24] But the "slimy rat's" fault is not basically moral culpability, nor the misjudgment of ultimately desirable political ends. Rather he errs in refusing to come to grips with certain harsh, immediate political realities: the actual influence of the CP on the working class, the fact that the latter is not about to desert the former, and the consideration that "smiles from the Right" can make one a traitor overnight.[25] Do these facts indicate, as a matter of tactics, that the truly slippery one must go out of his way to provoke frowns from the Right, through rhetorical exaggeration? Sartre suggests as much in a footnote, where he characterizes the "slimy rat" as the wrongfully reproached culprit.[26] Moreover, if the fact of the workers' loyalty is a settled matter for Sartre, the character of that loyalty is not. For while they do indeed seem unwilling to desert the CP in favor of another political party, Sartre's central apprehension is that they are about to fall into a lasting state of political apathy, that their loyalty toward the CP will become merely the formal and ineffective loyalty of parliamentary elections. Thus, he later opines, in the current situation the CP must desire alliances with independent Leftists because of their differences.[27]

It should not surprise us, in light of this rhetorical context, that Sartre most conspicuously defends the CP by attacking anti-Communist positions and actions. He convincingly argues, for instance, that the conservative opposition to political strikes, because politics should not intrude into economics, itself conceals a prior political judgment on the relation of polity to economy. He shows with some plausibility that the electoral and parliamentary mechanisms of the Fourth Republic so weaken and isolate the CP that it must employ extra-parliamentary tactics in order to be politically effective. Somewhat less persuasive are his demonstration of the USSR's peaceful intentions from its failure to overrun Western Europe immediately, before NATO gets any stronger; and his inference, from the differences between the French and Italian Parties, that Moscow permits regional leaders a wide margin of initiative as a general policy. But he signals the weakness of these arguments himself by acknowledging the extent of existing NATO military power in 1952, and by stating that the French workers know and accept the fact of the CP's subservience to Comminform. (It is in the course of these arguments that he also mentions in passing that Russia has not yet achieved socialism.)[28] Perfectly plausible on its face, however, is his evident indignation at the Pinay government's attempts to repress the CP, an episode of Fourth Republic history which deserves some description.

The CP had called for a street demonstration on May 28, 1952, to protest a state visit by General Ridgway, and felt obliged to carry through on these plans despite advance indications that the workers' response would be disappointing. The demonstration did indeed prove to be a failure, accompanied by some minor violence. Antoine Pinay's government, however, took the occasion to round up and imprison 250 Communists afterward, including Jacques Duclos, the CP's leader in the National Assembly, in violation of his privilege of parliamentary immunity, fabricating the imaginative explanation that the squabs which he was at the time carrying home to have for dinner were carrier pigeons trained to fly state secrets to Moscow. The move had every appearance of a full-scale blunder which was only aggravated by the government's strained efforts to justify it. In the end, the French judiciary drew upon 150 years of traditional independence and threw the cases out, reprimanding the government for its disregard of the Constitution.

Sartre conjectures that behind this Keystone Cops facade there might lurk a Machiavellian design by

Pinay to use the attack on the Communists as a way
to capture the political Right from the Gaullists,[29]
but he does not press this hypothesis. Instead, he
expresses his disturbance at the failure of the non-
Communist Left and the workers to rally to the CP's
support. For in the former he claims to see the relinquishing of class solidarity and constitutional
guarantees (which are at least useful tactically) for
the sake of pressing a political rivalry; and in the
latter an ominous sign of the dissolution of the pro-[30]
letariat into a mere mass. This observation goes to
the heart of the essay. The demise or serious weakening of the CP would, under current conditions, lead to
the demise of the proletariat. In what he apparently
regards as a self-answering question, Sartre asks
his non-Communist readers, "Can you see us without a
proletariat?" The implicit cutting edge of this question is the presumed undesirability of the prospect
which it evokes: The general tone of life in a France
consisting of a depressed mass beneath a depressing
bourgeoisie, the most backward bourgeoisie in Europe,[31]
would be insufferable. Here is a fuller political
judgment than the Moscow apologetics alone would
suggest.

This implication receives expression in a short
but touching, and surprisingly nationalistic, set of
remarks which Sartre addresses to the Right, to the
believers in "eternal France," at the start of the
essay's third part. Far from being immortal, he says,
France is dying. It is a nation with no great hopes,
ambitions, or undertakings. Its standard of living is
poor. Its government rules by lies, preventing social
mobility, precluding social reforms, oppressing the
colonies, and abdicating its sovereignty in international relations to the United States and to recon-
structed Germany. The bourgeoisie is beset by political apathy. Amid all this decay, the working class
is the only locus of a doctrine; of a political party
whose program calls for democratic institutions,
national sovereignty, and economic rebirth; of vita-[32]
lity. It is not evident whether this nationalist
concern points Sartre toward a nationalist solution.
In the RDR discussions, he and his colleagues had
longed for union among the nations of a socialist
Western Europe, but it was unclear whether this implied[33]
anything more than regional economic cooperation.
His current chagrin at France's eclipse within Europe
by Germany suggests a more narrow nationalism. But

158

it need not preclude a longer range trans-national vision of political sovereignty. What his plaint does presage is the peculiar character of his ensuing "Marxian" political analysis, as an account not of a universal class struggle but of France's peculiar class struggle. His analysis thus remains substantively inconclusive on the issue of Marxism's universal validity. What it in effect demonstrates is that the French class struggle gains its peculiar virulence not from its conformity to, but consequent upon its crucial aberrations from, the classic Marxian model of capitalist development.

The two historical factors which Sartre regards as crucial to an understanding of French political society are the peculiar brutality with which the bourgeoisie suppressed proletarian insurgency in 1848 and 1871, and what he calls the bourgeoisie's "Malthusian" economic policy in the twentieth century. The suppressions, which reportedly made the French bourgeois pariahs among the bourgeois of Europe, drove the proletariat from French political society, precluding future parliamentary co-optation, and gave the class struggle there the aspect of a protracted civil war. The workers, permanently embittered against the organs of "legitimate" society, organized their power bases outside of parliament, in trade unions which felt free to make more extreme and polarizing demands than did the workers' representatives in other countries.[34]

"Malthusianism" is Sartre's peculiar conspiracy theory of the French economy, according to which the French capitalists, disspirited at the end of World War I by the proletariat's steady growth and the example of the Russian Revolution, and considering the "healthy" fascist reaction to be futile, determined instead to undertake a defensive, bridge-burning strategy. They would permanently depress the economy in order both to slow down the trends which strengthen the proletariat and to rob the workers of the fruits of their eventual victory. By checking their own competitive instincts and refusing to modernize the means of production, they would "maintain the national economy in a state of latent crisis," "darken(ing) the workers' consciousness by dimming themselves." They would do what they could to keep the proletariat relatively small and isolated. Small, by inducing a decline in the working class birth rate through the

159

depressed living standard and the development of
birth control technology. Isolated, by cultivating a
large class of poor peasants, white collar workers,
and small businessmen, who would regard their interests
as threatened by a militant proletariat. This was
accomplished through monopolistic collusion and a
series of government price support, tax, and tariff
programs which prevented the consolidation, moderni-
zation, and diversification of agriculture and industry. The result is a stratified society, in which
the non-proletarian poor cling to their illusory
privileges while "the big boys direct everything."
"French employers weigh down two-thirds of the nation
in order to reduce the other third to impotence."[35]

While the account of this conspiracy's orchestra-
tion seems a bit dubious, the basic accuracy of the
picture which Sartre paints is attested to by so
moderate a historian as Gordon Wright. Wright grants
that there is "much truth" to the view that the Paris
Commune is "the key" to contemporary French history;
that "the episode left a kind of psychological scar;
that it permanently divided republicans, embittered
the workers, and intensified class conflict." Its
"long-range effects," he concludes, "were deep and
severe." Likewise, he confirms two of Sartre's chief
observations on the French bourgeoisie's character.
First, he refers to the widespread social values of
uncongeniality to monetary success and "a genteel
pattern of entrepreneurship" in the nineteenth century
to explain the acknowledged failure of French business
to strengthen industrial production and to keep pace
with foreign competition. (He cites the case of
André Citroën, whose attempts to Americanize the
French automotive industry won him the deadly wrath of
the more tradition-minded industrial and banking cartel.
The latter ruined him in 1934 by refusing him a
crucial credit extension which might have kept his
enterprise solvent.) Secondly, he confirms the failure
of French labor to receive a proportionate share of
the post-World War I national prosperity, and French
employers' general lack of "social conscience." The
latter's "central interest in the 1920s," he says,
"seemed to be to secure the repeal of labor's single
gain, the eight-hour day, on the ground that it was
responsible for the high cost of production in
France." Finally, his observations on the government's
role in maintaining agricultural and industrial backwardness agree with Sartre's, although he traces this

no further than to the domination of Parliament by
small-town and rural electorates. On the other hand,
he regards the Fourth Republic years (with six years'
worth of hindsight over "The Communists and Peace")
as a time of significant economic reorganization and
development. The extent to which French business
atavism was the result of a general class conspiracy
rather than a more deeply ingrained national character
remains a question. The fact, however, that the French
economy could undergo rapid reorganization under the
Fifth Republic lends some support to Sartre's thesis
that the basic cause of its former depressed state was
political.[36]

The pertinent consequence of this Malthusianism,
Sartre continues, has been to "massify" the workers,
to persuade them of the futility of attempting to
better their lot by collective action, while preserving
a sub-class rivalry between skilled and unskilled
workers which reflects a frozen transitional stage of
industrial development. This division has been exa-
cerbated by the rift within the union movement between
Socialists and Communists. The existence of rival
union organizations removes from the decisions of the
union leadership the aura of infallibility which they
might otherwise have in the workers' eyes. It makes
them merely matters of opinion, having no necessary
relation to the course of History. And without a
sense of Self-within-history the worker becomes isolated, discouraged, selfish, and powerless.[37]

In opposition to this prospect of despair, the
CP offers a world view capable of exciting and sustaining the worker's self-affirmation as a human being,
his experience of society, and his exercise of the
redeeming attitudes of generosity and joyousness. But
this requires that the CP union operative be a special
functionary and that he make use of such radical tactics as permanent agitation, the extension of strikes
to whole industries, and the radicalization of opposition through political strikes. All this, because
the nature of modern work renders the workers themselves inert, because "the very essence of the masses
forbids them from thinking and acting politically."
Thus, the neo-proletariat requires a neo-unionism,
the leadership of which is, frankly, demagogic, subject to the masses' control "as the sea controls the
helmsman." Intellectuals should not be offended that
this entails the sacrifice of bourgeois democracy, the

democracy of the secret ballot, within the unions. For
that democracy, which polls the opinions of men in
isolation rather than through collective deliberation,
is both a sham for its lack of public responsibility,
and especially inappropriate to the masses, for whom
collective enthusiasm is the sine qua non of political
action. That the new union democracy involves coercion
and silencing of minority voices is apparently the
price one must be willing to pay for political vitality.[38]

We should note that History, in Sartre's account,
is not an absolute truth but a necessary energizing
belief. Far from the Revolution's being inevitable,
it would appear from his analysis that any country
which is willing to undergo economic stagnation can
stave it off indefinitely. As far as France is concerned, he indicates at the end of the part of the
essay written in 1952 that if the CP's influence on the
masses is allowed to disintegrate, if France's proletariat becomes a mere mass, the country could remain
static for the next twenty, or even fifty, years.[39]
Nor is it certain he regards the Revolution, as an
event, to be the decisive desideratum. The most positive objects of his attention are the moral qualities
which the proletariat manifests when in a state of
revolt, the implied benefits which the existence of an
active proletariat is apt to have on France's moral
climate, and the economic benefits which might follow
from an overturning of the country's Malthusianism.
The all-important consideration is to foster among the
workers a sense of class consciousness, without which
even a revolution could go awry. (A full generation
after the Russian Revolution, after all, socialism
still exists nowhere in the world.) What Sartre demonstrably seeks is not the proletariat's ultimate victory but its present existence.[40]

But that he recognizes something dubious in the
project of promoting its existence is suggested by the
peculiar terms in which he describes the psychology of
the worker's relation to the Party. The worker needs
to act in order to give meaning to his life and death,
and he needs unity of direction in order to act. He
needs to believe that there is an architectonic truth,
and to trust his class's leaders enough to believe
that the truth comes from them. He needs, in un-
Sartrean language, a civil religion of the insurgent
class. He must experience his praxis as "a call"

162

within History, as a "dying to be reborn" with the historical identity of Proletarian. While ideally the linkage of class-solidarity should occur "whenever two workers are together," the overwhelming fact of the workers' fatigue requires the Party to constitute itself as a secular Church. And in return for its gift to them of a class identity, the workers are to be released from what would for them be the burden of deliberative politics.[41] In an obvious echo from The Flies, he signals the Party's status by calling its authority "an order which makes order reign and which gives orders."[42] The Church-like Party must be Aegisthian. But while Aegisthus' project, as we have seen, is far from ridiculous, it is unsatisfactory from the higher Orestian perspective. Sartre thus retains toward commitment to the proper political project of the CP the same personal reservation which Orestes maintains toward Argos. What "The Communists and Peace" prescribes, in fulfillment of the task announced in "Materialism and Revolution," is Marxism as political myth.

## V. The Hervé Affair

A short but telling indicator of the various directions of Sartre's pro-Communism in the early 1950s is his editorial in the February 1956 issue of Les Temps Modernes concerning Pierre Hervé's break with the CP. Hervé had been a major Party figure. He was, in fact, one of Sartre's chief detractors during the CP's post-war assault on Existentialism. In 1955, however, he fell out with the other Party leaders, for concrete reasons which remain obscure, but making public his complaint over the exclusivity of Party deliberations. Sartre, joining in the fray, criticized Hervé for attempting to pressure the CP from the outside, that is, through a public appeal to the non-Communist Left, and for framing his critique of the CP in abstract, "idealist," terms.[43]

Thomas Molnar, perhaps the harshest of Sartre's academic critics, regards this editorial as the locus classicus of his blind pro-Communism during this period.[44] But Molnar disregards the high personal irony of Sartre's remarks. For while he does criticize Hervé for the indiscretion of publicizing the fact of his dispute, by characterizing his arguments as "idealist" he is in substance accusing him of being too discreet, of welshing on the details of his

163

differences with the CP. Moreover, Sartre goes on
substantively to join Hervé's criticism, by stating
that it is precisely the CP's closed attitude toward
Marxism as an intellectual system that is responsible
for spawning renegades like Hervé. It would be difficult for someone who is acquainted with the events
of 1947 to miss the ironic glee in Sartre's observation that Hervé surely exaggerates when he accuses the
CP of subjecting its critics to "the most dishonorable
accusations."[45] The chickens had come home to roost!

But behind his flattery of the CP's "extraordinary objective intelligence," which makes it "rare for
it to be mistaken"--which may mean no more than that
the CP happens to do the correct things without really
knowing why they are correct--, it is Sartre's wish
for the transformation of Marxism which comprises
this article's core. He muses:

> Men of my age know it well: even more than
> the two world wars, the great affair of their
> life was a perpetual confrontation with the
> working class and its ideology, which offered
> them an unimpeachable vision of the world
> and of themselves. For us Marxism is not
> only a philosophy: it is the climate of our
> ideas, the milieu where they are nourished,
> it is the true movement of what Hegel calls
> the Objective Spirit.[46]

But the CP has kept Marxism under too close a guard;
it has not allowed it to fructify the entire intellectual climate, to become a Culture. This is today
Marxism's great potential, for "the bourgeoisie is in
the course of evacuating culture: it no longer thinks
at all." Thus, he calls upon Marxism to be, not an
"open philosophy," but the "living" context for intellectual initiatives in philosophy, economics, history,[47]
sociology, psychology, and literary theory. In
criticizing Hervé, Sartre expands upon, perhaps even
radicalizes, Hervé's position.

## VI. "The Ghost of Stalin"

Nineteen fifty-six was a momentous year for
European Communism, and for Sartre's relations with
the CP. Pierre Hervé's dissension paralleled events
occurring within the Soviet Union itself over the issue
of de-Stalinization. Sartre's article on Hervé

coincided with Khrushchev's Secret Speech before the
Twentieth Party Congress--"Polichinelle's secret,"
Sartre called it, because of the rapidity with which
it spread[48]--, the repercussions of which were felt
through the remainder of the year, in Poland, in
Rumania, and finally in Hungary.  According to Simone
de Beauvoir, Sartre was seriously shaken by the news
of the Russian intervention in Hungary, feeling that
it called into question the previous several years'
efforts at rapprochement with the CP.[49]  Still, he
lost no time in publicly condemning the move.  In a
lengthy article, "The Ghost of Stalin," which appeared
in January 1957, he gave his account of the October
events and their background, and explained why, after
twelve years of increasingly friendly debate with the
Communists, he was now "return(ing) to the opposition."[50]

      Sartre minces no words in issuing a moral condem-
nation of the Hungarian repression as a detestable
"slaughter," as "massacres," "barbarity," and "monstrosities and crimes."  But the chief thrust of his
criticism is, to use his own distinction, political
rather than moral.[51]  Thus, he condemns the Russian
action for retarding socialism and for increasing the
probability of war.  Its retardation of socialism is
two-fold.  First, it represents an attempt by the
Soviet Union to continue to impose upon the satellite
countries of Eastern Europe a Stalinist political
and economic order whose proper time has passed, or
indeed may never have been.  The salient characteristics of that order are the breakneck development of
heavy industry and the collectivization of agriculture,
at the cost of considerable economic sacrifice and dis-
location, in order to fashion each country after the
Russian "socialism in a single country" model; and
the imposition from above of repressive political
leadership, subservient to Moscow, in disregard of the
countries' pre-existing political institutions.  But,
Sartre argues, once de-Stalinization has become the
official policy of the USSR, as it must once the need
for Stalinism has passed, there is no principled way
for the USSR to deny to the People's Democracies the
right to rid themselves of their imported Stalinism.
The Soviet Union's denial must therefore be a matter,
not of principle, but of expediency.[52]  Thus, the
second, and chief, weakening of socialism consists of
the fact that this unprincipled act by socialism's
chief sponsor discredits socialism everywhere.  In

France, for instance, the institution of a socialist program depends upon the possibility of a revived United Front between the CP and the SFIO. But the Hungarian intervention, by reasserting Moscow's supremacy over national Communist movements, has revived Socialist mistrust of the CP, and so ruined chances for a United Front.[53]

In additon to retarding socialism, the Russian action also implicitly endorses the division of Europe into two hostile blocs, discourages neutralist tendencies, and so increases the likelihood of war. As a strictly military move, this might have been valid at an earlier time, when the USSR was weaker and the US more aggressive. But in 1956, improved Russian defenses and the slackening of American aggressiveness make the bloc psychology inappropriate. The repression which sacrificed principle for expediency, Sartre concludes, was also inexpedient. He grants that to have let Hungary go its own way would have involved serious risks, but he assesses the pro-socialist forces there and elsewhere in Eastern Europe as strong enough to have made it worth the gamble.[54]

This political account helpfully establishes a retrospective context for Sartre's wooing of the CP, and shores up an obvious gap in what he calls a simply moral argument, by which he seems to mean a universal a priori rule respecting a given species of concrete act. Thus, he approvingly quotes a correspondent who denies him recourse to a simplistic condemnation of all killing and violence.[55] Sartre is aware that his position requires a more precise justification. Moreover, his objection to the Hungarian suppression could not consistently be a function of the magnitude of its violence, since he had some years earlier condemned only in the most subdued tones the existence of forced labor camps within the USSR, the raw atrocity level of which rivals that of the Hungarian events.[56]

But there are three political factors which distinguish the two cases. First, the labor camps and other examples of Russian Stalinist terror might have plausibly appeared to be a peculiarly Russian phenomenon, sanctioned by the Russian national character and by the exigencies of safeguarding the rapid development of "socialism in a single country," especially given that country's backwardness and military vulnerability. The Eastern European case, on the other hand, presents not indigenous but imposed atrocity, a distinction which implies the primacy of national political cultures.[57] Secondly, Stalinism is a system of the past, outdated by the USSR's achievement of industrialization and military security. One may therefore have cherished the hope that such terroristic devices as labor camps were transitional phenomena, which were, at the moment of their discovery to the West, at the point of becoming forever obsolete. But the Hungarian intervention would then be a regressive policy, designed to re-impose an obsolete order. It thus raises the possibility of a fundamental failure of judgment at the top, a failure by the Kremlin to discern socialism's true teleology.[58] And thirdly, the entire political climate on the Left had changed since 1950. The process of de-Stalinization had taken such a firm hold in 1956 as to be irreversible. The traditionally independent Italian CP condemned the invasion. The more orthodox French Party defended it, but suffered significant defections. This time Sartre could count on having renegade Communist allies in his opposition to the CP.[59] Without impugning the sincerity of this opposition, it seems just to observe that if his earlier silence had been politic, circumstances conspired to make this a politic protest.

Sartre's surprise at the Soviet invasion is not based upon a naive trust in the goodness of the formerly Stalinist Russian leadership, the kind of trust which he had disparaged in the "Humanism" essay.[60] Rather, he offers an analysis of Soviet society, according to which it would have been reasonable to expect the post-Stalin ascendency of a technocratic group within the regime, who would orient policy away from personality cultism, heavy industry, and the foreign policy of the bloc, and toward consumer-oriented production and socialist pluralism.[61] If Sartre can be accused of naiveté, it might be for placing an excessive faith in the purity of technocratic intentions (or rather in their peculiar impurity), for assuming that Soviet technocrats would be devoted to socialist internationalism rather than, say, to the pursuit of Russian hegemony. (Possibly the French Fifth Republic taught Sartre something about the political availability of technocrats.) Sartre, that is, had taken a calculated gamble, probably along with a number of Communists in the Western European Parties, on a probable relaxation within the world socialist movement, which would open the way to a variety of socialisms along national lines.

In this light, and in the light of his comments on the necessity for a United Front in France, his pro-Communist position in "The Communists and Peace" emerges as the first stage of a two-part strategy. The rehabilitation of the CP in non-Communist eyes would have been followed, when circumstances allowed, by efforts to re-align the CP into co-operation, and perhaps eventual unity, with the SFIO. The climate for such an alliance had been enhanced in 1956 by widespread Socialist disenchantment over Premier Guy Mollet's attempts to ally the SFIO with parties to its right.[62] History might indeed look kindly upon the intellectual who had comprehended, and helped bring about, the ruling political configuration of the Leftist Fifth Republic. The Hungarian invasion altered this calculation and forced Sartre's hand. But the calculation's basic premise, that there were present within the Communist movement sizable elements having a stake in de-Stalinization, remained intact. A modification of tactics was therefore in order. The 1957 "return to the opposition" was a movement back toward (but not to) the position of the RDR, but this time made in the company of a cadre of disenchanted Communists.[63]

Granting Sartre's political sophistication, we may still wonder whether this movement does not, ironically perhaps, betoken his more decisive collapse into ideology. For despite his vehement attack on the Soviet Union's policy, he does not question socialism itself as the proper end of human endeavor. He even criticizes Merleau-Ponty for seeking an intellectually neutral ground, for "appeal(ing) implicitly to some eagle's nest from which one would evaluate jointly the evolution of peoples regimes and that of capitalist democracies." "To which," Sartre continues, "it is necessary to respond: either this transcendent point of view does not exist, or else it is socialism itself."[64] But what does he mean by "socialism"? Manifestly, he does not mean whatever the Soviet Union may happen to do. But neither is his description of it as "an historic reality, concrete, positive and total" especially helpful.[65] For after all, is not the brute fact of Russian tanks in Budapest a "concrete, positive and total" historical reality? While "The

168

Ghost of Stalin" abounds with appeals to "socialism,"
Sartre is notably reticent at defining the term. But
his comments on its attributes permit the construction
of a composite picture.

The aspect which he emphasizes most is commonality.
Socialism is characterized by common endeavor, based
on needs which are "as true as" their possessors; it
alone "intends to give liberty and justice to all men."
In China, it is a "concerted effort . . . to suppress
misery and hunger," and the collectivity's "élan
towards the future, (its) conscious and sustained
action, (its) living unity." The apparent issue here
is that there be a feeling of care and vital fellow-
ship in actively confronting obstacles, the "experience
of society." This is what makes socialism "men's
hope," in contrast to the kind of decadent insouciance
which permits Merleau-Ponty not to become especially
upset--"to cultivate (his) garden"-- in the face of the
Soviet intervention. But he also describes it, in
terms which hark back to his early writings, as a kind
of perpetual becoming, "man in the process of making
himself." Further, the socialist project is circumscribed by the political community, such that "(e)ach
socialist nation is a singular undertaking." Thus,
"in the final count, (the French Communist leaders) are
responsible only before the working masses of their
country." Finally, while it is the only self-compre-
hending ideology, its means define its end. The dis-
tillate of these various attributes makes of socialism
an open-ended shared endeavor, based on commonly felt
needs, circumscribed by nationality, but having recourse
to universal ends the concrete content of which is
given by whatever a given people, collectivity, or
regime in fact does. What Sartre seems at bottom to
offer is a politicized version of Existentialist
humanism.[66]

VII. "Search for a Method"[66a]

i.

Search for a Method, published in 1957, is probably Sartre's most authoritative statement on his
relation to Marxism. Although he says that its claims
can only be substantiated by the much larger Critique
of Dialectical Reason, of which it forms the prefatory
section, it was in fact published separately some three
years earlier and thus in some sense stands on its own.
The Search has an explicitly limited scope, addressing

169

itself to the single question, "Do we today have the means to constitute a structural, historical anthropology?" As his self-consciously provisional answer, Sartre offers the "'comprehensive'" method of "the ideology of existence," which has the status of "an enclave inside Marxism."[67] That is, he offers a kind of existentialized Marxism. But the explanation of this method engages him in two important and long-standing subsidiary projects: the refinement and revision of Existentialism and the attempt to influence contemporary Marxism.

The refinement of Existentialism consists of a refutation of its subjectivist image. It might be thought that such a refutation would be unnecessary. Being and Nothingness, for example, made considerable concessions to the objective. The elaboration of freedom's situatedness is consistent with a far-reaching, but necessarily not a thoroughgoing, acceptance of universal determinism; and the phenomenological description of proletariat and bourgeoisie is suggestive, even at that early date (1943), of an attempt to integrate existential philosophy with Marxist philosophy of history.[68] But, in general, the emphasis of Being and Nothingness does not lead toward objectivism. Rather, its chief rhetorical purpose seems to be the saving of human subjectivity from absorption into one or another of the crude determinisms current during the early 1940s. Moreover, nothing in Being and Nothingness suggests that its claim on behalf of existential phenomenology fell short of a claim to transhistoric validity.

The Search's objectivism, however, does not merely restate Sartre's 1943 position with shifted emphasis. It contains elements new for Sartre and peculiar to him. Its fundamental concession seems to be made to Marxist historicism. "Philosophy," Sartre tells us, "does not exist." Rather, there are philosophies which serve as the successive cultural milieux for, and give expression to, the general movement of society. History displaces Truth. But the relevant categories of History are philosophic rather than economic epochs. Thus, he speaks of three periods between the seventeenth and twentieth centuries, designated by "the names of the men who dominated them: there is the 'moment' of Descartes and Locke, that of Kant and Hegel, finally that of Marx." Because Marxism today constitutes "the humus of every particular thought and and the horizon of all culture," because it "is one

170

with the general movement of society," there can be
no "going beyond" it so long as man has not surpassed
the historical moment it expresses. All intellection
today will be undertaken in relation to Marx. Existentialism, as a secondary development within the
Marxist "movement," is therefore a Marxist "ideology"--
"a parasitical system living on the margin of Knowledge." But Marxism, to be truly philosophical, must
be "the totalization of contemporary Knowledge." Insofar as Existentialism can provide the method for such
totalization, Marxism needs it for its own completion
as Philosophy. And insofar as Marxism ignores this
method, it will remain in a state of infancy. Upon
this point Sartre takes up his second subsidiary project, that of influencing Marxism.[69]

This project immediately plunges Sartre into certain long-standing critiques of orthodox Marxism, as
informed by the then recent Hungarian events of 1956.
The Soviet Union's historical need for security and
rapid industrialization resulted in the subordination
of ideology to "praxis." At the same time, Party
leaders, in order to integrate the group fully, and
out of mistrust that experience would not "provide its
own clarities," arrogated to themselves the formulation
of Marxist doctrine. Sartre calls the result "idealism"--a disjunction between theory and practice that
"transform(ed) the latter into an empiricism without
principles, the former into a pure, fixed knowledge."
And the empiricism itself became subordinated to the
"absolute idealism" of an obstinate bureaucracy:

Men and things had to yield to ideas--a
priori; experience, when it did not verify
the predictions, could only be wrong. Budapest's subway was real in Rakosi's head. If
Budapest's subsoil did not allow him to construct the subway, this was because the subsoil was counter-revolutionary.[69a]

In addition to being subordinated to practice,
Marxist theory was impoverished by the effective eli-
mination of its unique analytical element, the dialectic, and the substitution of a crude economic
determinism. Thus, Marxist analysis has become a
matter of "simple ceremony," which

consists solely in getting rid of detail, in
forcing the signification of certain events,
in denaturing facts or even in inventing a

171

nature for them in order to discover it later underneath them, as their substance, as unchangeable, fetishized "synthetic notions."

Against this modus operandi Sartre cites the synthetic accounts that Marx gave in The Eighteenth Brumaire of Louis Bonaparte and in his articles on India.[70]

Sartre's antidote for these faults in contemporary Marxist theory consists of revivifying the dialectic through the introduction of "mediations" into descriptive accounts of reality. He speaks of three such mediations: the political, the psychological, and the sociological. The mediations become necessary because Marxism's primary data about a given society's economic state at a given time permit us only to "situate" an event, not to explain it. To explain it, we must account for the particular way in which universal history is filtered through the individual historical actor. Thus, Marxists must take seriously, as they have not done, the actor's self-perception.

To understand a political figure like Robespierre, we must see his attempts to obtain and to wield power in terms of his conscious goals; we must not transform his actual intentions too quickly into their ultimate economic significance. Political motives must be granted a "relative irreducibility," for "Marxism ought to study real men in depth, not dissolve them in a bath of sulphuric acid." Marxists too often treat men as though they were "avalanches" and yet continue to hold them responsible as men. Such Marxists are in bad faith.[71] Second, the anthropologist must take account of the experience of childhood, rather than treat men as if "born at the age when we earn our first wages." But since only psychoanalysis attempts seriously to study childhood, anthropology needs psychoanalysis. In particular, it needs Existentialism, which

> believes that it can integrate the psychoanalytic method which discovers the point of insertion for man and his class--that is, the particular family--as a mediation between the universal class and the individual.[71a]

Finally, Marxism must understand the person's lived experience through his membership in, and relations to, various groups that act as "a screen between the individual and the general interests of his class." In all these cases, however, Marxist philosophy of history provides a privileged ground and point of departure. It tells us that a certain family structure is "appropriate to such and such a class under such and such conditions," or that existential psychoanalysis "can study today only situations in which man has been lost since childhood, for there are no others in a society founded on exploitation." By keeping us alert to the real historical relations among men, it preserves us from the error of some sociologists--that of giving the group a "metaphysical existence." Most important perhaps, it provides normative ends to which a committed social science may contribute its understanding.[72]

Sartre calls the product of these reflections the "progressive-regressive method." The anthropology served by this method, it seems fair to surmise from Sartre's elaborations on Robespierre, de Sade, and Flaubert, is to be fundamentally the study neither of Man nor of collectivities but of individuals.[73] This focus itself implies a prior decision about levels of historical significance. Social science must "(rise) from the abstract to the concrete," and the individual is the ultimate locus of concreteness. The method itself consists of a series of repeated and ever more comprehensive cross-references between the general-and-exterior and the particular-and-interior. In order to understand anyone thoroughly, the anthropologist must begin with the prereflective interiorization of the external that occurs in childhood. Later, the anthropologist must reconstruct the individual through his personal project across the instrumental field that is the world.

It is this project, or succession of projects, that defines the man. For purposes of this reconstruction, the world must be taken, not as the idealized description of its objective substratum, but as it appears to the historical subject himself--as the "reciprocal interpenetration and the relative autonomy of significations." Finally, the anthropologist would look at this project as a practical work within the world--as the subject's attempt to objectify himself in things. The result of this continually repeated process would be a better understanding of how history works within the individual and of how the individual makes history.[74]

173

There are a number of peculiarities in the Marxism of the Search. First, and most fundamentally, Sartre's apparent submission to Marxist historicism opens him to the reproach that he renders knowledge of man hopelessly problematic. Hegel claimed to have obviated this endemic problem of historicism by attaining the perspective of Absolute Knowledge, from which man's historicity becomes an evident truth--a perspective that can occur only at the end of history. Whatever this cryptic solution may have meant for Hegel, it calls into grave moral question the thoughts and actions of his successors, whom it seems to reduce to the status of mere epigoni. Once the past has flowered in an absolute moment that has also become past, the present and the future seem doomed to fall into either absolute meaninglessness or a dogmatic copying of the absolute moment.

Marx's positing of the absolute event, the Revolution, as still in the future and to be made, may have provisionally redressed this moral grievance, but at the cost of intellectual coherence. Men could, for the nonce, still have significant projects, or at least one significant project. But if the absolute moment has not yet arrived, then we are not yet at history's privileged vantage point. The character of that absolute moment is not something that, strictly speaking, we can yet know. At best, we can only surmise it from the course of past and contemporary events, based upon evidence the true character of which has yet to be revealed. Sartre sees this difficulty and draws the necessary consequence from it. There is no Philosophy, Hegel is only a moment in the succession of philosophies, and even Marxism is provisional. Under these circumstances the totalization of Marxism, which Existentialism attempts to effect, can only be a "partial totalization," only a matter of sophisticated guesswork. Thus he refers to the ideology of existence's method not as comprehensive but as "comprehensive."[75] But this limitation is not intrinsic to Existentialism. Rather Existentialism inherits it from its Marxist philosophic framework.

A second, related, peculiarity lies in the Search's terminology. Less than two years earlier, Sartre had referred to Marxism as "not only a philosophy," but "the climate of our ideas, the milieu where they nourish themselves. . .the true movement of what Hegel calls the Objective Spirit."[76] We are confronted in the Search with a change in the meaning of terms. "Philosophy," formerly distinct from "cultural milieu," has come to mean "cultural milieu." It is a thought become an action or the context for a set of actions over a long period of time--a general orientation or Weltanschauung. The truth-content of philosophy has become a distinctly secondary matter. Philosophy has become what in ordinary parlance might be called "ideology." And "ideology," in turn, is a parasitic growth within a philosophy. But this statement expresses merely a cultural or historical truth. Kierkegaard's thought becomes part of Hegelianism because it addresses a climate of opinion that takes its fundamental cues from Hegel; it is a response to Hegel, and its originality is thus subsumed under the rubric "anti-Hegel." And because Hegelianism, as a philosophy, remains in some sense an open horizon, it incorporates this criticism and is enriched by it.[77]

But why is the same not true of Marx's relation to Hegel? Why are we not all still Hegelians, or Cartesians, or indeed Platonists? What transforms a movement that begins as an ideology into a philosophy in its own right? The answer seems to lie not in the thought itself but in events in the world. It is not Marx's expression of his own thought that makes the world Marxist but the Russian Revolution and its aftermath. Sartre even suggests that the status of Marxism as a philosophy was vouchsafed only very recently indeed, for he says:

It took the whole bloody history of this
half century to make us grasp the reality of
the class struggle and to situate us in a
split society. It was the war which shattered the worn structures of our thought--
War, Occupation, Resistance, the years which
followed. We wanted to fight at the side of
the working class; we finally understood
that the concrete is history and dialectical
action.[78]

Until the middle of the twentieth century the status of Marxism as philosophy could still plausibly seem to be an open question. The post-Hegelian philosophy could conceivably have been something else--a version of Nietzschean heroism, for instance, or Existentialist humanism.

175

However this may have been, it has now become apparent to Sartre that there is no alternative to Marxism, for bourgeois culture is as good as dead. The alternatives that may have been available formerly have either been thoroughly discredited or have simply not caught on. It is, therefore, only a matter of time before all the world becomes Marxist. But when all the world, and every thought that arises within it, is "Marxist," what indeed shall have become of Marxism? Is it to be merely a rhetorical point of reference--a ritualistic touchstone to which all must pay due homage in the course of saying whatever they would have said in any case, much as Church and imperial publicans in the Middle Ages always made a point of referring their respective positions to Scripture? Or is there a substantive core to Marxism that will render some thought legitimate and other illegitimate? It seems significant that in all of the Search Sartre calls Marx "absolutely right" (his emphasis) on only one point--that "the ideas of the dominant class are the dominant ideas"--an observation that borders on truism and predates Marx by several millenia.[79]

It may, therefore, be helpful to consider some of Sartre's comments on Marx and on contemporary Marxism's theoretical formulations. His starting point seems to be the generally plausible notion that Marx himself is a good deal richer than orthodox Marxism, which has taken its cues from Engels, Lenin, and Stalin, has made him appear--that there is a proto-Existentialist "humanistic" side which the ideology of "economism" has tended to obscure. That there is more to Marx than the theory of surplus-value is suggested by such things as his expressed concern for "species man" in the recently discovered "early writings."[80] But Sartre, for his part, seems to overstate his case. Thus, for instance, he says:

> When Marx writes: "Just as we do not judge an individual by his own idea of himself, so we cannot judge a...period of revolutionary upheaval by its own self-consciousness," he is indicating the priority of action (work and social praxis) over knowledge as well as their heterogeneity.[81]

Examination of this passage's context, however, reveals Marx to be making a somewhat different point--one more in line with orthodox Marxism. Speaking of "an epoch

176

of social revolution," Marx says,

> With the change of the economic foundations
> the entire immense superstructure is more
> or less rapidly transformed. In considering
> such transformations a distinction should
> always be made between the material trans-
> formation of the economic conditions of pro-
> duction, which can be determined with the
> precision of natural science, and the legal,
> political, religious, esthetic or philoso-
> phic--in short, ideological forms in which
> men become conscious of this conflict and
> fight it out. Just as our opinion of an
> individual is not based on what he thinks
> of himself, so we cannot judge of such a
> period of transformation by its own con-
> sciousness; on the contrary, this conscious-
> ness must be explained rather from the con-
> tradictions of material life, from the
> existing conflict between the social pro-
> ductive forces and the relations of pro-
> duction.[82]

What Marx seems to be pointing out is not the
priority of existence over knowledge but rather indeed
the priority of knowledge, based upon a true understanding of the wellsprings of history, over what he
calls "ideology," or the false consciousness that an
epoch has of itself. Yet, Sartre leads us to doubt
Marx's ability to provide the factual foundation for
historical knowledge. For in one interesting footnote
he praises both the much-acclaimed Eighteenth Brumaire
of Louis Bonaparte and also Marx's articles on British
rule in India for their alertness to historical peculiarities. But, referring to Marx's description of
Hindustan, he mades the following remark: "Whether
Hindustan is actually this or something else matters
little to us; what counts here is the synthetic view
which gives life to the objects of the analysis."[83]
Marx is, it appears, even of doubtful reliability as
a descriptive source. His value lies chiefly in the
inspiration provided by his attitude. Of what use,
then, are Marxist economic categories? At the start
of Chapter II of the Search, Sartre states that they
allow us to "situate" an historical event. But even
then, "everything remains to be done."[84] And this
doing, the explaining of specific events, requires
recurrence to Sartre's mediations and to his progressive-regressive method.

177

When do the refinements, which supposedly perfect
a theory, come to supersede that theory itself? It
is to this question, upon which the issue of Sartre's
Marxism ultimately turns, that reflection on his mediations leads us. The political mediation, for instance, aims at reconstituting the projects of political actors as self-conscious motivations. These
motivations are, therefore, granted a "relative autonomy." Presumably, this autonomy is relative to the
absolute autonomy of Marxist historicism, which presents the true general schema for understanding at
least the past. Thus, Sartre criticizes Marxists not
for effecting a reduction of ideology to economics
but for being "too quick" to reduce, for instance, all
motives of generosity to class interests. For example,
he asserts, in a comparison which is questionable for
its own economism, that, unlike the American Civil War,
the French Revolution "is not directly reducible" to
economic motives.[85] Decisive to this comparison is
what the people of these respective times "were themselves aware of"--the particular history-for-itself.

> What is necessary is simply to reject aprio-
> rism. The unprejudiced examination of the
> historical object will be able by itself to
> determine in each case whether the action or
> the work reflects the superstructural motives
> of groups or of individuals formed by certain
> basic conditionings, or whether one can ex-
> plain them only by referring immediately to
> economic contradictions and to conflicts of
> material interests.[86]

But if Sartre really calls for the rejection of
all apriorism, for the unprejudiced examination of the
historical object in itself, does he not also thereby
reject a priori designations of false consciousness?
That is, must he not relinquish Marxism's claim to a
privileged historical perspective? Sartre waffles
here. He admits, for instance, that the men of 1792
"commit the error of ignoring the action of other
forces, more muffled, less clearly descernible,
infinitely more powerful" than those upon which they
act. "But," he says, "that is exactly what defines
these men as the bourgeois of 1792."[87] However, he
describes this conception of false consciousness as
"by no means specifically Marxist." It merely

restat(es) what everybody has always known:
the consequences of our acts always end up
by escaping us, since every concerted enterprise, as soon as it is realized, enters into relation with the entire universe, and
since this infinite multiplicity of relations goes beyond our intention.[88]

The value of Marxist interpretation of history
lies in its ability to "situate" a concrete person or
act in terms of his or its most fundamental structures,
namely, "the direction and character of a society, the
development of its productive forces, and its relations
of production."[89] But this characterization of "situation" seems too narrow to encompass some persons or
events. Speaking of Lukács' attempt to explain
Heidegger's existentialism as "an activism under the
influence of the Nazis," Sartre observes:

> There has existed a whole dialectic--and a
> very complex one--from Brentano to Husserl
> and from Husserl to Heidegger: influences,
> oppositions, agreements, new oppositions,
> misunderstandings, distortions, denials,
> surpassings, etc. All this adds up to what
> one could call an area history. Ought we to
> consider it a pure epiphenomenon? According
> to what Lukacs says, yes. Or does there
> exist some kind of movement of ideas, and
> does Husserl's phenomenology--as a moment
> preserved and surpassed--enter into
> Heidegger's system? In this case the prin-
> ciples of Marxism are not changed, but the
> situation becomes much more complex.[90]

Sartre does not limit the technical term "situation" to the categories of Marxist historical interpretation. He fails, however, to honor his own call
for an unprejudiced examination of history, for he
will not credit such historical actors as the bourgeois
politicians of 1792 with the kind of ideational validity he will grant to Heidegger, a fellow philosopher.
Granted that this distinction is not altogether unrea-
sonable--that political actors rarely examine their
beliefs with philosophic thoroughness--, still Sartre's
notion of politics as a kind of power-brokerage seems
unduly restrictive. While politicians do seek and
wield power, they also seek to justify their particular
uses of power by invoking principles of justice or

179

right. A phenomenological approach that failed or refused to examine this most familiar of political phenomena betrays the first principle of phenomenology--to examine the things themselves. As in Being and Nothingness, Sartre goes to the brink of political philosophy but refuses, apparently on the basis of a dogmatism, to take normative arguments seriously in their own right.[91]

The psychological mediation raises the question of the extent to which childhood experiences decide a person's project, rather than merely influence it. Sartre's position in Being and Nothingness is fairly clear. There are human passions and habits, but in the decisive respect we stand toward them as we stand toward our own past. They are Being-in-itself, and we are free either to acquiesce in them or to oppose them.[92] This judgment implies the nondecisiveness of childhood experience and, in particular, of the class alienation experienced in childhood prereflectively and at second hand, as the alienation of our parents' labors. But here too, Sartre wavers. He speaks of childhood as setting up "unsurpassable prejudices" and of "the childhood we never wholly surpass."[93] Taken emphatically, this characterization renders the Revolution a radically problematic venture. For even if we assume a change in the institutions of property, the revolutionary generation would remain within the unsurpassable grip of its prerevolutionary childhood. The fundamental attitude and habits of alienation and "lostness," imbibed in childhood, would tend to create resistances both to the initial occurrence of revolution and, thereafter, to the fulfillment of a revolutionary program.

We might, of course, posit a tendency in human nature to revolt avainst alienation, but Sartre regards as the chief strength of existential psychoanalysis its claim "to put History in place of nature in each person."[94] Such a displacement of nature by individual history seems to negate the value of psychoanalysis for a revolutionary theory as such. Psychoanalysis would become a purely speculative endeavor--a mere piecing together of idiosyncratic descriptions.

iv.

Again, despite Sartre's insistence on the situating of groups to be studied within the Marxist historical framework, the sociological mediation ends in

180

difficulty.  For Sartre, in The Critique of Dialectical
Reason, sets up a typology of groups that appears independent of that theoretical framework, and indeed to
rival it.  Sartre's theory presents a succession of
four apparently comprehensive group configurations:
the series, the group-in-fusion, the group-under-oath,
and the institution.[95]

Seriality is the relation of alienated individuals
under conditions of scarcity.  Sartre gives as an
example of this configuration a queue of people waiting
for a bus.  There are not enough seats for everyone;
each is in competition with all; anyone at all (n'im-
porte qui) will serve the same function as anyone else
with respect to the given social role--anybody can
occupy any seat.  This situation resembles a Hobbesian
state of nature.  It is the general condition of man
within capitalist society.[96]

The group-in-fusion forms when scarcity or the
threat from some outside force causes the members of a
collectivity to drop their competitive relations and
spontaneously to fuse into a common action.  The Paris
rabble of 1789, upon hearing the rumor that royal
troops are about to surround and massacre them, suddenly transform themselves into a revolutionary mob
motivated by the single desire to survive.  They storm
the Bastille, not as isolated individuals but as a
fused group.  Once the danger is past, however, diffu-
sion of the group becomes an ever-present possibility.
It therefore places itself under oath, to remain
Group, imposing sanctions upon those who would pursue
self-interests at the expense of group solidarity.

Later still, when the danger has disappeared, or
when the group-under-oath has become victorious, the
centrifugal forces increase, and the group must insti-
tutionalize itself by imposing a reign of terror, at
the outset at least, in order to hold itself together.
The terror pits some against others, those who rule
against the ruled, and places the ruled back into a
kind of serial relation.  When the terror subsides,
the institution remains, and seriality has reemerged.
The succession of configurations is circular and, to
all appearances, eternal.

Both these categories themselves and their circularity seem foreign to Marxism.  Its recurrent aspect
especially seems to jar with Marxism's known mille-
narianism.[97]  This scheme certainly can accommodate

181

revolutions--indeed, it is built around the idea of
revolutions--but can it accommodate the Revolution?
Under what conditions would it be possible to break
through its circularity, to prevent a return to the
series?  Since scarcity is central to seriality, we
are tempted to say that the circularity will be overcome when scarcity is overcome.  This resolution would
break the circle at the point of the institution and
would maintain, actually or incipiently, a reign of
terror in order to assure the continuation of esprit
de corps.  Such a remedy appears worse than the disease.
Moreover, if the institution and terror tend to distinguish the ruler from the ruled and to reduce the
ruled to seriality, then the overcoming of scarcity
will not suffice.  It would be necessary to halt the
cycle at an earlier point, either that of the group-
under-oath or the group-in-fusion.  Of these two, the
group-in-fusion is the purer form.  It is to remedy
the falling away from it, consequent upon the disap-
pearance of external danger, that the oath is insti-
tuted at all.

Thus, in order to maintain the fused group,
danger, or the appearance of danger, must be imminent.[98]
In an older language, the far must be brought near.
But the presence of danger is not enough, for a danger
of sufficient magnitude is as likely to cause total
dissolution as fusion.  Some additional source of co-
hesion is thus required, some source of inspiration in
conjunction with a kind of situation engineering.  That
is, there is a need for political leadership that
stands radically outside of the community and that comprehends and guides it benevolently but inconspicuously.[99]   Argos still needs Orestes.

v.

The progressive-regressive method, as a way of
reconstituting the projects of particular persons,
also implicitly emphasizes the Great Individual--or
at least the interesting individual--but from the perspective of the social scientist.  The stake for the
meaning of history is indicated by Sartre's reaction
to Plekhanov's statement that if Napoleon had not
lived, and a more conciliatory general had taken charge
of the French Revolution, "the final outcome of the
revolutionary movement would not have been contrary to
what it was."  Sartre agrees with this conclusion, in
Plekhanov's meaning, but he disputes the statement's

182

implicit definition of reality.  What Plekhanov "disdainfully toss(es) over to the ranks of chance"--the
pace of economic and social life, the conflict between
liberal bourgeoisdom and the religious fanaticism of
the Bourbon restoration, the political milieu that
gave birth to Hugo, Musset, and Flaubert--Sartre
identifies as "the whole life of men."  He continues:

> If after this we are told that these changes
> cannot modify the development of productive
> forces and the relations of production in
> the course of the last century, this is a
> truism.  But if this development is to be
> made the sole object of human history, we
> simply fall back into the "economism" which
> we wanted to avoid; and Marxism becomes an
> "inhumanism."[100]

The true reality of history, then, is "the whole life
of men."

     In a Marxist age the projects of individual men
will be informed by the expectation of the Revolution,
which exists as a call to the future.  It is itself
part of a dialectic, and, to be fully self-conscious,
it must see itself as such.  Thus, Sartre urges Marxists to give up the bourgeois notions of time and pro-
gress--that "homogeneous and infinitely divisible con-
tinuum which is nothing other than the 'time' of
Cartesian rationalism"--for a "dialectical" notion of
temporality.[101]  This somewhat mysterious recommendation suggests that Marxism cease to regard the
Revolution "objectively," as an event in history that
happens not yet to have occurred, and that it instead
take it existentially, as a call to the future.  But
it can only do so in relation to a present "praxis,"
as the implicit horizon that every revolutionary act
posits or, better still, affirms.  So long as the
Revolution remains to be made, so long as it remains
a call, so long as it confronts a hostile and threatening world, for so long may Marxism be the climate for
groups-in-fusion, with their attendant virtues.  Does
Sartre, then, wish the Revolution as an event not to
occur?  It would be difficult to say.  But in a world
in which scarcity had been overcome, the losses with
respect to those attitudes which Sartre evidently
values would be great and the gains uncertain.  One
ironic gain would be the demise of Marxism itself,
for Sartre says:

As soon as there will exist for everyone a margin of real freedom beyond the production of life, Marxism will have lived out its span; a philosophy of freedom will take its place. But we have no means, no intellectual instrument, no concrete experience which allows us to conceive of this freedom or of this philosophy.[102]

If the succession of systems that Sartre calls "philosophies" may guide us, Marxism itself will give rise to this philosophy. (It is tempting to apply to Sartre himself his description of Robespierre as a man acting across an instrumental field not of his own making and accommodating himself to it accordingly; or of Flaubert as someone the meaning of whose project has been reinterpreted, in fact reversed, by subsequent readers, because of a change in situation.)[103]

vi.

I have spoken at some length "around" Sartre's method. But what of the method itself? Quite apart from its problematic relation to Marxism, it appears to be essentially a complex attempt to formalize common sense. We are all born into a world not of our own making; each of us is shaped and influenced by events that occur during childhood before we fully recognize their meaning; each of us has specific projects, which define us in some sense for others and for ourselves. The complex relation between a person and "his" world may change, either suddenly or gradually. An understanding of it thus requires constant cross reference between person and world.

All this seems unobjectionable enough. Insofar as it can correct Marxist economistic fanaticism, it may prove helpful to Marxism as a way of broadening its horizon. It may be similarly helpful as a corrective to any kind of analytic or methodological fanaticism. Indeed, the method may be found objectionable for its extreme "moderation"--for a degree of openness that invites the admission of any and all materials as evidence in the reconstruction of a person as a project. Consider for example, the prodigious, indeed the monstrous, length of Sartre's biography of Flaubert, which attempts to explain an enormous amount of data, often in agonizing detail.[104]

184

What Marxism apparently can contribute to this method is an ultimate judgment on whether the project of the person studied is a success or a failure--on its conformability to the tendency of history.[105] But such a contribution is subject to two objections. First, it runs afoul of the priority of the subjective project. Is St. Paul, whose project of universalizing a new religion did not seek to alter the relations of material production, to be accounted a success or a failure?[106] The judgment of Marxism in this case would seem to be irrelevant. Second, more fundamentally, if Marxism is itself a historical phenomenon--the standard of judgment for this age, but this age only-- then Marxism's judgment of the project of a person in another age will also have only this relative value. Marxism's judgment on St. Paul's success or failure is of value only insofar as it may orient men of the twentieth century toward St. Paul. But it will not necessarily--indeed, Sartre suggests that it will not at all--serve even this function for men of the twenty- first century.

What will serve this function for them Sartre declines to say. But if Existentialism is designed to outlive Marxism, if Sartre's method is to be a carrier of his values, then it is essentially as a teacher of values that we must regard him in order to obtain an answer to this question.

## VIII. Continuities

Our review of Sartre's Marxist writings has provided occasional glimpses into a moral teaching, but these have been largely incidental to more imme- diate tasks of polemics and explication. Thus, we noted of "The Communists and Peace," what seems fin- ally to justify the insurgent proletariat is its mani- festation of vitality, generosity, and joyous self- affirmation, qualities which are to be neither found nor expected among the bourgeoisie. Again, in "The Ghost of Stalin," the ultimate recommendation for socialism lay in the image of a people's determined engagement in a common endeavor. The Search for a Method's criticism of an economistic approach which turns Marxism into an "inhumanism" implicitly invokes the thought that Marxism ought to be a "humanism." This invocation in turn refers us to the "Humanism" essay, with its exoteric teaching of a quasi-Kantian ethic modified by the ambiance of spontaneity, and its

hidden implication of the ethical Founder who promul-
gates that ethic.  Finally, we drew from The Critique
of Dialectical Reason's sociological configurations
the implication of an Orestian political Founder,
working, somehow inconspicuously, to assure the efficacy and the longevity of the most desirable of these
configurations.  In doing so, we took for granted such
desirability.  But we ought now to look more closely
at this question, for it indicates both the continuity
and the modifications of Sartre's early political
teaching of heroism.

In positing the four-fold typology and in re-
garding the group-in-fusion as the peculiar locus of
virtue, we followed the lead of Howard R. Burkle, who
argues that this configuration embodies a Sartrean
ideal of social unity.  But Burkle's justification for
this social ideal does not itself lie in the notion
of sociality.  Rather, he refers it to certain more
traditional, individualistic Sartrean qualities:

> (T)he group-in-fusion is more in accord with
> the ontology of human freedom:  it provides
> a more creative outlet for human energies,
> permits individual choice to have a greater
> impact on the course of public affairs, and
> is more hospitable to individual diversity.[107]

Burkle also refers the group-in-fusion to the so-
called "third man" principle.  This is the mechanism
whereby an outside observer, a "third man," unifies
the otherwise disjoined praxeis of individual actors.[108]
In the case of the group-in-fusion, such as the crowd
storming the Bastille, each is both observer and actor.
Thus, each serves as "third man" for all the others:

> Each by his awareness of the others and by
> his striving with them for the same goal,
> unifies them with himself and with each
> other.  There are many centers of conscious-
> ness overlapping and interlocking, and many
> paths of activity converging and co-operating.
> The many become one without ceasing in the
> least to be individuals; on the contrary,
> they remain distinct centers with all their
> independence and personal difference intact
> and enhanced.  They are one not as a thing
> is one, but functionally:  they think,
> intend, and struggle as one.  All relations--

186

individual to individual, individual to group, group to individual--are direct and open. In this sense there are both individuals and an Individual.[109]

An intimate social bond of imitations is thus established among the actors. Each acts as all act, beholding the others and being beheld by them. The group-in-fusion thus satisfies the condition set down in the "Humanism" essay's definition of "anguish."

Likewise, the qualities of creativity and individual impact on events, to which Burkle points, seem to represent attempts to capture "forlornness" and to redress "despair." The actors in the group-in-fusion are forlorn in that they no longer refer their actions to a received and established social role. All such roles have collapsed in the exigencies of the moment. Their imitations of each other are spontaneous. Again, they act in despair. No established roles vouchsafe the success of their attempts. But because they act in a critical historical moment, their actions may have a greater chance of success than otherwise. This in some way answers the problem of despair. In all these respects, the group-in-fusion contrasts with the series, in which individuals are characterized by alienation and isolation. Each regards himself and others through the mediation of an established role, which prescribes for them uniform appearance and behavior. Each is thus both isolated and undistinguished.[110] The series recapitulates Sartrean bad faith, this time as a social rather than as an ontological structure.

To this account of Burkle's I enter two reservations. First, Burkle seems to exaggerate the importance of the group-in-fusion as a locus of individual diversities. Judging from Sartre's chosen example, the storming of the Bastille, the choice which the members of the group-in-fusion make is apt to be severely limited by circumstances. Its virtue lies in its intensity rather than its extensiveness. Offhand, there seems to be more room for diversity, or at least for eccentricity, within the interstices of the serial society. Secondly, although Burkle is aware of the heroic aspect of the group-in-fusion, he does not emphasize it sufficiently. Again, it seems significant that Sartre uses the example of the French Revolution, instead of something innocuous, like an anglers' club. [111] The group-in-fusion is a rare and privileged historical moment, requiring "a conjunction of historical circumstances; . . . an historical change in the situation, a risk of death, violence." [112]

Burkle correctly takes note of two problems of the group-in-fusion. First, there is the practical problem of its transitoriness. "Compared with the institution," he says, it "and the group-under-oath are so short-lived that they seem less societies than stages in social change. At one point Sartre actually says that the group-in-fusion is seriality in the course of dissolving." [113] Taken in its strongest sense, this identification yields the second problem, that the group-in-fusion is not merely short-lived but non-lived, because it claims to do something which is ontologically impossible. This impossibility may be raised as an objection to the earlier remarks on the "third man" principle. The "third man" of the group-in-fusion is both observer and actor. But, it may be objected, insofar as he is one of these he is not the other, although he may be both in rapid interstitial succession. More, the argument of the "Bad Faith" chapter of Being and Nothingness may be read against the analysis here. We are not any of our chosen attitudes. [114] Thus, the observer, insofar as he merely observes, is neither the observer-for-himself nor the actor-observer. The membership in the group-in-fusion of the group-in-fusion's individual members cannot be established for-itself, but only for-others, or by the members for-themselves when they stand to themselves in the relation of the Other, latterly, post hoc.

It is with considerations such as these in mind that Burkle characterizes the group-in-fusion as an "ideal," the value of which is to inform the more stable subsequent structure of the institution, to "add a dimension of infinity to the world of objects," to "make the present with its dead weight of pastness receptive to the future." Thus, the revolutionary groups "exist, have their moment of being, and afterward can be remembered, held up as ideal, and used to judge the society then in being." [115] The Paris mob of July 14 does not think of itself as the makers of the French Revolution, but that identity is its political value. The group-in-fusion thus has the political status of edifying myth, and the Founder whom we earlier inferred to be waiting in the wings, prolonging the group-in-fusion's life, is the political myth-maker and myth-perpetuator.

Whether truly or mythically, the group-in-fusion embodies a kind of heroism. But what kind of heroism? However bright the colors and however bold the sweeps with which the pictures of the storming of the Bastille may be painted, the Paris mob will never have those qualities that give Orestes his peculiar attractiveness --his intellect, his _eros_, his youthful pride, and his romantic longing for horizons. Rather, the mob is moved by the basest of drives: hunger, self-preservation, and unthinking mutual emulation. Conformably to Sartre's general accommodation to the demands of democracy, his latter-day heroism is an impoverishment of its former self.

Indicative of this debased heroism is Sartre's 1961 preface to Frantz Fanon's The Wretched of the Earth, an earnest (albeit an unfortunately self-flagellatory) statement of sympathy for the plight of Third World peoples, coming at the end of France's futile eight-year attempt to suppress the Algerian independence movement. The concept of heroism implicit in this statement has five characteristics. First, it is anti-bourgeois. True to his longest-held political conviction, Sartre assails the bourgeois way of life, especially as it appears in a colony, as "sham from beginning to end." Secondly, it is, in the crucial respect and at the crucial moment, an attitude of defiance and an act of saying No to an established role. It is a rejection, in yet another context, of bad faith. Thirdly, it involves confronting death. It is because the native revolutionary has come to regard himself as already a dead man, "a potential corpse," that he is free to engage himself in acts of daring. Fourthly, it exhibits a kind of fascination with violence, which has both instrumental value, as a way of constituting a new society, and, more importantly, intrinsic value, as the mode of being in which a man constitutes himself as Man. Sartre distinguishes, in passing, the self-constituting violence of decolonization which Fanon describes from "the fascistic utterances" of Sorel; but the substance of this distinction remains obscure. Finally, Sartre's statement brings to fruition the democratic imperative which was always a part of his thought. His heroism now embraces a formerly-disregarded three-quarters of mankind.

One consequence of this broadened scope is the

shift in this long-time urbanite's perspective from city to countryside. In marked contrast to Marx himself, Sartre touts the only kind of socialism which can take root in the Third World, rural socialism, and he promotes the most backward of people into the true repositories of the socialist revolution.[116] Orestes' imperative--"every man must invent his (own) way"[117]-- seems in the end to have reached its fulfillment only at the expense of what Orestes himself does and is. His heroism has become universal only through striking heroism's lowest common denominator.

## IX. Epilogue

In a 1975 interview with Michel Rybalka, which was released to the English-reading public in 1981, Sartre reflected on his career generally and on his former relation to Marxism in particular. He recalled his youthful interest in Nietzsche's life; and ranked him, along with Marx and Kierkegaard, as a philosopher "who could be taken as a point of departure for understanding twentieth century thought." This, relative to the "great change" in his own thinking during World War II, when he moved "beyond traditional philosophic thinking to thinking in which philosophy and action are connected, in which theory and practice are joined."[118]

Concerning Marxism, he admitted to having used the word "Marxist" "a bit lightly" in the Critique of Dialectical Reason, and asserted that while the Critique was "close to Marxism" in some respects, "it is not a Marxist work." Such Sartrean notions as "seriality" and the "practico-inert" "have come out of Marxism but . . . are different from it." His earlier characterization of Existentialism as an enclave of Marxism was a "mistake":

> It cannot be an enclave, because of my idea
> of freedom, and therefore it is ultimately a
> separate philosophy, . . . linked to (Marxism),
> . . . (but not) contained by (it).

The Marxist concepts which he retained, like "surplus value" and "class" are valid as "elements of research," but even so they must be "reworked" "because the working class was never defined by Marx or the Marxists." Moreover, the "Marxism of today" cannot be preserved because "(t)he analysis of national and international capitalism in 1848 has little to do with the capitalism

190

of today." Thus, Marxism is moving "toward death."
"We are witnessing the end of Marxism; . . . in the
next hundred years Marxism will no longer take the
form in which we know it."[119]

As for Sartre himself, even though he did not
originally choose the label, he would in the end have
preferred to be called an Existentialist.[120] What he
might have been called, or wished to be called, had
that name not stuck we can only conjecture.

## NOTES

[1]Hereinafter abbreviated as "CP." We designate
the French Socialist Part and the Democratic Revolutionary Assembly by their respective French abbrevia-
tions, SFIO (Section Française de l'Internationale
Ouvrière) and RDR (Rassemblement Démocratique Révolu-
tionaire).

[2]See, e.g., Adam Schaff, A Philosophy of Man (New
York: Monthly Review Press, 1963).

[3]Simone de Beauvoir, Force of Circumstance, p. 45.

[4]For Sartre's own account of these events, see
Jean-Paul Sartre, David Rousset, and Gérard Rosenthal,
Entretiens sur la politique (Paris: Gallimard, 1949),
pp. 70-78.

[5]Ibid., pp. 13-14, 16, 18-22, 32-36; 165, 170 ff.;
59-64, 84-87.

[6]Contat and Rybalka, vol. 1, p. 17.

[7]Jean-Paul Sartre, The Communists and Peace, trans.
Martha H. Fletcher and John R. Kleinschmidt (New York:
George Braziller, Inc., 1968), pp. 9-21, 90-131. This
article first appeared in Les Temps Modernes, nos. 81,
84-85, 100 (1952, 1954), under the title "Les Commu-
nistes et la paix."

[8]Contat and Rybalka, vol. 1, p. 17; Simone de
Beauvoir, Force of Circumstance, pp. 304-305; Jean-Paul
Sartre, "Le Réformisme et les fétiches," Les Temps
Modernes, no. 122 (1956), pp. 1153-64; Maurice Merleau-
Ponty, Adventures of the Dialectic, trans. Joseph Bien
(Evanston: Northwestern University Press, 1973 (orig.

Paris: Gallimard, 1955)), chap. 5: "Sartre and Ultra-bolshevism."

[9] Jean-Paul Sartre, The Ghost of Stalin, trans. Martha H. Fletcher and John R. Kleinschmidt (New York: George Braziller, Inc., 1968). This article first appeared in Les Temps Modernes, nos. 129-31 (1956-57), under the title "Le Fantôme de Staline."

[10] See, e.g., Sartre on Cuba (New York: Ballantine Books, 1961); and the interviews and lectures reprinted in Between Existentialism and Marxism. For the basic social theory, see the selections from The Critique of Dialectical Reason in Cumming, pp. 415-83.

[11] See, e.g., Molnar passim.

[12] See, e.g., The Communists and Peace, pp. 67-68.

[13] "Foreword," in Paul Nizan, Aden, Arabie, trans. Joan Pinkham (New York: Monthly Review Press, 1960), pp. 9, 10.

[14] Cf. supra, p. 2 ("pebbles").

[15] Originally published in Les Temps Modernes, nos. 9, 10 (1946). The first part of this article, upon which I base my remarks, is reprinted in Novack, pp. 85-109.

[16] Cf. supra, pp. 103-106.

[17] "Materialism and Revolution," pp. 88-93, 97-99, 103-109.

[18] Entretiens sur la politique, pp. 12, 22-23, 109, 120-22, 125, 128, 139-41, 204, 205.

[19] Ibid., pp. 40, 37.

[20] Ibid., p. 106.

[21] Cf. "Existentialism Is a Humanism," p. 78.

[22] The Communists and Peace, pp. 4, 5, 7, 208-30.

[23] Cf., e.g., Entretiens sur la politique, pp. 103, 204.

[24] The Communists and Peace, p. 7.

$^{25}$Ibid., p. 8.

$^{26}$Ibid., p. 9 n. Note also the disjunction between the end of part 2 and the beginning of part 3, concerning what Sartre has or has not shown about Communist responsibility for worker discouragement (pp. 131, 133).

$^{27}$Ibid., pp. 67, 80-82, 86-88, 104; 68.

$^{28}$Ibid., pp. 32-33; 42-45; 16, 9-10; 15, 9, 12.

$^{29}$Ibid., pp. 57-59, 62, 70.

$^{30}$Ibid., pp. 67, 69-70, 75, 95-100.

$^{31}$Ibid., pp. 104, 84-85.

$^{32}$Ibid., pp. 136-37. That Sartre did not become a Gaullist after 1958 is compatible with a number of explanations: that this chronicle of complaints is either not comprehensive or not decisive, that Sartre was by 1958 so practically committed to the Left that a shift to Gaullism was tactically unfeasible, or that he (rightly or wrongly) regarded de Gaulle's solutions to these problems as at best only a kind of makeshift trickery. Cf. Entretiens sur la politique, pp. 51-57, 138, 182-83; "Preface" to Frantz Fanon, The Wretched of the Earth, trans. Constance Farrington (New York: Grove Press, Inc., 1963), p. 29.

$^{33}$Entretiens sur la politique, p. 64.

$^{34}$The Communists and Peace, pp. 148-54.

$^{35}$Ibid., pp. 143-47, 156-74, 179.

$^{36}$Gordon Wright, France in Modern Times (Chicago: Rand McNally, 1960), pp. 280, 347 ff., 468, 462, 466 ff., chap. 34 ("Silent Revolution or Quiet Stagnation? Social and Economic Trends, 1945-1960").

$^{37}$The Communists and Peace, pp. 181-82, 198-99, 204, 78-82.

$^{38}$Ibid., pp. 98-99, 208, 212, 215, 219-26.

$^{39}$Ibid., p. 132.

[40]Ibid., pp. 99, 104, 85, 90-95, 12.

[41]Ibid., pp. 127-131.

[42]Ibid., p. 128; cf. Les Mouches, p. 87:11-15.

[43]"Le Réformisme et les fétiches," pp. 1155-56; cf. Entretiens sur la politique, pp. 75-77.

[44]Molnar, pp. 91-93.

[45]"Le Réformisme et les fétiches," pp. 1163, 1161.

[46]Ibid., p. 1158.

[47]Ibid., pp. 1159-60, 1164; cf. Entretiens sur la politique, p. 37.

[48]The Ghost of Stalin, p. 109.

[49]Simone de Beauvoir, Force of Circumstance, p. 357.

[50]The Ghost of Stalin, p. 142.

[51]Ibid., pp. 1, 10, 121, 122; 3-4.

[52]Ibid., pp. 81-93; 13, 16, 17, 29 n., 39, 40, 51 n., 55-56; 99-100, 107-109, 117.

[53]Ibid., pp. 45, 64-65, 80-81, 115-18, 120; 142, 125-29, 134, 136-37.

[54]Ibid., pp. 25, 41, 65, 94, 113, 114, 117; 53-62.

[55]Ibid., p. 3.

[56]See Jean-Paul Sartre, "Reply to Albert Camus" (1952), in Situations, trans. Benita Eisler (New York: George Braziller, Inc., 1965), pp. 80-88; Molnar, pp. 82-83.

[57]The Ghost of Stalin, pp. 65-81.

[58]Ibid., pp. 99-106, 122.

[59]Ibid., pp. 128-29, 138, 123, 149; cf. also pp. 35, 130-32 on the "sclerosis" of the French CP.

[60]"Existentialism Is a Humanism," p. 82.

[61]The Ghost of Stalin, pp. 96-99, 101-102.

[62]Ibid., pp. 7-9.

[63]Ibid., pp. 138-41; cf. Entretiens sur la politique, pp. 22, 30-31, 109, 120-22, 139.

[64]Ibid., p. 120.

[65]Ibid.

[66]Ibid., pp. 115, 119, 122, 121, 5, 126, 139, 4, 116.

[66a]This section has been previously published as "Search for a Marxism: Some Questions on Sartre's Method," Marxist Perspectives 7 (Fall, 1979): 142, (c)1979 The Cliomar Corporation.

[67]Jean-Paul Sartre, Search for a Method, trans. Hazel E. Barnes (New York: Alfred A. Knopf, Inc., Random House, 1963), pp. xxxiii-xxxv. This work first appeared under the title "Questions de méthode."

[68]Being and Nothingness, pp. 619-707, 66, 544-46, 554-55.

[69]Search for a Method, pp. 3, 7, 8, 6, 30.

[69a]Ibid., pp. 22, 23.

[70]Ibid., pp. 27, 26n.

[71]Ibid., pp. 35, 41, 43-44, 48; cf. pp. 45-46.

[71a]Ibid., p. 62.

[72]Ibid., pp. 67, 61, 65, 74, 68; cf. p. 69.

[73]Ibid., pp. 135-40, 113-15, 57-65, 106-108, 140-50, 130.

[74]Ibid., pp. 49, 135, 62, 100-101, 111, 150.

[75]Ibid., p. xxxiv.

[76]"Le Réformisme et les fétiches," p. 1158.

[77] Search for a Method, pp. 10-13, 14-17.

[78] Ibid., pp. 20-21.

[79] Ibid., p. 17. Cf. Karl Marx and Friedrich Engels, The German Ideology (New York: International Publishers, 1947), p. 39; cf. also p. 43 with Search for a Method, pp. 6-7. Cf. Aristotle Politics 1279b17-1280a7. Of course, Aristotle does not explicitly relate "class" to those who control the means of production as such. But an untutored non-Marxist may at least wonder whether Marx's description of the contention among various groups under the Second French Republic--groups defined not only by control or non-control of the means of production, but by kinds of property, social and dynastic attachments, and the political skill of individual leaders--tends to support or to refute this basic definition of class and the two-fold division of capitalist society that Marx builds around it. See Karl Marx, The Eighteenth Brumaire of Louis Bonaparte, in Robert C. Tucker (ed.), The Marx-Engels Reader (New York: W. W. Norton & Company, Inc., 1972), pp. 447-50, 459-60, 463, 479-80, 495-97, 515-25. Does Marx implicitly recur to the Aristotelian solution when he adds to the "ruling class-ruling ideas" formula the qualification "insofar . . . as they (i.e. the individuals composing the ruling class) rule as a class and determine the extent and compass of an epoch"? The German Ideology, p. 39.

[80] See, e.g., Karl Marx, "On the Jewish Question," in Early Writings, trans. and ed. T. B. Bottomore (New York: McGraw-Hill Book Company, 1963); Erich Fromm, Marx's Concept of Man (New York: Frederick Ungar Publishing Co., 1961).

[81] Search for a Method, p. 13. Sartre's emphasis.

[82] Karl Marx, "Preface" to A Contribution to a Critique of Political Economy, as quoted in Fromm, pp. 17-18.

[83] Search for a Method, p. 27n.

[84] Ibid., p. 35.

[85] Ibid., p. 42.

[86] Ibid.

[87] Ibid., p. 41.

[88] Ibid., p. 47.

[89] Ibid., p. 50.

[90] Ibid., pp. 37, 38-39. Emphasis in original.

[91] See Being and Nothingness, pp. 65-76; but cf. p. 24. Cf. Edmund Husserl, "Philosophy as Rigorous Science," in Phenomenology and the Crisis of Philosophy, trans. Quentin Lauer (New York: Harper & Row, 1965), p. 129; supra, pp. 19-20.

[92] Being and Nothingness, pp. 16-17.

[93] Search for a Method, pp. 60, 64.

[94] Ibid., p. 62.

[95] See the selections from the Critique in Cumming, pp. 456-80. The present analysis largely follows Howard R. Burkle, "Sartre's 'Ideal' of Social Unity," in Warnock, pp. 315-36.

[96] But this description is not, of course, limited to capitalist society. Cf. Search for a Method, pp. 72-73.

[97] I do not mean by my use of the term "millenarian" necessarily to imply that Marxism is a mystic or "unscientific" doctrine. Rather, I refer merely to its prophetic, or predictive, character as a teaching that looks toward the radical reconstitution of history through a crucial event--the revolutionary advent of the classless society.

[98] Aristotle Politics 1308a24-31.

[99] "During a revolution everyone's actions are determined by the revolution itself. The most one could hope for (to constrain revolutionary violence) would be the emergence of heroes capable of interceding to maintain respect for democratic debate between the revolutionary forces and keep discussion free and open. This is the most one can say, the most one can hope for." "A Conversation with Jean-Paul Sartre," Ramparts 12 (February, 1974), p. 38.

197

[100] _Search for a Method_, pp. 131, 130, 132.

[101] Ibid., pp. 91-92 n.

[102] Ibid., p. 34. Emphasis in original.

[103] Ibid., pp. 135-36, 149-50; cf. supra, p. 2.

[104] _L'Idiot de la famille_, vols. 1 and 2: _Gustave Flaubert de 1821 à 1857_ (Paris: Editions Gallimard, 1971), 2136 pp.

[105] _Search for a Method_, p. 65.

[106] See Rom. 13:1-7; 14:3. One might, however, raise the opposite conjecture, that St. Paul's project was the profoundly political one of defusing the revolutionary potential implicit in the teaching of Jesus. But while such a hypothesis might prove quite fruitful for some future work, its assumption here would be extravagant.

[107] Burkle, p. 317.

[108] _Being and Nothingness_, pp. 534-56.

[109] Burkle, pp. 322-23. Emphasis in original.

[110] Cumming, pp. 456-58.

[111] Cf. _Search for a Method_, pp. 76-77.

[112] Cumming, p. 472.

[113] Burkle, p. 329.

[114] _Being and Nothingness_, pp. 103-104

[115] Burkle, pp. 335, 330.

[116] "Preface" to Fanon, pp. 7, 10; 17; 23-24; 21, 14; 7, 11. Cf. Karl Marx and Friedrich Engels, _The Communist Manifesto_, in Tucker, p. 339; Marx, _The Eighteenth Brumaire_, pp. 515-19.

[117] _Les Mouches_, p. 105:29.

[118] "An Interview with Jean-Paul Sartre," in Paul Arthur Schilpp (ed.), _The Philosophy of Jean-Paul_

<u>Sartre</u> (La Salle, Illinois: Open Court Publishing Company, 1981), pp. 9, 12.  In light of the latter statement, I believe that we must regard Sartre's earlier assertion that Nietzsche "never stood for anything particular in my eyes" (p. 9) as referring, in context, only to his student days.  But cf. Simone de Beauvoir's report that Sartre and Paul Nizan, at the age of seventeen, "decided they were both supermen."  <u>Force of Circumstance</u>, p. 77.

[119]Schilpp, pp. 20-21; cf. supra, n. 79.

[120]Schilpp, p. 22; cf. supra, pp. 124-25.

# 6. CONCLUDING REMARKS

The danger of those who always give is that
they lose their sense of shame.

Nietzsche <u>Zarathustra</u> 2. 9.

I

We have found that political heroism, in one version or another, is a constant, albeit not always
predominant, strand running through the several successive phases of Sartre's career as a political teacher.
These heroisms rest on three grounds: first, as a way
of incarnating the elusive ontological truth of existential anguish; secondly, as an esthetically preferable alternative to the drab and uninspiring patterns
of bad faith which typify bourgeois life; and thirdly,
as the necessary instrument for the political salvation
of modern men, from bourgeois life on the one hand and
from their own diabolic potentialities on the other.
But the premises of these several heroic projects are
both individually dubious and, at least implicitly,
mutually contradictory.

The concept of heroic anguish is two-fold. As a
stepping back from everyday experience, and therewith
as an assessment and a rejection of everyday values,
anguish poses the challenge to constitute an alternative order, either in deed or in speech, which would
not merit condemnation. Anguish would thus be a kind
of prolegomenon to one of the traditional tasks of
political philosophy. We have seen how the ethical
critique implicit in Sartre's discussion of anguish
and bad faith seems to indicate such a project of political reconstitution. But officially the anguished
rejection of everyday values is not undertaken from the
perspective of the rightful political order or the
Good City, but rather from that of the very being of
man as the being by whom alone values have their being.
This perspective leads to the condemnation of all
Order, as contaminated with bad faith, and appears to
exclude a priori the political philosophic project.
Fundamental to this view seems to be an acceptance of
the fact-value distinction of positivist social science,
a distinction which accords to values the being of fan-
tasms. This premise, however, which no doubt reflects
the earnest wish to pursue a rigorously scientific inquiry into Being, is probably not necessary to, and is

perhaps even inconsistent with, the phenomenological
method which Sartre attempts to ply.  This difficulty
is especially evident in Sartre's examples of anguish,
which implicitly appeal to a realm of basic human
values.  Acceptance of the official account, however,
requires us to characterize the more practical heroic
teachings as merely ameliorative, as attempts to introduce redeeming graces into an essentially corrupt
reality.

As an alternative to a bourgeois way of life, then,
the invocation of heroism involves the criticism of
particular moral qualities and the substitution for
them of other particular qualities.  Under the rubric
"bad faith" Sartre castigates the contemptible inclination toward unwarranted self-assurance in the fixed
character of particular beings, be it for the sake of
sustaining a glib complacency in things as they are or
in order to promote oppression of others.[1]  Beneath
this lies a kind of mental laxity, especially the absence of self-examination.

The Flies gives this cluster of qualities several
mythic expressions:  the Argives' guilt and their death
cult mummery, which fixes their being and preserves
them from serious reflection on their mortality;
Electra's obsession with destiny, which shields her
from facing a virgin future; and the ambiguous character of the "tyrannic" regime, which in its very oppressiveness releases the citizens from the responsibility
of determining their own lives.  By contrast, Orestes
presents the image of proud self-assertion coupled
with openness to the future, and hence to his own
being; of direct confrontation with death, in an unusual and violent act; and of estrangement from the
principle of Order, signified by what for him may be
called the death of God.  But he is also, through his
founding myth, an order-establisher; and he speaks of
being constituted, and thus in a sense contained, by
his act.  While these seem to be lapses into bad faith,
the example of Orestes' resolution, introspection, and
intensity may well be, in the absence of an explicit
Sartrean discussion of authenticity, as close as one
can practically come to that vaunted "self-recovery of
corrupted being."[2]

Moving beyond these individual qualities, Sartre's
subsequent writings attempt to remedy bourgeois asoci-
ality by promoting egalitarianism and common endeavor,

be it through the willing-for-all-humanity of "human-ist" anguish or through participation in a mass histor-ical movement. But these remedies somewhat strain the heroic content. This, not only because the social con-sciousness is clouded by the hallucinations of humanism and historicism, but also because it abstracts from and seeks to suppress the very possibilities of distinction and human conflict which are heroism's preconditions. The evident ludicrousness of lauding a hypothetical anonymous mass's "heroic" struggle to build the White Sea Canal must make one doubt that the creator of Orestes could have been entirely candid in his latter-day Marxian rhapsodizing.

Politically, heroism is instrumental both to sal-vation from overt oppression and to moderation of the many's worse possibilities. Orestes expresses the probable truth that at the most critical moments only the intellectual outsider can assume the detachment from the everyday life and premises of a political community that is prerequisite to radical prescription for it. But such salvation can only be provisional. Both because the actual presence of an Orestian hero would be too awesome to permit everyday political life and because the practical requirements of ruling would draw him into unrewarding patterns of play-acting, the community must be allowed to fend for itself under the inspiring myth of the Savior. The heroic influence, however, cannot be merely inspiring, and indeed it must guard against its own random emulation. Thus, Orestes' myth to the Argives conjoins admonition with inspira-tion, and he enunciates for the audience a universalist teaching at odds with his own actions. Thus too, Sartre later conceals the extreme possibilities of existential anguish beneath a cover of "humanism." And, later still, revolutionary leaders are said to be needed both to maintain the élan of the group-in-fusion and to preserve some modicum of group respect for indi-vidual rights and dignity.

II

We have provisionally assumed, as a working hypo-thesis, that Sartre may indeed have been a political philosopher. But is that assumption in truth warranted? Manifestly, Sartre was a political teacher. Manifestly too, he did not decline, in his politicking, to ex-ploit his reputation as a philosopher in order to pro-mote his positions. While probably no-one would accord him the philosophic rank of a Plato, it would certainly be uncharitable, and also unjust, to deny to Sartre a credential which this generous age has bestowed upon Bertrand Russell, Mao Tse Tung, and innumerable members of academic philosophy departments. Being and Nothingness undeniably probes questions of philosophic dimension. And if our method of reading Sartre's works is at all valid, then there is beneath their bold and vehement exterior a craft and subtlety of expression suggestive of that peculiar kind of intelligence characteristic of philosophy-in-the-world, that is, of political philosophy.

But substantively, such political philosophy as we can piece together from these works seems both deficient and distressing, founded upon an apparent philosophic dogmatism and tending practically to the promotion of both fanatic immoderation and vulgarity. In fairness to Sartre, it is necessary to ask whether the political conditions of the twentieth century, this peculiarly immoderate and democratic age, might not have made these qualities indispensable preconditions to the efficacy of any political teaching. In the extreme, this is to deny that political philosophy is at present possible. Short of this dismal conclusion, one litmus test of a political teaching might be to ask whether its concessions to the spirit of the time are reasonably selective and tempered, and whether some valuable contrary truth lies beneath them.

However we may ultimately decide this question, Sartre should still be of interest to the student of politics and philosophy. Historically, he provides a valuable guage of the temper of our time. Philosophically, he is a kind of battleground upon which various political and philosophic currents of modernity contend, and thus also a bridge to and commentary upon his possibly more profound antecedents. And more personally, more existentially, he presents the rare and awesome spectacle of the man who earnestly attempts to pursue all three of the kinds of lives of which Aristotle speaks.[3] His successes thus offer solace and inspiration, that even a clay-footed mortal may profitably cast his mark far and wide. And his failure provides a sobering object lesson for us all.

# NOTES

[1] See Jean-Paul Sartre, _Anti-Semite and Jew_, trans. George J. Becker (New York: Schocken Books, 1965).

[2] Cf. Hazel E. Barnes, "Translator's Introduction," in _Being and Nothingness_, pp. li-lii.

[3] _Nicomachean Ethics_   1095b13-1096a5.

# INDEX